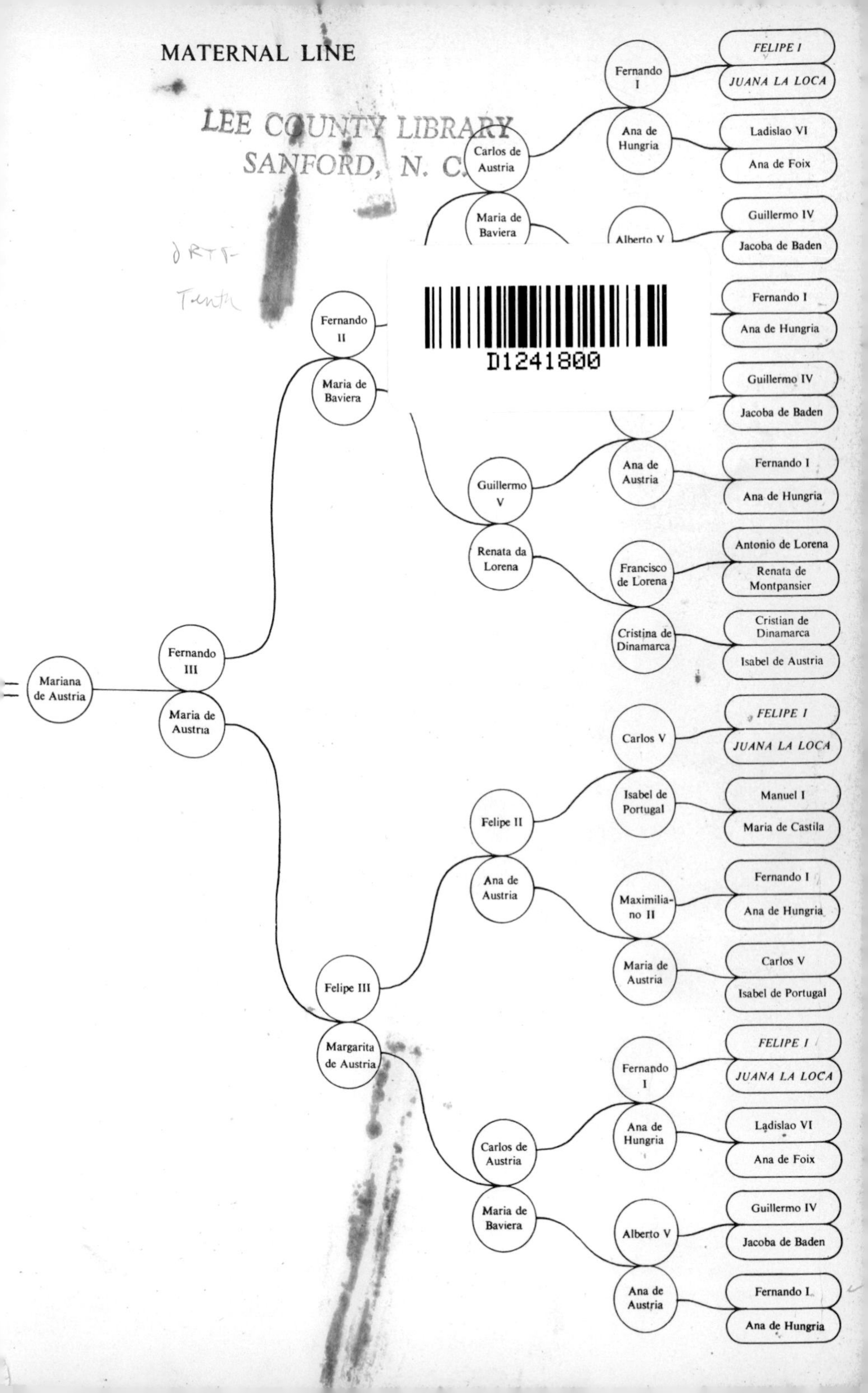
MATERNAL LINE
Mariana de Austria
Fernando III
Maria de Austria
Fernando II
Maria de Baviera
Carlos de Austria
Maria de Baviera
Fernando I
Ana de Hungria
FELIPE I
JUANA LA LOCA
Ladislao VI
Ana de Foix
Alberto V
Guillermo IV
Jacoba de Baden
Fernando I
Ana de Hungria
Guillermo IV
Jacoba de Baden
Guillermo V
Renata da Lorena
Ana de Austria
Fernando I
Ana de Hungria
Francisco de Lorena
Antonio de Lorena
Renata de Montpansier
Cristina de Dinamarca
Cristian de Dinamarca
Isabel de Austria
Felipe III
Margarita de Austria
Felipe II
Ana de Austria
Carlos V
FELIPE I
JUANA LA LOCA
Isabel de Portugal
Manuel I
Maria de Castila
Maximiliano II
Fernando I
Ana de Hungria
Maria de Austria
Carlos V
Isabel de Portugal
Carlos de Austria
Maria de Baviera
Fernando I
FELIPE I
JUANA LA LOCA
Ana de Hungria
Ladislao VI
Ana de Foix
Alberto V
Guillermo IV
Jacoba de Baden
Ana de Austria
Fernando I
Ana de Hungria

CARLOS

The King Who Would Not Die

JOHN LANGDON-DAVIES

CARLOS

The King Who Would Not Die

PRENTICE-HALL, INC.
Englewood Cliffs, N. J.

First American Edition 1963

Library of Congress Catalog Card Number:
63-16580

Printed in the United States of America

11480-T

Prentice-Hall International, Inc.
(London, Tokyo, Sydney, Paris)
Prentice-Hall of Canada, Ltd.
Prentice-Hall de Mexico, S. A.

CONTENTS

ILLUSTRATIONS

A Genealogical Tree is printed on the endpapers

To my friend of fifty years
Hugo Vere Hodge

'This king's life being of such importance in this conjuncture as to all the affairs of Europe, I thought might excuse these particulars, which otherwise might seem impertinent.'

Stanhope to the Duke of Shrewsbury
Madrid, September 19th, 1696

CHAPTER ONE

A CHILD IS BORN

On November 6th, 1661, a Sunday, as she sat down to her midday meal, the Queen of Spain, Doña Mariana, felt certain symptoms which she had been expecting for two anxious days.

She left the table and hurried to the Tower Chamber, which had been prepared for the event. The royal collection of sacred relics occupied every corner, the three thorns from Christ's crown, one of the nails from His Cross, a fragment of the Cross itself, a piece of Our Lady's mantle, and dozens of treasures only less rare. To these had been added other very special ones, known to be most helpful on such occasions. Father Juan de Ojalvo had hurried to Madrid with the walking-stick of Santo Domingo, Abbot of Silos; and from San Juan de Ortega's convent, his miraculous belt had been brought by the Prior himself.

To reinforce the spiritual aids, there was gathered together a notable team of medical experts: the royal obstetrician who had delivered the royal babies ever since the last king's time, forty years ago; the royal midwife, Inés Ayala, who for a quarter of a century had assisted at the birth of nearly all Philip IV's[1] children, both legitimate and bastard. In case of emergency there were present five other doctors, including Dr Bravo, portentously learned and long-winded, from whose interminable folios the details of these intimate moments can be gleaned.

Although most of the royal bastards had done well, six out of Doña Mariana's previous eight children had been born dead, or had died almost immediately. The other two were Margarita,

[1] It is impossible to achieve uniformity in the use of names. They will usually be given their Spanish form, but it would seem artificial to most English readers to call the four royal Philips, Felipe, or the Emperor Charles, Carlos. On the other hand our hero will be called Carlos, as the anglicized Charles II so easily brings to mind his English contemporary.

who was painted by Velazquez for our eternal delight in her blue and her pink guarda-infantes, and Felipe Próspero who had died a few days before these present events, at the comparatively ripe age of almost four. As against this, several of the bastards were growing up, a matter of bitterness for a Queen so invariably unlucky in motherhood.

The King had not eaten with Doña Mariana. It would have been a breach of etiquette for him to do so. He had gone straight from mass to his own study to answer Sor Maria de Agreda's last letter. He had sat down at eleven o'clock, his mind full of the recent death of Felipe Próspero.

> With the long illness of my son, and the continuous help I was giving in his room, I have not been able to answer your letter of last month ... I assure you that what has most exhausted me, much more than the loss, is to see clearly that I have vexed God and that he sent this punishment to castigate my sins ...
>
> Help me as a friend with your prayers to placate God's just anger and to beg Our Lord that, as he has taken my son from me, He may make His light shine on the Queen, whose confinement we await hourly, and give her good health and guard what is to be born, if this is His will, for otherwise I do not wish it ...
>
> Ah, Sor Maria, if I had succeeded in following your teachings, perhaps I would not have found myself thus. Pray to Our Lord that He may open my eyes, that I may perform His holy will in all things ... There is nothing new in the English situation. I, thank God, am in good health ...

At this point Philip was interrupted and told of what was going on in the Tower Chamber.

His was not the only anxious mind. It can be imagined with what impatience the whole Royal Court of Madrid was awaiting the outcome of this latest confinement. And not only Madrid: all Europe knew that its future was dependent upon what happened in the next few hours.

In Madrid, those who relied most on spiritual remedies had become a little despondent. Not that they were weak in faith: they remained unshaken in their devotion to the Triune God and especially to the Mother of God; but it seemed increasingly doubtful whether God cared very much for Spain. Certainly a whole battery of sacred relics, reinforced to the utmost, had not helped poor little Felipe Próspero. Had they not carried Nuestra Señora de la Soledad from one sacred dwelling place to another? Had not Nuestra Señora de Atocha made the journey from her church to the convent of the Barefoot Nuns, accompanied by prayerful multitudes? And the peripatetic body of San Isidro, always brought to the sick beds of the great, had been carried into the child's bedroom, while San Diego of Alcalá himself, in his open urn, had been placed contiguous to the cot. None of it had availed; Felipe Próspero had died, leaving Spain and Philip, his father, without an heir, and naked, therefore, to their enemies.

And Philip knew the reason for these tragedies, these dead royal children, Spain's military disasters, the poverty of the country, the plagues, pestilences and famines. Possessed of the greatest capacity for sexual pleasure recorded of any modern monarch, he was also gifted (alas!) with the most acutely guilty conscience on mornings after. It was clear to him that his incessant womanizing provoked the deity to reprisals and, unfortunately, instead of punishing him for his sins, God punished Spain.

This was the subject matter of almost every letter which passed between the King and his astonishing confidante, that simple but very subtle nun, Sor Maria de Agreda, who, in some inscrutable manner, had learned worldly wisdom without ever knowing anything of the world outside her convent. In politics, Sor Maria was the only person capable of giving Philip good advice; she was as near to being a statesman as anyone in Spain at the time, and far nearer than most of the Council of State. And it was to her that Philip unburdened his soul. She, with her nuns, prayed for him incessantly; they begged God to give their king the gift of continence.

It must be admitted that for many years their success was only sufficient to bring Philip a little comfort without much of the desired continence. He begged Sor Maria to help him stop his adulteries; he begged her to beg Our Lady, with whom she had so many close conversations tête-à-tête, to beg her Son to show His forgiveness by allowing him to provide Spain with a healthy male heir. At last, age and decrepitude had come to reinforce the power of prayer.

Philip's salad-days had come to an end, and he could hardly take any pleasure in women; rheumatism and worse diseases were giving him the gift which he had sought for so long in vain; nevertheless he retained his sense of duty. He told an indiscreet, gossiping courtier, who has passed the information on to us, that he had resolved to make one last legitimate procreative effort with little or no natural concupiscence to help him. It was a sacrifice not so much to Venus as to his beloved Spain. And it had succeeded. But the events of the next few hours in the Tower Chamber would tell to what extent God had actually relented.

At this moment the doctors were disagreeing over natural forms of treatment. Anxiety for a living heir was coupled with anxiety for the mother's life. In the past, Mariana had not had happy experiences. Each of her last three children had nearly cost her her life, and Dr Bravo, as one would expect, had a theory which explained this. At the births of Ambrosia, of Felipe Próspero, and of Fernando, the mother had had terrible epileptic seizures, and the infants had either died at once or lived only a very short time. On the other hand, at the birth of Margarita, the only child to survive, the mother had been perfectly well. Now why was this? To Dr Bravo the reason was plain. Just before Margarita was born, Doña Mariana had suffered several violent nose-bleeds. Therefore, what she required now was to be bled. Some of the doctors disputed this, and as things turned out they would hardly have had time to give the treatment.

For one thing is certain: the birth was easy. In a very short time Philip found himself once more a father, and Spain had a male heir. Philip's last throw had won a prize. Not only Madrid, but all Europe was to be influenced by this event, for the consequences had there been no viable male heir would have been cataclysmic. Spain, the greatest empire the world had known, would have been thrown to the wolves and divided piecemeal. To pious and patriotic Spaniards it would have seemed that a sacred and seamless garment had been partitioned, an act of sacrilege which even the Roman centurions abstained from when Christ hung on the Cross.

The official Gazette published a description of the new-born child, 'most beautiful in features, large head, dark skin, and somewhat overplump'. This officially perfect specimen was soon found to have been born with the most satisfactory auguries. The parturition was of the shortest, it took place at full moon, on a Sunday, which was under Our Lady's patronage. The astrologers were of course consulted and reported most favourably; the child had been born when the first minute of Aquarius ascended to the horizon of the Spanish Court, with Saturn in the angle of the tenth Royal House, free from malicious aspects, in the sign of Scorpio, in conjunction with Mercury 'all of which promised a happy and fortunate life and reign'.

Those who put a greater trust in doctors than in astrologers (who had promised long life and joy to little Felipe Próspero) may have been interested in certain learned researches being carried out by Dr Bravo. When Carlos was born he was two days overdue. Dr Bravo set to work to answer the question which surely only a fool would ask: could the prince's birth be regarded as natural? After many paragraphs, he answered it in the affirmative and, moreover, pointed out, with a wealth of references to classical literature as well as to Christian sources, that the tendency is for heroes and other outstanding characters to exceed the limits which are found sufficient for ordinary mortals. It was, therefore, almost certain that the Serene Carlos José, Principe de las Españas, would be a hero with outstanding qualities. Ominously enough, Dr Bravo's next thesis in the third edition of his folio is entitled *De Impotentia Viri ex Maleficio* – On Male Impotence due to Witchcraft.

Other fortunate prognostications were that Carlos was born on the sixth day of the month, the very same date as the Emperor Trajan. Moreover the Cherubim seen by Isaiah in attendance on God had six wings;[1] doctors divided the hexameter into six feet; there were six Vestal Virgins; the tides run for six hours each way; the sixth Spanish King was Beto who founded Cadiz; the sixth Gothic king was Theodoric and 'the sixth generation of the House of Austria is our newborn prince.'

The sixth generation of the House of Austria! Aye, there was the rub. Philip I, Carlos I, Philip II, Philip III, Philip IV, and

[1] The optimist who mentioned this evidently did not know his Bible as well as he should have.

now Carlos II. As his expectant parents, already stricken by disease and repeated disappointments, prayed and hoped through those last hours for the infant who would save Spain, they could not know that the gods had made up their minds long ago; the ruthless chain of biological cause and effect could only bring disease out of disease, and they themselves were a link in a chain of which the last link was already irreparably broken.

This Sunday's child, born so easily with the help of the saintly walking-stick and the miraculous belt, described so cheerfully in the official Gazette, awaited so eagerly by despairing parents, grew up to be the pivot of European history for at least a quarter of a century. But for him we might never have heard of Marlborough or of Blenheim. He is a perennial reminder that history is not made by only the strong men, but that weaknesses shape human destiny as surely as do the supermen and heroes. His life was a misery, his debilities beyond all help either of San Diego dead or of Dr Bravo alive. Not even the Devil himself, whom we shall later see called in as chief consultant when others failed, could save him.

But it was far more than a personal tragedy, this life of Carlos II of Spain. It was the whimper with which a great historical theory came to an end. We shall see them searching the back streets of Madrid for the witches who had stirred the brew; they had been better employed retracing the highroad of European history.

Two days later, Philip returned to his desk and finished his letter to Sor Maria:

> Thus far I wrote to you on Sunday at eleven o'clock, and at one o'clock Our Lord was pleased to give me back the son he had taken from me ... Help me to throw myself at His feet and to pray that He conserves this pledge, if He so desire, and if not, I do not want it so, but that He do His will. The Queen and child are well.

facing: CARLOS SEGUNDO

THE EMPEROR MAXIMILIAN AND HIS FAMILY

back row: MAXIMILIAN I, PHILIP I THE FAIR, AND MARIA OF BURGUNDY

front row: FERNANDO, CHARLES V, AND THEIR COUSIN, LUIS II OF HUNGARY

CHAPTER TWO

HAPSBURG AND BURGUNDY

A NORMAL biography proceeds from the birth to the baptism to the weaning, thence to nursery days and the putting away of childish things. For us this would be an impossible progress, for we are dealing with a man who died of poison two hundred years before he was born. If birth is a beginning, of no man was it more true to say that in his beginning was his end. Carlos was history's 'I told you so' to the proud Emperor Maximilian.

The sixth generation of the House of Austria. Mankind has not taken very seriously the warnings that the sins and ignorances of the fathers are visited upon the children unto the third and fourth, yes and unto the sixth generations, and certainly the great ones of the earth have paid little attention to that part of a man's life during which he remains hidden in the loins of his forebears. But in Carlos's case, so important was this part of his life that the baptism must be left until later.

Carlos II, Philip IV, Philip III, Philip II, Carlos I, Philip I, the six generations of the Spanish Hapsburgs, bodies and minds thrown out by the continuing life process for its own inscrutable purpose. What was the fatality, the serialized murder mystery, which ended in the creation at one o'clock on Sunday, November 6th, 1661, of a man whose whole life was a dying, whose very passion was a sterility, whose utter weakness forced all Europe into a terrible war? In order to see the situation in its proper historical context, we must trace the growing horror from one day in 1477.

It was in 1477 that the eighteen-year-old Archduke Maximilian of Hapsburg, later Emperor Maximilian I, married Marie of Burgundy. It was a splendid match for both. For the Hapsburgs it was the beginning of future political greatness, for Burgundy the revival of a court which for courtliness had known no rival; a court whose manners were those of the books which turned Don Quixote's head.

The Emperor Maximilian has been a legendary figure for so long that it is difficult to submit him to historical assessment. The mainsprings of his conduct were often so different from any motives we can readily interpret today. As Mr Waas, an American historian, says: 'though the things he did have long been a matter of record, there has never been complete agreement as to why he did them.'

He was in fact unpredictable, and his motives, in so far as we can guess them, were often surprising; for example, there is his desire, which cannot but endear him to us, to become Pope as well as Emperor.

> I am sending tomorrow to Rome [he wrote to his daughter on September 15th, 1511] to find a way for the Pope to make me his partner, so that, after his death, I can be sure of the Papacy and of becoming a Priest and later a Saint. You will then have to worship me when I am dead, which will be delightful.

The seriousness of his ambition to be a saint has been questioned, for he was apt to mix frivolities with solemn matters. But there can be no doubt of his scheme to become Pope. He took the practical step of applying to the banking house of Fugger, the real rulers of Europe, for enough money to corrupt the Sacred College of Cardinals and half Rome besides. As usual he was short not only of ready cash but also of the normal forms of collateral, so he offered the Fuggers in pawn his Imperial Crown, the Sceptre of Charlemagne, and most of his crown jewels. The Fuggers would not play. They were hardly likely to regard papal, let alone saintly, aspirations from such a source as a sound basis for investment.

That Maximilian was superstitious and flighty cannot be denied, and yet he combined with a full share of these qualities an inquiring mind much above the standard of his age. His relationship with the Abbot Trithemius, Johannes von Trittenheim, illustrates both sides of his character.

The King and the Abbot were great holders of seances, the

accounts of which read very much like those described by trusting spiritualists today. At one of them Trithemius managed to persuade the deceased Marie of Burgundy, who had been killed at twenty-four in a hunting accident, to materialize before her remarried but still devoted relict. She walked past him and bowed and smiled, and Maximilian recognized her by a mole on the back of her neck. But he found the experience very distasteful and ordered the Abbot to get rid of the spirit as soon as possible.

On the other hand, Maximilian asked Trithemius some very shrewd questions which formed the basis of that scholar's most famous book. They are the questions which occupy the mind of any serious person to this day, but for any monarch to ask them more than four hundred years ago argues a more than usually inquiring mind.

Why does God want to be taken on faith by mortals rather than be clearly recognized? Can those who, by no fault of their own, know nothing of the Christian religion and are therefore without baptism and Christian belief, become blessed if they are faithful to the religion which they do know? Why are prophets of false religions also able to do wonders? How can the doctrine of the righteousness of God be reconciled with the allowance of so much evil, often to the damage of good and pious people? ...

These questions are all good, which is more than can be said for some of Trithemius' answers.

It was only natural that such a man should discover miracles taking place for his special benefit. On one occasion two stags and a pheasant came to do him homage, and, in 1492, when he wanted support for his policy of war with France, meteors fell. When, nine years later, he wished to start a Crusade, miraculous crosses appeared on people's clothing; and, to help him combat the luxurious living which militated against the crusading spirit, God, so Maximilian was convinced, sent syphilis.

At that time the air was heavy with miraculous material. The young Maximilian himself was hopefully regarded by many as the reincarnation of the great Emperor Frederick II who, as the common people knew, would come one day to right all wrongs, to remove the mighty from their seats and place the poor in them instead.

When he showed no sign of playing this messianic part, he

became anti-Christ. The mysterious but certainly elderly 'revolutionary of the Upper Rhine', who left the manuscript known as 'The Book of the Hundred Chapters', advocated the slaughter of the Emperor as a preliminary to a general massacre, in the interests of justice and righteousness. Indeed, nobody was willing to see Maximilian as an ordinary human being. The man of flesh and blood was merely raw material for myth and fantasy.

But Maximilian, sane and at times even sage, was rather more eccentric than most people, and his eccentricities in some cases appear to be shadows cast by coming events. Thus, he took to travelling about Europe with his coffin and could be heard addressing it at night in the quiet of his bedroom. Some said he slept in it. And these obsessions with coffins and death recur time and again in his descendants, for they would not leave their dead alone.

Maximilian spent almost as much time arranging for the comfort of his corpse as over his own lifetime needs. His will is full of detailed instructions for its disposal. It was to be shaved and depilated, and the teeth extracted, ground to powder and burned. Was this for fear that witches might otherwise use what were universally known to be favourite adjuncts to their nastiness? Above all, for decency's sake, the body was to be buried in a pair of breeches.

This misplaced modesty was part of Maximilian's abnormally ambivalent attitude towards sex, another eccentricity which he appears to have bequeathed to his heirs. After the death of his second wife he had been urged to marry again, but he refused, saying that the mere thought of a naked woman revolted him. Yet, besides his legitimate offspring he had at least eight acknowledged bastards.

Maximilian, therefore, can be labelled a Great Eccentric, delightful in a book, though no doubt difficult in life. But he had another characteristic perhaps even more important for his descendants.

In the portrait of this Emperor with his family (opp. page 17), we see at once that his lower jaw protrudes in such a way that its teeth must lie in front of the upper ones, instead of meeting them vertically or lying behind them. We may also notice that the nose is long without being aquiline, and the lips are rather thick.

Finally, there is a certain narrowing of the whole face, making it long in proportion to the width.

And if we look closely at Marie of Burgundy in the same picture, we are struck at once by the character of the lips, especially of the lower one. They are thicker than normal, and the lower one looks as if it needed strong musculature and a very firm purpose if the mouth is to remain shut. These lips did not originate with Marie; they were an inheritance, and fixed as a family trait by consanguineous marriages, so that later her grandson, the future Emperor Charles V, was to be so malformed that he had the greatest difficulty in keeping his mouth closed. The story is told that when first he came to Spain a Calatayud peasant shouted to him: 'Your Majesty, shut your mouth, the flies of this country are very insolent.'

Maximilian and his wife, then, both inherited certain physical abnormalities, but nobody in those days could have foretold what was latent beneath these two profiles now joined in holy matrimony. Subsequent events showed, however, that their marriage brought together undesirable elements which were to play havoc with the individuals who inherited them.

Nor was it only a distinctive profile that was involved. This set of the jaw is not found alone but usually with other facial and skeletal anomalies known collectively as acrocephaly. This condition is the result of inherited endocrine disfunction, and sometimes involves certain mental peculiarities which may be shown in a variety of ways, especially in a tendency to epilepsy, in the upset of normal sexual desire, and in a hypersensitive nervous temperament.

It was the son of this marriage who founded the Hapsburg dynasty in Spain, and it was this germ plasm which subsequently created Carlos the Bewitched.

CHAPTER THREE

THE MAD QUEEN

By his marriage to Marie of Burgundy, therefore, Maximilian appeared to have laid the foundations of Hapsburg greatness. Burgundy and the Empire could together look forward to a day when they would stand up to France, and in northern Europe prospects were at last bright. How could anyone imagine all this being jeopardized by the physical union of a lip and a jaw?

Long afterwards, the Hapsburgs were to be praised for winning empires by marriages rather than by wars, and the Emperor might well be proud of his next statesmanlike move, which brought his son Philip a Spanish princess for bride. In a few years this marriage was to become even more politically fruitful than Maximilian had dreamed. All he had hoped for was to strengthen his friendship with Castile and Aragon so as to carry one step further the encirclement of France. The Spanish princess was not heir to any Spanish Throne; there were three people between her and her parents' dominions. Yet, finally, she was to be queen of all the Spains in her own right, and Philip king.

Maximilian had never bargained for quite such good luck; nor could he know the price which would have to be paid for it – a price so great that it involved the ruin of the Hapsburgs and of Spain. And he could not have guessed that the evil thing which would eventually corrupt all his good fortune, and that of his descendants, would be contributed by that great woman, Isabella, the Catholic Queen.

Isabella the Catholic, by whom Granada was captured, and the Moors and their religion expelled from Europe, and through whom America was discovered, was without question one of the greatest rulers of her day, indeed of all time. The difficulties she overcame, the sheer physical energy with which she achieved her ends, never allowing hard campaigning and long journeys on horseback to interfere with her fertility as a woman, her vision as a statesman, all these set her apart. But this great Isabella was a genetical *femme fatale* with a death-dealing gift. She was a genius who carried madness in her seed.

Folk wisdom advises a man to take a good look at his prospective bride's mother before he ties any knots about him; but certainly no one could wish for a finer mother-in-law than Isabella, the Catholic Queen of Castile. It is true that her husband and second cousin Ferdinand, astute, devoted, energetic, was so deficient in honesty that only fools among his enemies trusted his word. Some think he was the model for Machiavelli's Prince. It was to him an Italian referred when he wrote of a certain Prince 'who preaches nothing but peace and good faith, and yet of both is the greatest enemy'; and Guicciardini wrote: 'I am certain that beyond all others he is a master of dissimulation.' Ferdinand was ruthless, his word was worthless, he was superstitious – so unsatisfactory a character indeed that even Spanish historians have occasional scruples about extending to him the sobriquet, Catholic King.

None of this, however, made him less acceptable as Maximilian's son's father-in-law. On the contrary, he was a good man to have as an ally, especially as he was suffused with the traditional hatred for France felt by every Aragonese.

It was not in Isabella or in Ferdinand, as individuals, that warning of future disaster could have been found. If someone endowed with the biological knowledge which humanity did not acquire for another four hundred years had considered their relatives, especially the three closest relatives of the Catholic Queen, he might have advised her to remain celibate. If Maximilian could have had Marañon, the great Spanish doctor and medical historian, at his elbow to help him assess Isabella's father, mother and half-brother, and if he could have been induced to believe that political expediency never justifies biological crime, Spanish history would have been different, for there would never have been a dynasty of Hapsburgs fated to destroy Spain.

Juan II, Isabella's father, came to the throne at the age of two, his father, a life-long invalid, having died before the age of thirty. Juan was a modern 'decadent intellectual' born out of due time. He cultivated the arts and artists, but refused to have anything to do with governing. His unquestionable aesthetic sensibilities were unfortunately coupled with a quite pathological incompetence in the things of everyday life. He was completely under the thumb of a favourite, Álvaro de Luna, who is presumed to have poisoned his first queen and known to have selected his second, as he thought, for his own purposes. Álvaro's choice, however, was his downfall. He had expected that Isabella of Portugal would be easy to manage, coming as she did from an inferior dynasty, but, with an obsessive determination not foreseen in her, she concentrated from the first on destroying him. Álvaro de Luna, thanks to her, met an ugly end, beheaded in public at Valladolid.

It was all she was ever able to do, for when next year Juan died and left her a widow at twenty, she became melancholic and very soon a hopeless schizophrenic. For forty years she remained in solitary confinement while first her stepson and then her own daughter occupied the throne.

The stepson, Henry IV, Isabella the Catholic's half-brother, took after his father in every unsatisfactory way, only in him the pathological tendencies were ten times more pronounced. He was schizoid, sexually perverted, semi-impotent. In fact, his sexual deficiency was considered by most people so great that his daughter was known as La Beltraneja, after her presumed father Beltran de la Cueva; but some believed she was really Henry's daughter and described the method of artificial insemination which had been necessary, involving the use of an apparatus of pure gold. Historians have quarrelled about this question ever since, but the best modern authority, Marañon, inclines to the opinion that La Beltraneja *was* Henry's daughter, though some method of artificial insemination may well have been necessary.

Whatever the truth about his potency, Henry was filthy in his person, liked the smell of burned horn and other odours even less attractive to normal people, and had a profile so concave that Alonso de Palencia, his chronicler, says it was as if a piece had been wrenched out of the centre. And it is this last physical feature, this same 'Hapsburg jaw' that is perhaps the most ominous. The visible sign of a degenerate inheritance, it meant that when Maximilian's son Philip married his Spanish princess they would hand on to their offspring a double dose of whatever poison these symptoms indicated.

With such a father and mother, such an execrable half-brother,

Isabella could only be regarded as an unrepeatable miracle. A degenerate father, a schizophrenic mother, and a schizoid and filthy brother were more reliable as presages of the future than her own genius. But the truth had not been revealed when Maximilian chose her daughter, Juana, for his son Philip the Fair.

For Juana promised well in her youth. She was gifted and educated. She could make speeches in Latin. Indeed she promised to take after her mother. Whether the subsequent disaster is to be attributed solely to her heredity, or, in part, to a series of catastrophes which would have tried the best balanced mind, cannot be usefully discussed. There is no doubt that she suffered, like her grandmother, from schizophrenia.

On the arrival of Juana in the Low Countries, Philip was so entranced at the first sight of her, and she with him, that rather than wait for the marriage arranged for two days later, he sought out a priest to give them his benediction, and they went to bed together on the same afternoon; but by the time she had become heir to the throne of Spain she had begun to make his life a misery with attacks of jealousy. Jealousy, no doubt, is a common failing of human beings, but there were few royal brides in those days who could reasonably expect their husbands to be entirely faithful or even to take any trouble to conceal their infidelities; and Juana's reactions surpassed normal limits. Moreover, an even more alarming trait began quite early to manifest itself. Juana was widely reported as being slipshod in her religious duties. In those days any tendency to unorthodoxy could only be pathological, only the mentally deranged could be free-thinkers. The screams and violence which punctuated her married life could have been forgiven in that uninhibited age, but this was serious. This, not her sexual eccentricities, nor her paroxysms of wrath, nor her growing melancholy, was the sign which first convinced her relatives that she was mad.

She had her legitimate grievances. Philip held the purse strings so tight that she was often without the money to pay the household wages, and no Spanish princess was likely to find the habits of a foreign court congenial. As for Philip, he did not find much relaxation in a moody wife who was always pregnant.

The marriage as a physical union lasted less than ten years, and between the birth of Leonor in November 1498, and of Catalina in January 1507, there were four other children. One of them was the future Emperor Charles V and Charles I of Spain. It was five months after Charles was born that Juana became heir to the throne of Spain. This involved her in a journey from the Low Countries to receive oaths of fidelity from the Castilian and Aragonese *cortes*.

Another pregnancy delayed the setting off, and it was not until the end of 1501, after almost a year's journey, that the royal pair arrived. Philip had not wanted to come, hated Spain when he got there and returned to Flanders as soon as he could, leaving Juana alone there, pregnant once more and racked with jealousy and frustrated desire.

It was at this time that unmistakable signs of mental trouble were revealed. She sat by the hour staring into vacancy, now and then breaking out into screaming and hysterical weeping. Only with difficulty could they keep her from setting off after her husband. Isabella, her mother, consigned her to the care of the Bishop of Córdoba who had the windows barred and the drawbridge up, but she countermanded his orders. The struggle lasted until the spring of 1504 when she had her way at last and started across Europe towards a husband who did not want her. Once arrived in Brussels she began to drive Philip to distraction, even, we are told, to thoughts of suicide. When she assaulted a court lady and left the marks of her nails, fists and a pair of scissors on her face her husband retaliated in kind.

She tried to dismiss all Flemish girls from her service, regarding them as potential rivals, and Philip could only prevent her by means once advocated by Lysistrata. These sufficed for one night's peace, but next day the struggle began again. Philip locked her in her room next door and she replied by beating all night on the dividing wall, and by shouting abuse. Philip threatened not to see her. She subsided. He relented and returned to her bed. And so it continued, the Court commonly calling their Queen the Terror, Philip writing to his parents-in-law telling them the truth, as he saw it.

But now Juana went from bad to worse. On their return to Spain she remained speechless and almost motionless all day, occasionally, Ophelia-like, trying on a small ornament or a sprig of flowers. Apathetic, lethargic, shut in from the world, she had only one activity; and soon once more she was pregnant – for the last time.

In 1504 Isabella died and her will contained instructions for the future government of Spain. On the assumption that Juana was too sick in mind to govern, Ferdinand was to be regent until Charles came of age. In 1506, after a very brief illness, Philip the Fair died. With him died the last shreds of his wife's sanity.

Philip's fair body was embalmed, his heart cut out and sent to Flanders as he had wished. And now began a hideous pilgrimage by night. Men carried torches, monks prayed, sword in hand. Juana, carrying his last child within her, kept the coffin ever in sight. At daylight they rested, but never at a nunnery; and the guard had orders to keep all women at a distance.

Whenever the whim returned, the coffin was opened to see if the slow march of corruption still tarried long enough for a last embrace. And as if this were not horrible enough, bubonic plague stalked behind, unseen but never forgotten, and hurried them from Burgos to Torquemada, from Torquemada to Hornillos, thence to Tortoles, and on to Arcos. By then the last child of Juana and Philip had seen the light of day, and Ferdinand had persuaded his daughter to surrender the government completely to him, which she did willingly, unprotestingly, being without a thought or a moment's leisure from her watch over the Fair Philip's corpse.

It is almost incredible, yet at this late stage her father Ferdinand and Henry VII of England wished to profit by this poor Juana, still an asset in their eyes, albeit a wasting asset, in the game of politics. It was suggested by the father and eagerly considered by Henry that a marriage be arranged between the mad woman and the Tudor King. Henry said that he was quite willing to overlook the madness, since Juana had well proved her fecundity, and it was a fecund woman that the Tudors most needed. Had the plan gone through we might have had Juana's son rather than her sister's daughter Mary on our throne. But Juana refused, for she was waiting hourly for the moment when the Fair Philip should rise from his coffin and resume marital relations.

At Arcos the deterioration in her condition continued. One day she would throw everything at hand into the faces of her maids-in-waiting; then for days on end she sat silent, refusing to change her clothing or bed linen, refusing to speak, waiting always for the decaying corpse to sit up in the coffin and return her kiss. Such were the latter days of this mother of two Emperors, two Queens of Portugal, and one of France, a Queen of Denmark, a Queen of Bohemia and Hungary. Such was the mother of all those crowned heads within whom was hidden the poison which devastated her life, the poison which mocked the Hapsburg dynasty and crucified all Europe for generations.

On the morning of Good Friday in 1555, after forty-six years of seclusion, having recited the Creed, cross in hand, helped by Francisco de Borja who administered all the consoling rites of the Church, this poor woman cried 'Jesus Crucified, help me', and died. But her germ-plasm lived on in her son, the future Emperor, and was so conserved and so concentrated by politically propitious and biologically disastrous marriages that Carlos the Bewitched had seven of his eight great-grandparents directly descended from Juana la Loca, the Mad, the original Crazy Jane.

CHAPTER FOUR

— ❧ —

CONCENTRATING THE POISON

MOST families have skeletons in the cupboard; most of us have an ancestor or two who was mad. That Juana la Loca was a schizophrenic is only half the tragedy which was to deprive the bewitched Carlos of his modicum of health and happiness. The other half of the tragedy can be stated most clearly in statistics.

A man's ancestors in the third, fourth and fifth generations comprise eight, sixteen and thirty-two relationships respectively. Thus Carlos's parents, like everyone else, each had fifty-six such relationships in their family trees, or one hundred and twelve between them.

These one hundred and twelve relationships in their case were shared between only thirty-eight individuals.

Of Carlos's mother's fifty-six ancestors, forty-eight were also ancestors of his father.

Of the thirty-two women in the fifth generation, that is the sixteen of one parent and sixteen of the other, twelve were descendants of the mad Isabella, mother of Isabella the Catholic.

In the two family trees the name of Juana la Loca occurs eight times, the names of her two sons nineteen times. Seven out of the eight great-grandparents of Carlos II descended from Juana la Loca. No wonder he was bewitched, possessed of devils — however primitive psychiatrists may have thought fit to explain his condition.

The Hapsburgs thought of their marriages as a key to political greatness; they did not realize that the key also fitted the gates of a biological hell. They founded their political strategy on a profound belief in the value of inbreeding, a habit which may of course bring good results. After all, Cleopatra was a remarkable woman, though not necessarily very like her Shakespearian or

Shavian portraits, and she was the product of generations of brother-sister marriages. Unfortunately, by the marriage of Juana la Loca and Philip the Fair, a poisonous brew had been concocted, and for generation after generation it was to be concentrated by habitual incest.

In the end, only when a passing favour to a country wench or to a still uncontaminated city ma'am diluted the poison, was there some chance of normal growth. The bastard, luckier than his legitimate brothers, received only half the dose of Hapsburg poison, and often survived in reasonable health.

This mingling of Juana's heredity with Philip's produced the strangest mixture of near-great and frankly pathological. Their son, the Emperor Charles V, might have been the man of destiny. If anyone could have prevented the splitting asunder of religious Europe it was probably he. Had his strength of will equalled his good intentions he might have forced the Church of Rome, inadequate Popes and infuriated friars notwithstanding, to reform itself in time.

But he had inherited a body worthy of his least satisfactory ancestors; backward as a child, defective in speech and subject to fits; teeth which would not meet to masticate the immense burdens that unnatural gluttony threw against them; chronic indigestion; horrible gout setting a barrier of excruciating pain between his intentions and his actions. All this worked together to produce a pathological inability to make up his mind and a tendency to religious gloom which militated against clear political thinking.

Yet with all this and with a full knowledge of the mistakes he made, we cannot but regard him as one of the greatest men of his time, for though the shadow of his mother and great-grandmother lay upon him, there was still something of his grandmother in him too. But the great unpremeditated crime which the Emperor Charles committed against posterity was his marriage.

This marriage was naturally of crucial importance to the Hapsburgs and to Europe. Nothing could show more clearly what marriage meant in those days than the catalogue of brides who were suggested, discussed, and rejected, before Isabella of Portugal finally won the prize. Negotiations began early, when Charles was a year and a few months old. He was already heir to the Spanish throne, and Louis XII of France offered his daughter,

Claude, with Milan, Naples and even Brittany as dowry. But this proposal was soon dropped.

By 1506 the Burgundians were negotiating an alliance with the English Royal House, and preliminaries were arranged in 1508 for the eight-year-old Charles to marry Mary, sister of the future Henry VIII. This was to strengthen their position when the Spanish succession came their way. By 1515 attention had once more swung towards France. Claude was now French Queen and wife of Francis I; the Burgundians therefore bargained for her sister, although they knew that Charles's grandfather Ferdinand was secretly trying to get her for Charles's brother. But a year later, by hinting at a close alliance with several of France's enemies, Charles's ambassadors made Francis I sufficiently uneasy to agree to a marriage between him and Louise, his infant daughter by Queen Claude. The mother being no longer available, no doubt her infant daughter would do as well! If the child died, Charles was to have a yet unborn sister, and, if both these failed, then Renée, Francis's sister-in-law. As Charles was now seventeen and his suggested bride less than a year old, to say nothing of her substitute being yet unborn, it is hard to take this plan very seriously, but, since it suited them politically, Francis I and the French pretended to do so, while even Charles himself had twinges of conscience about it later.

There followed a monstrous farce: at the Field of the Cloth of Gold, Henry VIII of England and Francis swore eternal loyalty and brotherhood, yet behind the scenes, in spite of Charles's existing betrothal to Francis's daughter, Henry discussed once more his marriage with an English princess.

Soon, however, the direction of Charles's matrimonial glances was to be completely and permanently changed. Though King of Spain, he was not yet Spanish. The true patriots of Spain were in revolt against him. The Comuneros in 1520 laid down the principles on which a Spanish king should live and govern, and, although they were crushed, it was on those principles for the most part that Charles became a truly Spanish ruler. The first of them was that Charles should marry according to the desire of his kingdoms; by which the Comuneros meant that a King of the Spains should not ally himself in marriage with hereditary enemies such as France and England, but with a princess nearer home.

This princess could only be Isabella of Portugal. They looked back, these rebels, to Ferdinand and Isabella and, in imitation of them, forward to Charles and another Isabella.

At this time there can be no doubt that Charles was still toying with the idea of an English marriage and that in doing so he had a guilty conscience about breaking the existing contract with the French King's daughter; and indeed he went so far as to request the Pope's absolution in advance for the 'possible future sin' of breaking his word, although he did not specify the contemplated breach of faith. Henry VIII, with Wolsey at his elbow, was using this promise of an English alliance to drive a wedge between the Emperor and the Francis with whom he had sworn eternal brotherhood on the Field of the Cloth of Gold. It was not to be; Spain was penetrating deeper every year into her King's mind and even into his heart.

Some time in 1525, Charles put down his thoughts on paper in order to clear his mind, and by great good luck the documents survive for us to read. After considering his difficult position with wars on his hands and no money to pay for them, he wrote:

> Taking all these things into account ... I can think of no better way in which to improve my condition than by going myself to Italy. Doubts may be raised because of the money needed ... In order to overcome these difficulties I think the best way would be to hurry on my marriage to the Infanta of Portugal ... For the money which is to be sent with her is a very large sum in actual bullion ... My marriage will be a good reason to demand a great sum of money from the Spanish kingdoms ... In this way I ought to be able to set out for Italy with the greatest splendour and honour this very autumn.

Thus, Charles considered his marriage as primarily a way of buying a first-class ticket to Italy. There were other considerations of course, and particularly that Isabella would be a regent acceptable to his Spanish subjects during his absence. Personal inclination did not enter at all into the transaction until afterwards, but in spite of the marriage being the result of the motives typical of the period, love was not excluded in the end. Charles and Isabella are a bright exception to the grim experiences of

facing: JUANA LA LOCA

most contemporary married royalty. That the marriage was far happier and more intimate than usual for the contracting parties, adds to the irony: alas, the bride and groom were first cousins. The marriage took place in Lent, and both the *incest* and the season required a papal dispensation. This presented no difficulty and nobody considered the incest any more important than the unsuitable season.

Thus Doña Juana la Loca's son married Doña Juana la Loca's niece, and made more of their marriage than most royal pairs. But the inexorable laws of heredity cannot be suspended by even the happiest marriages. Their son Philip II inherited every one of Charles's failings, both physical and mental, many times magnified. Nor should it be forgotten that in all these generations the offspring we describe is the best of the brood. Philip II's brother died young, and a sister suffered from hallucinations and puerperal insanity. Another sister, more nearly normal, unfortunately, permitted the inbreeding to continue.

Philip II, called the Prudent because he could never make up his mind about anything, had his father's jaw, gout, indecisive will, epilepsy, religious melancholy. What he did not inherit was his father's good fortune in advisers. The disciples of Erasmus had gone, their place taken by Jesuits and Inquisitors; this is probably why Philip's part in religious history is indefensible, although Charles's part had simply been indecisive. That he could never make up his mind was the secret of his seeming prudence. 'Leave it to the mercy of time no longer, Your Majesty,' cried Don Juan de Austria, 'for having done so has brought us to the pretty pass we are in.' 'Your Majesty spends so long considering your undertakings,' wrote Pope Pius V, 'that when the moment to perform them comes, the occasion has passed and the money all been spent.'

Dr Marañon sums up the case of Philip II as that of a man who, apart from the faults inevitably arising from his education and his epoch, had a special flaw in his character which came from his ancestors rather than from his environment.

> I refer to his hesitancy ... one can see a retiring disposition which came to him by psychological inheritance from his great-great-grandmother, Isabella of Portugal ... This trait

facing: THE EMPEROR CHARLES V

was aggravated in Juana the Mad, and was also very obvious in his father; the Emperor Charles V passed through phases of tremendous spiritual prostration ... Philip II inherited it from Charles ... He was continually in a state of hesitation, and had no expansive or optimistic moments ...

Philip II contracted four marriages, all of them consanguineous: two of his wives were cousins, one an aunt and one a niece. It is the last which concerns us, the marriage with his niece Maria, whose great-grandmother was of course the same person as her husband's grandmother, Juana la Loca. There were six children, five of whom died in childhood, while the sixth, our Carlos's grandfather, lived to become Philip III.

Of him nothing need be said here, save that in due course he too married a cousin, and produced Carlos's father, Philip IV.

CHAPTER FIVE

— ⁂ —

MOTHER AND FATHER

WE have followed Carlos through four generations in the loins of his forebears. Philip I, bringing with him the Hapsburg jaw and the Burgundian lip, marries Juana the Mad. Their son, the Emperor Charles V, with the burden of this inheritance keeping him from true greatness, concentrates the poison for his successors by marrying a cousin. Their son, Philip II, marries a niece and produces the useless Philip III who, in his turn, marries a cousin. Thus we come to Carlos's father, Philip IV, all four of whose grandparents are now seen to be direct descendants of the unfortunate Juana and of her grandparents, Isabella, the schizophrenic, and Juan II, the ineffectual.

Let us take up the father's life in 1643, eighteen years before Carlos, his last child, was born. Philip was then thirty-eight. We know what he was like from the 'Fraga portrait' which Velazquez painted in that Roman, fig-producing town on the borders of Aragon and Catalonia, where the King was campaigning in yet another disastrous civil war. It was painted as a gift to his beloved Queen, another Isabella, recovering at that time from the latest of her miscarriages.

On May 18th of that year, Spain's Golden Age came decisively to an end. The battle of Rocroy in the Ardennes saw her not merely defeated but annihilated for ever as a military power. The Spanish infantry formation, the *tercio*, had for generations been the finest in the world; on the other hand, the cavalry had been neglected; and as for artillery, for some reason the making of ordnance was regarded as an occupation for Jesuits, and at this time all the cannon at Spain's disposal were being produced by one Jesuit father with eight pupils. And now her infantry were gone. Those left alive at the end of the day at Rocroy owed their fortune to the chivalry of d'Enghien, later the Great Condé, who, unable to bear watching the useless slaughter any longer, sent trumpeters to offer the Spanish remnants honourable terms of surrender such as might be offered to the garrison of an invested town. This saved some lives but no honour.

The legend of Spanish superiority on the field of battle could not survive, and from that day the substance behind the Spanish façade vanished. Spain, still the most extensive empire in the world, was for anyone to plunder. Philip was still the Planet King, but, as Quevedo said, he was only Philip the Great in the same way as a hole becomes great as more and more earth is taken from it. And the only people who succeeded in remaining blind to what had happened were the Spaniards themselves.

Philip, prostrated by military defeat, worn out by domestic misfortune, torn by pangs of conscience, now stumbled upon spiritual help from an unexpected source. A humble but able nun who had gained considerable reputation by a series of works of devotion and mysticism, had founded a small nunnery in the poverty stricken village of Agreda in Aragon, of which she became the Abbess. On July 10th, 1643, seven weeks after Rocroy, Philip, on his way to repair the national unity in Aragon, paid Sor Maria de Agreda the visit which was destined to be the turning point of his life. We have already seen Philip writing to her on the death of one son and the birth of another.

In the King's first letter to her, he explains that he has written on the left-hand of a folded sheet of paper so that she may reply on the right-hand side, and send his letters back to him. In this way, says the King, he can be quite certain that the correspondence will never be seen by other eyes. Fortunately for us, and for Philip himself, he did not take into account that death almost always supervenes before the writer remembers to destroy such secret documents, nor, apparently, did he realize that even dedicated holy women take copies of interesting correspondence. In consequence, we know in intimate detail the pilgrimage, through more than twenty years, of one of the most shattered souls ever to stray from the narrow way and struggle to return. The psychiatrist's couch has seldom provided such a coherent account of the dark night through which so many human beings have to journey.

In this first letter, Philip expresses the main idea which

dominated his mind. The greatest favour God could give him, he tells Sor Maria, would be to afflict him personally rather than Spain, since it is his sins, his adulteries and sexual promiscuity, that have called down God's wrath; they are the true explanation of Rocroy, of Portugal's rebellion, of chaos at home. If only Sor Maria and her nuns will pray incessantly to keep him chaste, begging God to punish *him* and not the nation when he fails, things may still improve. Indeed there are signs of improvement already: the treasure fleet from Mexico has got home safely, Oran has been relieved, he has just enough money to pay for arms for the new campaign in Aragon – and for all this he thanks Sor Maria whose prayers are already doing what he cannot do. Alas, in spite of the devoted aid from Agreda, the God of Vengeance was scarcely ever to relax during the rest of Philip's life, and Spain as well as Philip was to be punished even more severely than before.

Nor was there to be any lasting improvement in Philip's personal conduct. Far from it; just a year after these events, the beloved Isabella died, and her broken-hearted widower plunged nightly into the most disreputable quarters of Madrid in a desperate effort to forget. Isabella had died very much alone; the King was still away, and she would not allow her son, Baltazar Carlos, nor her daughter, Maria Teresa, to approach her bed, lest they too should die. Spanish Queens are common, she said, but Spanish princes and princesses rare.

She had become ill on September 28th, and the symptoms were described as an erysipelas of the face and throat. The six doctors who wrestled with the disease attributed it to her having drunk chocolate and quintessence of cinnamon in an effort to increase the natural warmth of her stomach. In spite of bleeding her eight times, they did not succeed in killing her for seven days. Later medical opinion inclines to the belief that the disease was diphtheria.

When Philip wrote to Sor Maria about his loss, he contrasted it with the successful campaign he had just concluded in Aragon and seemed to find evidence that the punishment for his sins was already being transferred from Spain to himself. Both he and Sor Maria are satisfied, moreover, that God is just and that they should accept – nay, even rejoice in – His judgments; but one feels that Philip must even then have been waiting miserably for the next just judgment and wondering through whom he would be made to suffer.

He begged Sor Maria to commend to God 'those two angels which He has given me for children', and to ask God to enlighten him as to the best course he can take with them. With Isabella dead, it is clear that Baltazar Carlos and Maria Teresa were all that he had left, and of course now that no other son would be born the future of the Seamless Garment depended on Baltazar; and in two more years this only son, the seventeen-year-old heir of the Spanish Hapsburgs, was to die.

Only two months earlier, Baltazar had been betrothed to his cousin, daughter of the Emperor and his father's niece, and now this alliance between cousins was frustrated by death. It had been designed to keep the Spanish and Austrian branches of the Hapsburgs together; and so there was nothing for it now but that the uncle should marry the niece. Philip became betrothed to Mariana of Austria, so lately intended for his own son. It was satisfactory from two points of view: it kept France out and ensured a Spanish-Austrian matrimonial alliance; and it solved, or was a step on the way to solving, Philip's duty of replacing Baltazar Carlos with another male heir to the Spanish throne; but this uncle-niece marriage brought final biological destruction to the Spanish Hapsburgs, by concentrating still further what was already lethal in their germ-plasm.

When Philip married Mariana of Austria in 1647, the consummation of the marriage had of course to be delayed. The bride was only thirteen at the time of the espousal, but fear, lest France should step in, induced the Spanish Council of State to insist upon her being transported to Spain before she was nubile. Thereafter, from the time the marriage was known to have been consummated, the young Queen's oestrous cycle was watched and commented on by all the gossip-mongers of Madrid. If the natural course of events was delayed so much as a few days, speculation was rife, and false rumours circulated nearly every month.

What sort of person was Mariana, Philip's wife and niece, later to be Carlos's mother? Philip died when Carlos was only four, but Mariana lived on to dominate and bedevil most of his life.

When she arrived in Spain, a healthy girl of fifteen, she seems to have reacted very normally to her earliest experiences. We are told that she found the dwarfs and fools who accompanied the cortège sent to meet her very funny indeed, and that she laughed heartily. For this she was reproved and told that Spanish Queens were not allowed such noisy outlets to their amusement, and it is altogether to her credit that she found this reproval quite as funny as the dwarfs. She had probably not been told that the husband she was about to meet never let one muscle of his countenance relax in public, that Philip's face was a mask behind which every emotion was repressed. He is said to have smiled only three times in his life.

A curious custom which we will see repeated with Mariana's son decreed that Spanish Kings should meet their brides, and even marry them, in some dilapidated hamlet without amenities and without provender. It is sometimes stated that this custom was adopted because the place where a royal marriage took place was usually freed from all taxation for an unspecified future term of years, so that it would have been very deleterious to the royal exchequer if a reasonably wealthy town were chosen for the purpose.

Whatever the reason, the first meeting took place at the dreary desert village of Navalcarnero and, in conformity with Spanish custom, the bridegroom's presence was kept a secret from the bride-to-be. She was entertained at a comedy before supper, at which Philip, disguised so that everybody knew him immediately, spied on her and assessed her charms. He was well pleased.

Next day, surrounded by courtiers, he openly made his appearance, introduced himself, prevented Mariana from kneeling to him, led her to mass and marriage, and thence to bullfights and theatricals, and at last by coach to spend a honeymoon at the Escorial. Mariana, be it remembered, was fifteen, and her husband-uncle forty-four. There followed an endless round of court functions, hunting, comedies, masques, bullfights, illuminations. Philip wrote enthusiastically to Maria de Agreda promising to reform and to concentrate his remaining energies on producing a legitimate heir for Spain.

Mariana found court life amusing and particularly enjoyed the company of her husband's daughter Maria Teresa. It was soon clear that the five years between them could be bridged more easily than the twenty-nine between the young bride and Philip. The passage from niece to wife did not prove easy. Quite soon Philip was having to ask Maria de Agreda's spiritual help against his roving sexual instinct, and quite soon he was not describing Mariana in his letters as his wife but as his niece, and more often than not lumped her and Maria Teresa together as 'the girls'. How could a tired libertine suffering agonies from religious remorse get much companionship from a healthy, selfish 'teen-ager'?

Two years after the marriage, Margarita Maria was born, a bitter disappointment because of her sex. Philip was once more caught up in his night prowlings, and Mariana was by now longing for home. It was not a marriage of true minds. As so often happened, the shadows of Spain began to appear in the once rosy girl's countenance and character: she became cold, avaricious, unloving and unlovable. Even the Madrid rabble was quick to see the change and to substitute hate for love. And all the time, the wise, all-seeing nun knew what was bound to happen in spite of endless exhortations to the King and endless prayers to God.

Elsewhere, the strain might have resolved itself in a variety of ways. In some courts there would have been scenes, perhaps even unfaithfulness on both sides instead of on one side. Hot anger or hot passion might have poured out their streams of lava to relieve the inner tensions. Not so in the Spanish Court of Philip IV. Sexual intercourse must be maintained for the production of an heir, but no other incentive existed between the ill-matched couple, and no alternative was thinkable for the queen, now in her twenties. On her and in her an ice age descended, all the brood of chill bitterness proliferated in her soul.

Outside, the gossips continued their gossip: the Queen was a fortnight late; the Queen had miscarried; the Queen was definitely pregnant. The wars continued. There was no money. And then in 1657 Mariana, now a frigid politician with only her body in Spain, her soul, her desire, her hope back in Austria, produced a male child to whom was given the ironical name of Felipe Próspero. With his birth she had done all that could be expected of her; henceforth she had no interest except in her native land and no conception of duty but to thwart France in every way.

But she was only twenty-three and she was up against the wisest and, some would say, the wiliest of monarchs, the twenty-one-year-old Louis XIV.

In spite of the fact that the terrible Thirty Years War had ended long ago, Spain and France were still at war, though both countries equally longed for peace. By 1656 the French ambassadors were hinting that if Maria Teresa were married to Louis there might be an end to the traditional enmity. Mariana received letter after letter from her father begging her to prevent such a possibility. Against her cold will, reinforced by disillusion and hatred of the life she was for ever doomed to experience, she had nothing but the hesitancy of a husband, by now unable to make up his mind on anything. But she was defeated in this: the Peace of the Pyrenees ended the war, and the Spanish princess became Queen of France. Mariana was colder, bitterer, more withdrawn than ever.

During these years Mariana had to put up with poverty to a degree hardly credible had we not the contemporary accounts to prove it. The ubiquitous gossip-writer, Barrionuevo, reports on October 11th, 1656, that the normal rations for the staff at the palace have been suspended for two and a half months as the King has no money at all. He describes a deplorable meal served to the Infanta Maria Teresa on the feast of St Francis. First they served a capon which she ordered to be taken away as it stank like a dead dog. They substituted a chicken on pieces of bread, so covered with flies that she pushed it away, nearly upsetting it on to the floor.

A fortnight later Barrionuevo reports that the Queen one day asked for pastries and commented on their not having been served for some days. She was told that the pastrycook would not supply the palace until a large outstanding bill had been paid. She removed a ring from her finger and ordered a servant to exchange it for pastries wherever he could find them, whereat her buffoon, Manuelillo de Gante, told her to put the ring on again and gave the servant a copper to buy some tarts 'so that this lady can finish her dinner'.

On November 28th, 1657, the King, who normally ate fish on the Vigil of all the festivals of the Mother of God, could eat nothing but eggs; and more eggs on the Vigil of the Feast of the

Presentation, as his servants had not a single coin with which to buy anything. In May 1658, the King's victualler is reported to have said that he had not one penny to buy provisions for the royal table.

While this uncomfortable domestic situation continued, the disillusioned mother was in daily agony over the physical condition of Felipe Próspero. It is hard to assess the nature or the strength of the maternal instinct at a time when so large a proportion of children died and where their survival was chiefly valued, in these circles, for political reasons. But even so there must have been some animal feeling involved. To see the child daily clinging to life although afflicted in every limb and organ must have been yet a new reason for hardening her heart against all concerned in decreeing her fate. In letters to Maria de Agreda, the father, asking for the prayers of the nunnery that the child might be spared to reign, added the pathetic request that if God would not grant him this, at least let him die in childhood and not survive to manhood at all. Philip, unmoved by the massacre of innocents, could never get over the loss of the adolescent Baltazar Carlos.

But poor Felipe Próspero was doomed from birth to epilepsy, scabs and suppurations. We possess ample data about these: there are Philip's agonizing confidences to Maria de Agreda; the gossip paragraphs of the irrepressible Barrionuevo; and a long and well-written case history, full of good observation and description, in the folio of Dr Bravo. But we shall have so much to do with sickness later that it would be wearisome to linger now over Felipe Próspero's sufferings. In November 1661, he died. A few days later he was born again in Carlos.

We have reached the moment when Carlos's history as a separate being begins. We have sketched the conditions wherein the stuff of which his body and mind were composed had been carried in the bodies of his ancestors through almost two centuries. No stock-breeder, intent on breeding a worthy animal, would have mated any of his ancestors in the pairs which lust for political power had dictated. True, these marriages had brought into being a mighty empire, but it was a ramshackle affair which could only have been kept together by almost superhuman rulers. The very means by which it had been accumulated ensured that its rulers should be subhuman.

Nor was it only the tainted royal stock that was subhuman. The same mistaken ideals which led it to biological disaster existed among the aristocracy. Inbreeding had created a degraded sort of human animal unable to face the responsibilities of the real world.

It is almost impossible to believe that men behaved as the Spanish Court did throughout this period. Spain was starving, her armies were bleeding to death all over the world, and great areas of land were out of cultivation. The bread was inedible and meat too dear to be bought. A run of bad harvests and incessant bad weather brought illness to plants, beasts and men. Bubonic plague entered the ports and was fought by savage and ignorant means. In the midst of this tragic desert, a Court amused itself with incessant comedies, masques, bullfights, mass slaughters of wild animals; and vast sums of money were spent on festivities and religious occasions. Favoured courtiers amassed lucrative offices and rivalled one another in the extravagant presents they gave to the popular drabs of the moment.

Whereas most Courts have been articulated and organized with a view to carrying on the government and life of a State, so that the civilian chains of command have some relevance to the realities of existence and the necessities of everyday, the Court of Spain had no other articulation, no co-ordinating network combining man and man into a recognizable pattern, but etiquette. There were rights but no duties, and these rights were mostly concerned with unrealities; what men demanded of one another were obsessional acts; they lived together in a world of fantasy. Who sat on what and where, who shook hands and when, who took off his hat and in the presence of whom — these were the questions which concerned them, not defeats abroad and starvation at home. There was no disaster which could move even the more intelligent, or the less dishonest, to act. No one failed to see that the government was a disgrace to civilized man, but no one possessed the energy or the faith to go in search of change.

And in the centre there was Carlos. Not the least fantastic element in the general psychosis was that this almost imbecile nonentity occupied a vital position. In the world of reality he was less than nothing, but in the world of fantasy he was supreme. Nobody can understand how powerful over the human mind the belief in the divinity of kings can be, unless he has watched its effects where the king has been an idiot.

Fantasy is essential to nations as to men, for there is little point in possessing the gift of life except that it permits us to dream. But there is an inevitable rule binding all nations: their fantasy cannot be imposed on others except by the expenditure of blood and the use of steel. After Rocroy nobody took Spain at her own valuation, for a wakeful man does not fear the weapons which another dreams are in his possession. While Spain could win Lepanto, she could captivate the world with Don Quixote; but when she lost Rocroy no one took seriously her obsessive etiquette, her play-acting out of place; creativeness had become psychosis.

Thus Carlos inherited a problem without a solution. It was more than that, it was a sacred duty which could not be performed. He had to prevent the inviolable body of the Spanish Empire, the Seamless Garment, from being torn in pieces and distributed to the greedy robbers waiting for him to die. From the day of his birth they were waiting for his death.

He had nothing with which to fight, neither sound body nor sound mind, yet he blundered through his life trying to do what was right. He had so little brains or knowledge that he never knew there was no solution. *There* lay his inverted greatness.

CHAPTER SIX

CARLOS CHRISTENED

'MOST beautiful in features, large head, dark skin, and somewhat overplump.' The description went out to all the foreign capitals through the usual diplomatic channels.

It might be true! But to certain people, notably Louis XIV, it was essential to know whether it was true or not. If the infant Carlos was likely to grow up and propagate, then Louis's policies would follow one road, but if, as all the world had begun to take for granted, the Spanish dynasty was coming to an end from sheer physical debility, then Louis would have quite different plans for the future.

Louis himself and his wife, Philip IV of Spain's daughter, had recently rejoiced in the birth of an heir, whose sexual attributes had been given the full glare of publicity, usual in French royal circles, and shocking to Spanish opinion. The birth of Carlos had been quite another matter. Only the people most concerned had been present, and no one but the attendants had seen the naked infant. It might well be, thought Louis therefore, that the infant was not a boy after all. A male heir was so necessary to Spain that the Spaniards were quite capable of disguising their continued lack of one. Anyway, Louis was taking no chances. He sat down and wrote instructions to his ambassador; and he began to arrange for deputations to be dispatched to Madrid, seemingly for quite other purposes, really to find out the facts. Was Carlos a male? Was he healthy? Louis and all Europe must know.

Meanwhile, according to the doctrines of the day, everything was being done to secure a normal beginning for this precious life. Dr Bravo and the other court physicians had for some time been busy organizing the young prince's milk supplies. A posse of wet-nurses had been assembled. The authority relied upon in this matter was the great obstetrician, Aetius. A wet-nurse for a prince, he tells us, must not be less than twenty years old nor more than forty. She should have had two or three children. She must be healthy, of good habits and of a good size. Her breasts must be ample but only moderately productive, since if the supply is over-abundant some will be left and go bad. She must of course be chaste, sober, modest, cheerful and not subject to fits of melancholy. Spanish doctors added that there must be no Jewish or Moorish blood in her ancestry. It was not at all easy to find suitable candidates, and a great deal of research, particularly into genealogy, was involved.

While the chosen wet-nurse was installed in the palace, two or three substitute nurses called 'de respecto' were kept handy in case of emergency. Almost anything might indicate the advisability of a change, and by the time Carlos was weaned four years later he had had thirty-one donors in all. Any upset, however far removed from the infant's alimentary system, was apt to be laid at the door of the wet-nurse of the moment, and the palace had already suffered from inconveniences of this nature. Philip, who took the greatest interest in these matters, had had a scene with one of Felipe Próspero's nurses in which the nurse had stood up to him with admirable spirit.

Poor little Felipe Próspero had been having bad nights, which is not surprising, since from birth he had been no more than a cluster of diseases; and his father accused the nurse of being responsible.

> Sire [she replied], I have three children, the loveliest in the court, nurtured at my breasts, flourishing on my milk and care; when they cried I rocked them; I cured their rashes and pimples with my saliva; they slept on my breast, and I gave them love; I ate at my usual time seasoned food. Here they give me everything without spices, seasoning or salt; I spend the nights awake, and if I must rest I am forced to retire to an attic; they lift up my skirts to see if I have my periods; the fuss and noise is great; my milk, with so many annoyances, cannot be so good. This is how things are, and it seems there is no remedy; as far as I am concerned, I do what I ought and all I want is to serve Your Majesty.

Barrionuevo the gossip-writer who reports this, adds his comment: 'All I say is certain; the nurse is no fool.'

In spite of the disagreeable conditions, there were always

plenty of candidates for so honourable a position. They put up with the fidgeting of the King and the numerous inspections of the doctors. It is only to be expected that Dr Bravo once again found occasion to ask a question which really needed no answer, and to answer it at very great length. One of the chosen ladies who took up her duties forty-four days after she had herself become a mother, was found six days later to have a slight discharge altogether normal in the circumstances. Should she be allowed to continue? Might she not endanger the health, if not the life, of her charge? After many paragraphs of well-balanced argument, Dr Bravo decided that no harm could be done.

Meanwhile, preparations for Carlos's christening were being feverishly completed. Every detail must be performed in accordance with protocol. The slightest deviation might mean that someone would take offence, and it was hoped that there would be no repetition of the disagreeable mishaps which had clouded the baptism of Felipe Próspero.

Everybody had his own traditional role. Thus, certain grandees had the privilege of carrying one or other of the objects required for the ceremony; the Duque de Medina de las Torres, head of the Guzmans and the richest and most intelligent of the grandees, carried the baptismal cup. Next came the Almirante de Castilla, another intellectual who disliked politics and kept as far as he could from anything to do with government. He carried the sacred candle. He had earned fame a few years before by giving a banquet to the Duke of Gramont, when the Duke came from Louis XIV to arrange the marriage with Maria Teresa which was to abolish the Pyrenees. There were served five hundred dishes of meat and three hundred entrées and sweets; according to the Spanish account the French were astonished at the ceremonial courtesy, the cleanliness and neatness displayed by the Spanish cuisine; but Gramont's own account was that it had been 'a superb and magnificent feast, Spanish style, that is to say, pernicious and quite uneatable'.

The ceremonial napkin was carried by the Condestable de Castilla, an unpopular young military officer, who had once been incarcerated for eight years in the common jail for killing a man and freeing two of his servants from prison. He had made a scene at Felipe Próspero's baptism in the following manner: it seems that the crush of people was so great that a staircase gave way; this disarranged the procession as it left the Chapel, and in particular prevented the Duque de Bejar from taking his place and bearing away the 'mazapan'. The mazapan was not a sweetmeat, but a lump of breadcrumb on which the officiating ecclesiastic wiped his fingers after anointing the child with holy oil. The bread was enclosed in a highly decorated receptacle made of marzipan and carried on a richly worked piece of needlework. It seems to have been an object which evoked singular curiosity though little reverence. As the Duque de Bejar was unable to be its bearer, Philip was asked what should be done, and he told the master of ceremonies to ask the Condestable de Castilla to substitute. This gentleman replied that he was sorry but he had an injured arm. Philip, furious, repeated his order, whereupon he replied that 'the Condestables de Castilla are too exalted to fill the gaps and voids left by others.' That night the Court Mayor called on him with a royal decree of banishment to the town of Berlanga; but he was soon forgiven, since Philip was always partial to those who committed sins of pride.

The Duque de Alburquerque carried the ewer, and the Duque de Terranova the salt-cellar. Last came the Duque de Pastrana carrying on this occasion the famous mazapan. It was made in the shape of a castle with gold and silver ornamentation. So assiduous had Pastrana been in showing it to the ladies, and so meddlesome had the ladies been, that by the time it reached the Chapel this masterpiece of the pastrycooks' art had fallen into ruin.

We are not told in the account of the baptism where the mazapan was eventually deposited, but we may suppose that the grandee responsible for its safety had to take particular care that, until he handed it over to the priest to put it under lock and key, or perhaps to dispose of it in the handiest way, viz. by eating it, nobody appropriated it for improper purposes.

The chrism is a mixture of oil and balm used to anoint the infant. Owing to its sacrosanct character, it was in those days much coveted by certain ill-intentioned persons; hence, the drops of chrism deposited on the breadcrumb within the mazapan might well be stolen. Those who, having been spurned, wanted to transform hate into love, might achieve this, according to Martinez Delrio, by kissing the person in question either with a

facing: PHILIP IV OF SPAIN

morsel of the Blessed Sacrament in the mouth or by first anointing the lips with chrism. How the reluctant person was to be brought near enough to the morsel of wafer or the inunction of chrism, we are not told.

Philip's place in the Royal Chapel was inside a tabernacle of rich curtains, whence he could see all without being seen. This seclusion was in part a tribute to his rank, but also, alas, a necessity arising from the inconveniences involved in his numerous diseases. Near him were three silk cushions for the disrobing and robing of the prince.

The arrival of the grandees, courtiers, gentlemen, and fair ladies must have been as tedious as it was superb, and it was with as much relief as excitement that the resplendent congregation finally saw entering the aisle a glazed chair, carried by six attendants, in which sat the prince's nurse, Doña Maria Engracia de Toledo, Marquesa de los Vélez, with the infant Carlos himself, swathed in blue, resting upon her knees. And after her came the godmother, the prettiest sight of all, the ten-year-old Infanta Doña Margarita, not dressed as Velazquez painted her but still a picture of gracefulness, grave, petite. Behind her came the greatest aristocrat, the Duque de Alba, side by side with the prince's *menina* (court attendant), exquisitely dressed.

Now all eyes were on the font. Santo Domingo had been baptized at this font, and it was always transported hither and thither on royal occasions. The Patriarch of the Indies, a harmless old man of the highest dignities, who was performing the ceremony, asked the Infanta godmother in what name the child was to be baptized, and she replied: 'Carlos José and the other names on this paper.' The Master of Ceremonies unfolded the paper and read the sixteen further names chosen with the greatest care to honour those whose benevolence was hoped for, whether among the heavenly hosts or the church militant. Jordan water was poured over the wizened head, the Duque de Alba helping Margarita to sustain the infant's weight. Margarita, kneeling by the altar, offered her brother to God; the procession reformed and the Chapel emptied. Carlos Segundo had been made a child of God, a member of Christ and an inheritor of the kingdom of heaven.

Philip, his father, continued to believe in the infant's good health and good prospects.

facing: MARIANA OF AUSTRIA, WIFE OF PHILIP IV

CHAPTER SEVEN

A FATHER DIES

HAD Philip become blinded to the possibility of further disaster? Or were the reports sent out by ambassadors to their respective sovereigns prejudiced in the other direction?

For Philip it was essential that Carlos should be healthy; for Louis and others a great deal depended on his being fragile and unlikely to grow up. We cannot believe that Philip was deliberately lying when he reported to Sor Maria de Agreda, for it is most unlikely that a man in the habit of confessing all sins and withholding no confidences would falsify such a matter. A month after the birth he was writing of Carlos as 'famoso y lucido', a month later 'muy sano y lucido', and from then on 'muy sanico', 'en buena disposición', 'lindo, lucido y sano', and 'todos buenos'.

On the other hand, the special investigators sent by Louis on all manner of pretexts told quite a different story. Three weeks after Carlos was born, the first attempt was made to ascertain the truth. Louis sent Jean Joubert to Madrid to convey his deep regrets at the death of Felipe Próspero. He was courteously received and had no less than three audiences with the King. He had brought a picture of the new Dauphin to show his uncle. Philip admired it very much and gave Joubert a jewel worth five hundred ducats for his trouble; but all hints that Joubert would so like to see little Carlos fell on deaf ears. Joubert left Madrid with no information whatsoever.

Next month, it was Philip's move. He sent to Paris a certain Don Cristóbal de Gaviria to congratulate Louis on the birth of the Dauphin, and Don Cristóbal was evidently charged to paint Carlos's health in glowing terms. This he seems to have overdone to such an extent that Louis became more dubious than ever. Although it was just possible that the unhealthy Philip had finally produced a viable offspring, it was hard to believe that it was such a paragon of health. In any case, it was now Louis's move.

It was high time someone went to Madrid to congratulate Philip and Mariana on their male heir, and this time there must be no doubt that the said male heir should be brought from its secret hiding-place and exposed to a critical view. Louis therefore sent Jacob Sanguin armed with a carefully contrived piece of bait. In his congratulatory letter, Louis referred to an absurd rumour which, he said, was circulating among ill-disposed people in Paris that Carlos was not a boy at all, and that a female child had been christened as a male for reasons of state.

Whether it was this that decided Philip to allow M. Sanguin and the French ambassador to have an audience with the infant prince, we do not know – probably not, since no steps were taken at the interview to prove the question of sex. No such omission had taken place on other occasions: thus Louis's wife, Maria Teresa, would surely remember how at the baptism of her brother Felipe Próspero, the infant was handed to her naked for presentation at the font. She had called out loudly, 'Why have you put no clothes on him? Why do you give me him naked?' And the answer had been: 'That is done on purpose, so that all may see he is a male.'

M. Sanguin and the French ambassador were received by the prince's nurse, and a menina carried the prince in her arms. While two pairs of lips were saying all the things usual on such occasions, two pairs of eyes were taking in the realities. The Frenchmen prolonged their praiseful platitudes as long as they decently could, and when the interview could be continued no longer, hurried away to make their report to Louis.

> He appears very feeble, he has a rash on both cheeks, caused by the inflammation called here *empeine* [eczema]; his head is covered with scales; but what was not visible, though we knew of it from other sources, is that for a fortnight or three weeks matter has exuded from below his right ear, where there is a suppurating opening; this side was cleverly concealed by a turned-up bonnet.

The account added that the doctors did not regard the discharge from the neck as a serious symptom 'since it pertains to the category of evils which are considered good because they remedy a worse evil'; in short this was 'laudable pus'.

Finally the Frenchmen made a vague reference to hereditary evil; it had not been considered necessary, they said, to change the wet-nurse, as these symptoms were due to 'anterior causes, observed in the last sons of the King'.

It was perhaps a pity that the prince's nurse did not expose his sex, since for years afterwards Frenchmen firmly believed that he was female; but the important point for Louis was now cleared up: his plans must all assume that it was more than likely that the Spanish Hapsburgs would soon come to a dead end. Carlos did not promise a long life, nor a continuing dynasty.

And then what would happen? Carlos was too young to realize the insoluble problem that his wretched hold on life entailed. When he died, childless, who would rule Spain? From now on, all the diplomats of Europe would concern themselves with this enigma, and in the Court of Madrid, Carlos would grow up with double-dealing and intrigue poisoning his every breath. There would be one extraordinary element in the situation: though Carlos would be moribund all his life, and would remain utterly uneducated, without will or understanding, a weak puppet in the hands of scheming women, venial courtiers, lying diplomats, fanatical confessors, it was he himself who would have to make the crucial decision. So powerful was the divinity hedging a Spanish King, so undisputed the belief that his signature was needed to the document which would settle Spain's future, that in the long run his word must prevail. All his life this unfortunate infant was to be martyrized by contending interests, each wanting him to make a will in its favour, each realizing that only thus could it hope to prevail.

It is early days, however, to talk of wills. What Louis wanted to know from his emissaries was whether Carlos was likely to grow up at all. It is clear that he counted with certainty on his early death. Once this living corpse was out of the way, Louis could attempt one or other of two possibilities, either he could gain the Spanish empire in its entirety for himself or his heirs, or he could agree with other European powers to partition the Spanish possessions between them, making sure that France should have the greater share.

Louis was always careful to have several strings to his bow. His first string was implicit in his marriage to Maria Teresa, Carlos's half-sister. If Carlos died without an heir of his body, it was obvious that Maria Teresa or her children would be the nearest claimants to the Spanish throne, and precisely to prevent this, Philip and Louis had agreed as part of her marriage contract that she renounced her rights to the Spanish throne for herself and her children. But Louis had insisted upon one proviso: this renunciation only became effective after Spain had paid him Maria Teresa's promised dowry. The dowry, as usual, had never been paid. Louis therefore had this trump card up his sleeve.

Next, Louis was expert in the tactics of war, both cold and hot. When he made peace with Spain in 1659, he nevertheless continued to help Portugal to revolt. His one objective was to weaken both the Austrian and the Spanish Hapsburgs, so that even when he married Philip's daughter he continued to help Philip's enemies.

In this process of weakening Spain before the final showdown, Louis had recourse to purely legal quibbles. Thus, he found that the customs of Brabant could be interpreted as meaning that Flanders should pass by inheritance to the child, male *or* female, of Philip's first marriage, and not to the child of a second marriage. He claimed Flanders on legal grounds for his wife, Maria Teresa. Spain denied that this custom had anything to do with political inheritance, and after eighteen months spent in arranging alliances which would give him a free hand, Louis declared righteous war 'to protect his legal rights'.

Thus, as the grey dawn of his twilight intellect broke, Carlos found himself the victim of intrigues. His mother, being Austrian, was determined to yield nothing to Louis, and most of the Spanish Court, regarding France as the traditional enemy, were on her side. In the face of this atmosphere of permanent dissension, Carlos through his confessors grew up to hold one dogma above all else – there must never be a partitioning of Spain. It was his sacred duty to pass on, intact, the land which was above all lands God's and the Virgin Mary's. The best way of securing this was to have an heir. To fail was to betray God himself and to earn a just and eternal torment. All that was to happen later must be understood in the light of these fixed and unalterable beliefs:

Spain must not be divided; an heir must be provided. Failure was worse than all the deadly sins rolled into one.

Curiously enough Philip did not seem to fear disaster in his last years. Perhaps the mere fact that he now had an heir, with the belief that this meant that God had not altogether condemned him, was enough to lighten his burden. He did not often feel happy, but he showed a little more resignation, and, on one occasion, something approaching real joy.

This was when a Papal Bull arrived from Alexander VII speaking very favourably of the Immaculate Conception of the Virgin Mary, which had always been one of his chief interests, especially since his meeting with Sor Maria de Agreda. But soon after this an ugly rumour began to spread abroad that the harassed King had a new enemy, and one that was working hand-in-glove with the Devil himself.

It seems that the officials suspected a certain house of being used for coining, and raided it. They arrested a woman and seized the apparatus with which she was carrying on her criminal activities. In searching for hidden material they came upon two engraved plates, each having a heart transfixed by an arrow; on one were the words 'Philip IV son of Philip III and Margaret', and on the other 'Luis de Haro, son of (his parents' names)', and also some quotations from the Bible. Each heart had the motto 'Thou art mine and I am thine.'

These plates were taken to the Inquisitor General, who at once smelt heresy, claimed the woman as his prisoner and ordered her transferred from the secular prison to the custody of the Inquisition. This was quite enough to start the wildest rumours of a serious attempt to bewitch the King.

We hear no more until December, when we are told that the matter of the witchcraft against the King is very much alive, and that it is believed the objective was to dominate the will both of him and of Haro. In the following February, we are told that the Inquisitor General, with the King's consent, having arrested one of the dead Felipe Próspero's servants, everybody is led to believe that the arrest has something to do with witchcraft. In March there are complications, the Marqués de Liche has been behaving oddly, trying to set fire to the Madrid theatre and to poison various Moors who might give evidence against him. He had written and signed a letter to the prison governor asking him to arrange the poisoning and he had enclosed the poison with the letter. There was no attempt at concealment and when the Marqués was arrested he explained everything most candidly: he had arranged to burn the theatre because he did not wish the scenery, which was his property, to be used by a rival, and he had been afraid that the Moors would give him away, as he had once deprived one of them of his ears as a punishment.

These very bizarre actions on the part of the son of so high a person as the recently dead Duque de Haro could, in the opinion of many, be explained in only one way: he was possessed; and, what with devils and witches, the atmosphere at the Court was even more strained than usual. It is clear that while the invalid child sat on the laps of his female attendants and absorbed who knows what undertones from his grey environment, his parents and their attendants must have been worn out by these continued crises. There was more to come: in the early winter of 1664 one Fray Francisco Monteron who, if not mad, was at least unsatisfactorily exalted, published a corpus of most injudicious prophecies. Fortunately Philip was less taken in by his speciousness than most of the Court, but many important ministers and others, attracted by his reputation for mediumistic abilities, even went to Father Monteron for confession. It must be accounted against Sor Maria that in his first enthusiasm Philip had become not a little susceptible to mystical charlatanism and that she tended, perhaps unwittingly, to encourage this. The King soon recovered from his initial credulity in these matters, and, by the time Father Monteron presented himself, had very little use for prophets. Indeed in these last trying months of his life, with a body racked with pain, with nephritis, paralysis and other serious troubles creeping up on him, Philip showed more sense and even more energy than ever before. He attended to the business of governing. He made up his mind for himself. He disagreed with his councillors and stood by his opinions. He showed energy in ordering reforms long overdue.

It was natural that his methods were not always the best, and it was also natural that an exhausted libertine, hovering over the edge of death, looking back on a lifetime of sexual sins, should concentrate on preventing others from sinning sexually. He got his Confessor to write a number of letters to prominent councillors and courtiers ordering them to break off their illicit connections; and the Almirante de Castilla must have been surprised to get an order telling him to return a married woman he had taken away from her rightful dwelling and kept in his house for his own pleasure. He replied that he had long ago done much better than the King demanded and returned her not only to her home but to her husband.

The Almirante sent the King a memorial suggesting that as he was so eager to reform his morals perhaps he had better look to some much more notorious cases, and enclosed a list of offenders which was probably drawn up to embarrass the King, since, when he acted on it, he found that some of the accused were quite innocent. Thus, an exceedingly old gentleman, whose accumulated years were his assurance of innocence, replied that to keep a domestic servant was not the same as to keep a mistress.

While the Court was still in a flutter about the prophet, anxiety was increased by the appearance of a comet. This was in December 1664. Philip again was more sensible than most of his subjects and to those who with long faces suggested that the comet might mean his death, he grimly asked which they thought a greater danger to his life, the comet or his diseases. But it was the stoicism of utter despair, and soon after the comet and the prognosticator had come to disturb his quiet misery, he lost his one consolation: in April 1665 Sor Maria died.

Three months later, his last obsession reached its inevitable end at Villaviciosa, where the Portuguese confirmed their independence by slaying half the Spanish army and capturing all its artillery.

On Midsummer's Day he took his last carriage drive and could only make the habitual round once; in August the doctors reduced his diet to asses' milk, and soup; and the attendant ecclesiastics removed a small bag, said to contain relics, which he had always worn round his neck, took it to the chapel of the Virgin of Atocha, found it to contain a book of charms, his portrait transfixed with pins, and other sorceries, and burned it. But it was too late.

On October 14th, he confessed and heard mass at a portable altar in his bedroom; later he handed over his will to an assembly of his councillors and had it signed by one of them, as his own hand was paralysed. When asked if he would like the inevitable San Isidro brought along to join the already present body of San Diego, he replied: 'Where they have got it is more convenient for it and for what I can ask of it distance is no handicap.'

There next came a surprising episode. His bastard son Don Juan de Austria presented himself, having hastened from his place of exile in Consuegra to say farewell to his father. Three times a request for audience was made, three times it was refused: 'Tell him,' said his father, 'to go back to Consuegra. It is now time for nothing but death.' Next day he was too far gone to be moved, and lay with his eyes fixed on the crucifix which had been the last object seen by all his ancestors since Charles V. So passed the Planet King.

We are told that there were scarcely any but dry eyes in all the royal palace.

And now Carlos Segundo was King in his stead.

CHAPTER EIGHT

CARLOS KING

CARLOS had to be weaned. Etiquette rather than physiology dictated this change, for no King of Spain might be fed at the breast of a commoner. He was within a month of his fourth birthday.

While the nursery staff reorganized the new King's diet, the nobles and courtiers gathered to hear the dead King's will. It appointed his widow Governor and Tutor, with power to rule with the help of a Council, until Carlos was fourteen years old. The only surprise was that the Duque de Medina de las Torres was not among the councillors appointed, although he was generally considered by far the most able of the grandees. Philip dying counted against him, perhaps, his assistance in early sexual escapades.

With due ceremony, too, the late King lay in State, his body surrounded by altars where, without pause, masses were said for the repose of his soul. Twenty-one different religious orders assisted in this exercise. Then the corpse was carried, not without altercations about etiquette and precedence, to the Podridero, the place of corruption, in the Escorial, and everybody returned to the palace to render homage and adulation to the infant Carlos.

Before him filed ambassadors and foreign diplomats, grandees and titled folk, councillors and members of tribunals, ministers of every grade, civil servants, gentlemen of quality, knights of the orders, magistrates – a fatiguing procession, every member of which paused, bent and kissed the pallid hand. The whole thing had to be extended over several days, as the King could not stand the strain for long at a time.

Carlos indeed was not yet able to walk; he had to be carried everywhere by his menina, or his nurse; in Maura's phrase, he felt the weight of a crown upon his head before he felt the ground beneath his feet. Yet he showed signs of having already learned somewhat from his mother. Thus, when a grandee, bending to kiss his hand, said that he hoped to be as good a friend to him as he had been to his father, the child replied: 'Kings regard their vassals not as friends but as servants.'

It is believed that the grandee in question was the Duque de Medina de las Torres himself. If so we see the best read, the most intelligent, the most distinguished Spaniard of his age, a man whose library is still talked of today, put in his place by a rachitic infant who never achieved sufficient education to read more than a devotional tract, and who was to remain to his last days scarcely capable of writing legibly. Evidently Mariana, his mother, had begun to instruct him early in the things that really mattered and one of these was to avenge her for her dead husband's bastards.

Looking up from his nurse's knees at the crowd gathered to do him homage, Carlos noticed one who was not wearing Spanish court-dress. He asked who he was, and he was told that it was the representative of the Prince de Condé, wearing his national dress which he did not wish to change for the Spanish. Carlos ordered him out of the room. He had been taught thus early to tolerate nothing French.

Mariana herself, who was only just entering her thirties, now suffered the inevitable transformation that etiquette demanded of her. She cut off her hair and assumed the stern garments of a nun, accentuated by a thick veil over her face. For nine days she saw no one except an official who brought her documents for which her signature was essential. From the tenth day she received female visitors but no males, not even an ambassador.

When the days of strict seclusion were over, there followed the complicated ritual of 'Honras' for the late King. These obsequies must have been tedious to a degree. Though Mariana ordered the responsible officials to cut the preparations as short as possible, they took six weeks to organize. Poor Carlos, who could not know what any of it meant, sat through interminable religious exercises, a quite deplorable funeral sermon, lugubrious hymn singing, fatiguing processions. From time to time his blinking eyes rested in vague wonder on a temporary monument erected for these occasions, called a tumulus or catafalque. This monument, ablaze with candles, was adorned with bad allegorical pictures and worse mottoes and poetic verses, some of them alluding to the recent comet and how it had predicted the death of the Planet King. All over the country, similar obsequies were being held, the same brilliant catafalques were adorned with bad verses and futile allegories, the same sort of intolerable sermon was being spun out. But nowhere, surely, could there have been so wretched a spectator as here in Madrid, where a child King, sick in body and vague in mind, had to perform his part in a suffocating ritual which prescribed his clothes, his gestures, his facial expression. It was good practice for him, as throughout his life Carlos was to take part in a tragicomedy which he could never understand, to be moved like a puppet, to be used by other people for their own ends, and all the time to be obsessed with a fear of doing wrong without ever knowing what would have been right.

Due honours having been done to the dead King, it was once more the turn of the living to be the centre of symbolical play-acting. Carlos was now to be named a Knight of the Golden Fleece. One of Philip's last decrees, left unsigned, declared:

> I have elected the Prince Don Carlos, my son, Knight of the Golden Fleece, and I therefore order the Knight of the Order who is the oldest among those members to be found in this Court to give him the collar and Knight's accoutrements in the presence of the other Knights who can be assembled from among those who are here; with the customary forms and ceremonies.

On Sunday November 8th, in an antechamber covered with rich tapestries and carpets, the Order met, and the royal decree was read. Formality required that the proposed new Knight should signify his willingness. The Duque de Cardona and the Grefier, the keeper of the Rolls of the Golden Fleece, left the room and entered another near by where King Carlos waited in his nurse's arms – he could not yet walk. They asked him if he desired Knighthood, the nurse nudged him, and he gave an affirmative answer. Then the company filed in pairs before His Majesty and received his greetings, an inclination of the head and, to the one member who was also an ambassador and therefore entitled to special treatment, the request to cover his head with his hat.

All having returned to the antechamber, the King, still in the arms of his nurse who was seated in a covered chair, said, 'His Majesty commands that your Excellency be seated and covered, and that the Ministers be seated.' If the ambassador's hat had been forgotten, it is probable that an international incident would have followed.

The Grefier, bowing thrice, now approached Carlos, and there followed a dialogue in which the nurse said the King's part and he repeated it after her. He was asked thrice if he wished to be an armed Knight and when he answered yes, 'God and St Andrew, Patron of the Order, make you a good knight.' 'God give me grace to be it,' he replied after his nurse, and all with such solemn dignity, we are told, that he might have been much older than he was. In the same way he swore to guard the Constitution of the Order of the Golden Fleece and to maintain its grandeur and dignity and not to consent to any diminution of its honour and public esteem. He swore a number of similar oaths and was at last invested with the collar that had so recently been his father's. All his fellow Knights were delighted with the new Knight's bearing, as were his mother and sister who watched the proceedings concealed in a gallery. Moreover, as Knight of the Golden Fleece, he was now able to claim from the palace a roll of bread and a pottle of wine daily.

A week or so later he was able for the first time to hold a public ceremony with his feet to the ground, though it could scarcely be said that they supported his body. The occasion was the reception of French diplomats who had come, ostensibly, to bring Louis's condolence for Philip's death. Once more they had eyes for quite other purposes than were involved officially in their visit, and once more their master, the Most Christian King, received a gloomy report of the Catholic King's future prospects.

> We found time to examine the King of Spain carefully while Monsieur de Bellefonds transmitted in French your Majesty's compliments ... The King of Spain supported himself on his feet propped against the knees of his Menina who held him by the strings of his dress. He covered his head with an English-style bonnet, which he had not the energy to raise, as otherwise he would have done when I and the

> Marques de Bellefonds approached ... We could hear no other word from him except *cubrios* (cover yourself) addressed to me, and it was his nurse standing on the left of the Menina, who replied to our compliments. He seems extremely weak, with pale cheeks and very open mouth, a symptom, according to the unanimous opinion of the doctors, of some gastric upset, and though they say he walks on his own feet and that the cords with which the Menina guides him are simply in case he makes a false step, I doubt it, since I saw him take his nurse's hand to hold himself up when they retired. Be that as it may, the doctors do not foretell a long life, and this seems to be taken for granted in all calculations here.

Having received this report confirmatory of earlier ones, Louis XIV not unnaturally began to frame his policies on the assumption that Carlos might die at any minute. Curiously enough it may truly be said that the main factor which defeated Louis's grandest conceptions was that this moribund infant remained alive for thirty-five more years. For had he died much sooner, the rise of national feeling in northern Europe and the increasing strength of the Maritime Powers, Holland and England, would not have reached a stage at which they were too strong for Louis. By merely continuing to exist, Carlos was largely responsible for turning history in the way it went.

We have, therefore, the curious situation that a vacuum, or quintessence of weakness, was the centre around which men and women of strong will and fierce ambitions broke as against a granite rock. The plot is unusual: let us consider the dramatis personae.

First, there was Louis XIV after whom the whole age is not unjustly called, a man as brilliant as Carlos was negligible. It is worth recalling that Louis and Carlos, such opposites, were brothers-in-law. At this time it is unlikely that Carlos had ever heard of Louis; certainly he could have had no clear picture of him. Nevertheless, as we have seen, he was already being trained to regard as part of his *duty* towards God that he should hate France and that he should regard as sacrilege any plan to divide Spain. At this very moment, when his ambassadors were condoling with him for the death of his father, Louis was publicly claiming large parts of the Spanish Empire and preparing to back up his claims with open war, and privately carving up the Spanish Empire between himself and Carlos's other dear brother-in-law, the Emperor. Louis never appeared on the Spanish scene, of course; these two never met; it would be most accurate to call Louis the puppeteer rather than a puppet, but a puppeteer whose actions were in turn controlled by a stronger force still, the inevitable march of events, against which Louis was to prove as impotent as Carlos himself.

Next to Louis, of the people in the background, the Emperor was perhaps the most important. Not at all successful as a military leader against France, he represented the figurehead of opposition to French domination of Europe, and as the head of the Austrian branch of the Hapsburgs he was of course the natural ally of Spain. Moreover, he too was linked by marriage ties to the young sovereign, his wife being Margarita, Carlos's own sister.

Behind these two, Louis and the Emperor, there were growing up elsewhere in Europe men representing new forces and political tendencies. For generations Hapsburgs and Bourbons had waged dynastic war, but now there were emerging national entities and policies whose vital interest was in preventing either Hapsburg or Bourbon dominating Europe. The age of the Balance of Power was beginning, its leader and symbol William of Orange.

In the hands of these three men, Louis, Leopold and William, lay the fate of Spain, the sick man of Europe, the ramshackle empire.

At first it would seem that Leopold was better placed than anyone to intrigue and influence, for the Queen Mother, Mariana of Austria, was the regent and the sole person able to mould the child who in the last resort was the arbiter. It would seem that there would be little difficulty in brainwashing him into an assumption that, failing heirs of his own body, only Austrian successors could be considered. However, it was not going to be so easy. Even at this early date the Austrian Emperor, unknown to Mariana, or Carlos, or any of their Council, was planning a partition with the resourceful Louis. And besides this untoward treachery without, Mariana had an enemy within, Carlos's bastard brother, the thorn in her flesh.

CHAPTER NINE

THE BASTARD BROTHER

Out of more than thirty bastards known to history or to gossip, Philip recognized but one. Several others grew up to respectable positions in church and state, but only Don Juan de Austria was permitted to claim a royal father. Whether or not Philip deliberately chose to call him thus in memory of the great Don Juan de Austria, hero of Lepanto, beloved bastard of his ancestor the Emperor Charles V, resemblance ceased at the bar sinister and the name. This Don Juan cannot claim greatness. Compared with the offspring of the two Queens, however, he was at least healthy, for he had a healthy mother.

When Carlos came to the throne, this half-brother was thirty-six years old. Philip had almost loved him, in so far as such a sentiment can be associated with him; and it had been a great surprise to everyone that he had refused to see him on his deathbed. If we wonder why Don Juan had been singled out for recognition by his father, the most plausible guess is that there had been something rather more than animal lust in his feelings for the mother. Or perhaps there had been a better satisfied lust, for which Philip remained grateful.

La Calderona was an actress of some merit though of little physical beauty. It was the Duque de Medina de las Torres who first called Philip's attention to her. Being on confidential terms with the King in all that concerned their erotic careers, he told him that she possessed a physical peculiarity which had so far defeated the potency of all aspirants and hinted that with her even the King would find himself defeated. Philip, piqued and curious, entered the lists and found himself worsted. A minor operation was all that was necessary, however, and this Philip ordered, after which he enjoyed the lady and became not a little attached to her.

facing: MARIANA OF AUSTRIA, WIDOW OF PHILIP IV

In due course a son was born, and following the etiquette of the Spanish Court, which prohibited any woman who had been honoured by the King from being honoured by any other man, La Calderona entered an order and became a Bride of Christ. She is said to have taken her new career seriously and shown exemplary faithfulness to her vows.

That entertaining liar, Madame d'Aulnoy, in her famous but fictitious *Travels in Spain*, recounts that, the Queen being enceinte at the same time as La Calderona, the latter persuaded Philip to exchange babies, if they should both be male. This, she says, was done, and so Baltazar Carlos was really the actress's son, and Don Juan, Isabella's. This was supposed to explain why Don Juan was recognized, when even the son who was made Bishop of Málaga was not. If only because there were six months between the two births, the story, like most of Madame d'Aulnoy's, is ridiculous.

Don Juan was born on April 7th, 1629, and was baptized two weeks later. The palace midwife, Inés Ayala, who was later to assist Carlos into the world, was his godmother, but her signature in the parish register was erased. In the margin of the register was written 'hijo de la tierra', son of the soil (i.e., of unknown parents); but the crowd who attended this very public function was in no way deceived.

He was carefully brought up in a district remote from the capital, and his education was put in the hands of a mathematical Jesuit and a theological Inquisitor. There he might have remained, so it is said, until he could later be made Archbishop of Toledo, had not the Conde Duque de Olivares wished to legitimize one of his own bastards and prevailed upon Philip to do the same so as to make his action more respectable. However that may be, in May 1642, at the age of thirteen, Don Juan de Austria was recognized by his father and made Grand Prior of St John, with an almost royal household and a large income. The youth soon came to regard this as the lowest rung of a ladder by which he could climb to unknown heights, though not necessarily in the ecclesiastical field for which, with its accompanying vows, the young Prior felt less and less vocation as time went on.

The recognition of Don Juan involved a monumental piece of research into the correct etiquette to be observed by him and to

facing: CARLOS SEGUNDO

him. The results were incorporated in a Cédula Real which reads like a catalogue of obsessional acts imposed on some unfortunate by his psychosis.

His rank was to be that of potentates like the Electoral Princes, who were addressed as Brother by kings and Serenity by subjects. When he received cardinals it was to be in one half of the antechamber, and both he and they must keep hats on. He would offer them precedence through doors but would himself go first when they refused, as according to protocol they would be bound to do. He would remove his hat and hold it waist high to grandees of Castille, ambassadors of the first rank, the Archbishop of Toledo, so long as he was not a cardinal, and Presidents of the Council of the Kingdom in which he happened to be. He would receive these at the door of his chamber, and dismiss them there. When receiving titled people, eldest sons of grandees, bishops, representatives of foreign princes, viceroys, and captains general within the territory of their jurisdiction, Ministers of the Councils, representatives of cities with a vote in the cortes, and members of Cathedral Chapters, he would stand back two paces from the table where he had left his hat, so that when he ordered them to cover and he did not himself do so, as he would in the presence of grandees, they would not cover either.

After several pages of this sort of detail, the really delicate matters are discussed. His brother Baltazar Carlos is to call him 'my brother' or 'my brother Don Juan'. They can go to the theatre together alone in the same coach, but they are not to eat together. The Queen will end her letters to him 'To Don Juan de Austria, my son', while Baltazar will end 'my brother and friend'.

Don Juan de Austria began very shortly after his recognition to mount the ladder which might lead to power; at the age of fifteen he was already Governor General of Flanders, and two years later he was given the title of Prince of the Sea, chiefly because his namesake had been victor of Lepanto. His only sea-battle was the defeat of a small French boat accidentally met by his fleet of six galleys in the Straits of Gibraltar. Thenceforward he was to fight on land, and unfortunately with far less success against far more powerful foes. Although certainly not a military or naval genius, Don Juan was not altogether despicable. Indeed as a youth he was affable, brave, intelligent, hard-working, but the twin enemies of his ambition and his defective birth tended to make him lose what good qualities he possessed and to gain many others less admirable.

It was in the spring of 1665, when it had become clear that his father had few more months of life, that Don Juan made a proposal which shocked even Philip and led to his refusing ever again to see his bastard son, even on his deathbed.

As long ago as 1656, this very unsuitable plan must have taken shape in Don Juan's mind, for there is evidence that in that year he consulted the theologians of Louvain on a matter of high ecclesiastical policy. The question for which he wanted an expert answer was: if it were necessary for the salvation of a monarchy, would the Pope be willing to grant a dispensation for a brother-sister marriage? He added that he had in mind the political expediency of a marriage between himself and his half-sister Maria Teresa, at that time the sole heir to the Spanish throne.

However, with the birth of Felipe Próspero the plea of urgency was of diminished force, and Don Juan dropped the idea.

But now, nine years later, he revived the plan, substituting Margarita for Maria Teresa. Even more extraordinary than the plan itself was the method of presenting it to Philip. Don Juan was something of an amateur painter and he showed his father one of his works, a miniature representing Saturn contemplating with a smile the incestuous dallyings of his son and daughter, Jupiter and Juno. It was on the occasion of a visit to Aranjuez, whither he had been summoned by Philip to discuss whether he would prefer to be made Archbishop of Toledo or Inquisitor General, and the intention of the painting was singularly out of key with such a discussion, for the face of Saturn was unquestionably that of Philip, while Jupiter and Juno were recognizable portraits of the artist and his half-sister the Infanta Margarita. Philip understood, and was scandalized. He turned his back on his favourite bastard and never saw him again. An even more important and lasting result of this indiscretion was to accentuate the loathing that Mariana felt for its perpetrator.

Don Juan soon had another plan for his future, almost as extravagant as this one. It would be scarcely scientific to suggest that he had inherited from his mother a double dose of dramatic sense, but he cannot be denied a great gift for doing things in a highly theatrical manner. On this occasion he did not use the medium of painting, but cast himself in the character most likely to appeal to his selected audience, and his selected audience was none other than Father Nithard, the Queen's Confessor.

He had cultivated the Queen's Confessor for some time before his father's death, realizing that, whatever happened, this individual would certainly possess the key, if any existed, to unlock Mariana's heart to him. Moreover, Don Juan and Father Nithard had one bond of interest which was of great consequence: Don Juan professed himself, and may very well have been, an ardent crusader for the publication of the Dogma of the Immaculate Conception. This was of course the darling cause of the priest's heart and mind. Years before, they had knelt side by side in the Monastery of Montserrat pledging themselves to use all their strength in the service of this cause. Don Juan knew well how to use this devotion to ingratiate himself with the powerful fanatic.

About a month after Philip's death in October 1665, Don Juan got into his coach and drove out to a secret meeting place which Father Nithard was approaching from the opposite direction. Having both reached the spot, all their retainers were dismissed to some distance while the two consulted in one coach behind closed and curtained windows.

The Jesuit had not known at all clearly what Don Juan wished to propose and was greatly surprised to find him on his knees at his feet in earnest supplication. According to Don Juan, what troubled him was the vow of chastity which had of course gone with his receiving ecclesiastical status and would continue when he became Archbishop of Toledo or Inquisitor General. As the years went by, Don Juan had found that he had less and less vocation for chastity; indeed, in Naples he had disgracefully seduced the very young daughter of the painter Ribera, in circumstances that had called down on him strong criticism even in that epoch and place.

On the other hand he could not possibly do without the emoluments he got from his ecclesiastical appointments, so that he was in the horrible position of having to try to exercise a virtue which God had not given him, because otherwise he would be a poor man. What he wanted now was release from the vow, which must of course be made possible in the only way Don Juan could imagine, by a good income from a secular source.

Thus having explained his reasons for desiring such a change of vocation in a way likely to appeal to the ascetic Father Nithard, Don Juan proceeded to outline a possible solution which might well appeal to the Queen Mother, for it involved his removal not merely from Madrid, as she had always insisted, but from Spain. It was notorious that the reigning King of Poland was old, infirm and without heirs. This was a plum which might well fall on the plate of the Most Christian King of France, since the Duke d'Enghien was married to the Polish Queen's niece. The Queen had suggested, or so Don Juan thought, that if he was married to another Polish niece, Poland might fall to the House of Austria. The whole thing was a figment of Don Juan's imagination, since the Emperor had already two candidates of his own choosing in the field. To this plan Don Juan added an important rider: to be in a position to become a candidate for such honours he must no longer be banished from the Court.

In a very short time Don Juan found that the King of Poland's position was an unenviable one. He had no army with which to maintain himself against incessant revolutions. Don Juan thought it might be better, therefore, if he married the Archduchess Claudia Felicidad. Mariana and Nithard now made a mistake. The Queen Mother first agreed to request the Junta to revoke Don Juan's banishment from the Court, fully confident that they would refuse, which indeed they did. But while she thought herself so shrewd, she was in fact now setting a trap for herself into which she surely fell. She decided that it would be excellent to get Don Juan out of Spain by persuading the Emperor to marry him to the Archduchess Claudia Felicidad, therefore she agreed to Father Nithard's giving him an introduction to the Emperor's Ambassador Extraordinary, the Baron de Lisola, and also to his ordinary ambassador, Poetting. The consequence of this was that Don Juan had an opportunity, which he used successfully, of ingratiating himself with them and undermining their good will towards Father Nithard. Not only was he a more attractive personality than the sour, severe Jesuit, but the ambassadors were already offended with the Jesuit for his superiority over them in the eyes of the Queen. Their changing estimate of the two men, friends on the surface but bound ultimately to be rivals, was passed on to the Emperor. Thus Don Juan gained powerful allies for the struggle which was now beginning in earnest.

Carlos was of course ignorant of the hatreds gathering about him. As far as his retarded intellect would allow, he was the automaton of his mother, Mariana. A five-year-old is too young to understand anything of the world, but not too young, perhaps, to be unconsciously influenced by an atmosphere charged with hate and intrigue. Besides, an offshoot of the general struggle was shortly to appear in his own nursery.

CHAPTER TEN

INTRIGUE

FOR ten years the boy-king struggled into friendless youth amid dogs and dwarf buffoons; his sole companions, his aristocratic nurse and a bevy of adolescent debutantes who prized their positions as meninas for their snob value.

The ambassadors reported home from Madrid the details of his health, each according to his personal bias. If it were not pathetic, it would be absurd to note how the Austrians and their sympathizers claimed a steady improvement, while the French reported increasing debility. It was noted by a French observer, for example, that at the age of three the bones of Carlos's cranium had not yet closed, while he could certainly not stand on his own feet. The Venetian ambassador is in raptures about the child's promise, both physical and intellectual: he has escaped his father's ill health, he is good at lessons, his disposition is sweet. The French ambassador, Archbishop Embrun, sends a detailed diary of dilapidation. Carlos has made some progress, he admits, towards standing on his own feet, though certainly not towards using them for propulsion.

By July 1667, however, when Carlos was six, he could certainly stand alone, even if he could still not walk, a fact which seems to be proved by the unfortunate quarrel which was its immediate result — a quarrel which was to lead to quite serious consequences.

The Queen's Camarera Mayor, or chief Lady of the Bedchamber, was Doña Elvira Ponce de León, Marquesa de Villanueva de Valdueza, and very conscious of the dignity due to such a name and lineage. She had for some time been irritated by the fact that the King's nurse walked in front of her on state occasions, and on July 30th of that year, shortly after Carlos had received his Court's homage standing on his own feet at his mother's side with his nurse at a little distance, Doña Elvira Ponce de León gave notice that in future she would claim her right position on these occasions, seeing that the King no longer needed his nurse's support.

But the King's nurse had also name and lineage, for, it will be remembered, she was Doña Maria Engracia de Toledo, Marquesa de los Vélez; and the suggested change in etiquette was considered nothing less than an insult by her relatives and well-placed friends. The whole month of August, therefore, was taken up by the two sides writing memorials which Doña Mariana was forced to read. The harassed Queen Mother, whose natural preference was for the nurse as against her chief Lady of the Bedchamber, did not know what to do. Feeling was high. At last she referred the matter to the Council of State.

The Council held a grave discussion and it seemed likely that the decision would be unanimously in favour of the Camarera Mayor, when the whole matter was thrown in the melting pot by a violent explosion from the Duque de Alba. The Duque reminded the Council that he was in an excellent position to judge fairly, as he was related to both the ladies involved. For that matter, the Duques de Alba were related to everybody in Spain who had any claim to distinction of birth. Moreover, the Duque had unquestioned precedence over both the ladies, distinguished as they were; indeed, he had precedence over nearly everybody in Spain.

However, observed the Duque, facts were facts and whether the King was able to stand on his own feet or not, he clearly required the assistance of his nurse. This fact must override any normal rule of precedence which might be involved. Let the Camarera have precedence in a coach, where the immediate presence of the nurse was not indispensable, as Carlos would be sitting down, and let the nurse have it at receptions where she would be needed to move him about.

Medina de los Torres, Mortara, Ayala and Don Juan supported the Camarera; Peñaranda and Nithard suggested a compromise: the nurse should stand on the right of the Camarera but one step behind; but the Duque de Alba refused to accept the proposal. He did, however, introduce one gleam of common sense into the discussion by complaining that such a trivial matter should ever have been brought before the Council of State.

Mariana, having got no clear directive from her Council,

ordered that the nurse should continue to take precedence. At the palace, ladies took sides, the Nithardes for the nurse and the Austriacas for the Camarera. The Austriacas were led by an intolerable mischief-maker, Doña Leonor de Velasco, who was probably Don Juan's spy, though not, as insisted by rival mischief-makers, his lover.

This lady's career throws a scandalous light on the depths to which life among the court ladies had fallen. Etiquette had taken the place of common morality, and those who disputed bitterly who should stand to the right of whom were by no means so particular about whose bed they occupied, so long as they could avoid being found there. Doña Leonor had had a particularly scandalous intrigue and, in spite of it being common knowledge, she was asked in marriage by the bastard of her friend the Camarera's husband. Licence for this was refused by the Junta at the request, she believed, of the Queen Mother and the Confessor. Thus condemned to single blessedness, she did all she could to revenge herself on them by services to Don Juan.

These court intrigues had become almost a part of compulsory etiquette, and there was scarcely one of the ladies who did not carry on affairs which went further than innocent flirtation.

> From these *galanteos* [wrote an anonymous critic] arise very great offences to God: public scandals, sins against the laws of holy matrimony; signals and counter-signals even in the Chapel Royal and before the Blessed Sacrament; uneasiness of mind, perturbation of conscience; a wretched life for the wives of the gallants; ruin of fortunes spent in presents for these Ladies, instead of on the needs of their wives and households; sorrow and affliction for fathers and relations; blots on the sacredness of the royal palace; noises and screaming in its corridors; nocturnal disturbances; worry and intolerable work for its guards; loss of respect due to the royal person and house; numberless indecencies causing unbelievable grief to good God-fearing people and lovers of decency and honesty.

These signals and counter-signals indulged in even in the most sacred places were a peculiar sign language, not unlike our deaf and dumb language: a use of the fingers to convey amorous and often indecent suggestions between the court ladies and their gallants.

The futilities of the court ladies fitted into the more dangerous political plots and counter-plots of their husbands. Thus we note that Nithard and Don Juan appear on opposite sides in the affair of the nurse and the Camarera Mayor, and this has more significance than would at first appear. It meant that Don Juan had undermined the Jesuit's position as head of the Austrian party; but with his hatred of the Austrian Queen Mother this could only be a temporary and deceitful position for him to take up. His whole political objective was to thwart in every way everything that Doña Mariana desired. Thus he was fanning the flames of hate felt in the streets of Madrid for her favourite, the foreign Confessor, and for the moment, all his manoeuvres were concentrated on identifying himself in people's minds with the anti-Nithard party, but once Nithard was disposed of there was no knowing in what direction he would move.

Mariana had played into his hands by having Nithard made a Councillor of State, and a few months later sealed the fate of her favourite by appointing him Inquisitor General. The smear campaign against him was intensified and then for the moment Don Juan overplayed his hand. He hired a ruffian to assassinate the Jesuit. The plot failed and Mariana seized the opportunity to have Don Juan exiled; but, instead of leaving the country, he went to Barcelona where his supporters were strong, collected a small squadron of cavalry and returned towards Madrid gathering recruits along the way. Madrid was all excitement, the population, weak in lasting political faiths but strong in their desire for a quarrel, were divided into Afrancesados, Nithardistas and Donjuanistas. The Council of State was divided and futile, and a civil war seemed imminent when the Pope intervened and, begging the Queen Mother, Nithard and Don Juan severally to keep the peace, suggested that the best solution, whatever his merits or demerits, would be for the Jesuit to leave Spain.

When the Papal Nuncio approached Don Juan with a request for an amicable compromise, he got the one positive and unequivocal answer offered him by anyone: 'If by Monday the fellow has not left by the Palace door for ever, I shall go with my men on Tuesday and throw him out of the window.' Doña Mariana saw that she must sacrifice her favourite, and off he went to Rome where he was consoled with a Cardinal's hat and spent a studious life writing his autobiography in twenty-five manuscript volumes. The eight-year-old Carlos, on hearing of the Confessor's departure, is reported to have said: 'What evil there is in the world! Let him come back and punish the evildoers.'

There followed a period of pure melodrama. To hatred of Don Juan, Mariana now added a quite justifiable terror. She regarded him as the possible leader of a civil war against her as indeed he was. She was hated by the mob whose traditional cry of 'Long live the King, down with the evil government,' was at this time aimed against her.

Her first step was fatal. The Portuguese war had just ended and she had the returning soldiers formed into a private corps to protect her. She went further, she had them dressed in the foreign uniform of the troops commanded by Marshal Schomberg in the recent war, and this unnecessary copying of foreign custom gave the mob and Don Juan an easy avenue for the most bitter criticism. Her state of mind can be judged by the absurd incident which now occurred in the palace.

Mariana had gone to bed one night when she heard a suspicious noise. She called: 'Who goes there?' The noise stopped, only to begin again a moment later. This happened three times, then the Queen could stand it no longer. She called her servants and made them search the palace. They found nothing. She made the Duque de Aytona and his son sleep the rest of the night in her anteroom. General opinion put the noise down to a banging window or to a cat, but Mariana was convinced it was Don Juan come to murder her.

She reacted in a curious and injudicious way. Don Juan was kicked upstairs to a place as remote as possible from Madrid. To his intense surprise he found himself appointed Vicar General of Aragon with official residence at Zaragoza. But what was more surprising still, and what perhaps showed that the Queen Mother had not altogether lost her head was that in her official letter she called Don Juan 'mi primo'. Now this was the phrase which was used by Spanish Kings only to grandees, and Mariana must have known that its use to Don Juan would bring on his head all the jealous anger of which the grandees were capable. No better way of securing the dislike of the high aristocracy for Don Juan could have been conceived.

But Don Juan was in no way put out by his forced exile to Zaragoza. Not long after, he sent armed men to ransack the Viceroy of Aragon's house on the excuse that that official, the Count of Aranda, was plotting to poison him. He wrote a violent protest to Madrid accusing Mariana and her friends of being implicated. They were no less agitated by his letter when they realized that the plot was a figment of his imagination, for the whole thing was clear evidence of what he proposed to do in future. By all the means in his power he was determined to get Carlos away from his mother, which would be tantamount to achieving royal power for himself.

Mariana's immediate method of defending herself was to elevate to the highest honours a young man who had been left by the departing Nithard as a sort of go-between for his correspondence with the Queen Mother. This was Valenzuela, who ruled the palace for the next few years, but he is only of interest to us for his effect upon the young Carlos.

Carlos was now fourteen, in better health than at any time in his life, and under the tutelage of Valenzuela he began to take a serious interest in hunting. He was not very adept, and to his early efforts can be attributed Valenzuela's greatest honour: Carlos discharged his gun into the favourite's person, and though the wounds were not dangerous they were painful enough to need assuaging by making him a Grandee of Spain.

Soon after this event, which increased the already universal hatred of Valenzuela among the grandees, came the end of Carlos's minority, as laid down in his father's will. On November 6th, 1675, the regency of his mother officially came to an end, and Carlos was King indeed. It was at that very moment that the hatreds which made up the normal atmosphere of his Court reached their greatest intensity. The sickly youth of fourteen, brought up entirely by women, educated by incompetent elderly theologians, conditioned to hate certain powerful personages and certain powerful countries, devoid of physical strength or of mental stamina, and innocent of all knowledge of the world of politics and diplomacy, faced up to enemies at home and abroad, and a rotten state of his world in general.

CHAPTER ELEVEN

CARLOS COMES OF AGE

NOVEMBER 6th, 1675. There was to be a solemn Te Deum in the afternoon, for the happy day had arrived on which Carlos, fourteen years old, and come-of-age, was to take over in his own right the governance of the Spanish Empire. Things did not turn out as expected. Indeed, as the day ended, almost all the chief actors must have mingled astonishment with whatever other emotions possessed them.

In accordance with his father's will, Carlos was to be severed from his mother's apron-strings. In theory, he could now face the world and begin to rule a good portion of it himself. He did not know that there was merely the choice of remaining in one spider's web, or of falling into another. Nor did Mariana, sitting at the centre of one web, know the extent of the other. She feared that the rival spider, Don Juan, might construct one, but she had no idea that her son was almost enveloped in it already.

But two days before the crucial birthday, Mariana and her Valido had a most unexpected shock. They handed Carlos a simple document for signature, a mere matter of routine; Carlos always signed documents when he was told to. This one, taking into account the boy's backwardness, his lack of all necessary qualities for governing, extended the period of regency for two more years. It was the best way to save him, and themselves, from any possible rival web. How easy it would be for Don Juan to gain control over him, if their guiding hand were removed! Carlos glanced at the document and, probably, since his reading ability was small, asked someone to explain it. When he understood, he refused to sign it, refused indignantly and even violently.

Mariana and Valenzuela were dismayed, not so much that Carlos refused to sign away his freedom for two more years, but because there was evidently behind his obstinacy a hidden danger for them. Mariana knew very well that she was hated, moreover her own hatred of Don Juan was of a quality to cause her uneasy nights. She remembered, for instance, the night noises at the palace; she thought of the rumours going around the *mentideros*, the lie factories, of Madrid, during the last few days.

In particular it was being said that Don Pascual, Cardinal-Archbishop of Toledo, had arrived. Now Don Pascual could not have come for nothing. He had voluntarily exiled himself some time ago. Of all the members of the Junta appointed by Philip's will, he was the most consistent opponent of everything that Mariana desired. He had shown unswerving hostility to both Father Nithard and his successor Valenzuela. And now he was in Madrid, and Carlos was behaving very strangely. He could not have developed a will of his own overnight. Had his obstinacy any connection with the Cardinal's unexpected arrival?

Don Pascual came from an ancient and honoured family, but having the misfortune of being a younger son he had had to adopt an ecclesiastical career for which he was not entirely fitted. He had held all manner of high office, including that of Inquisitor General. He had yielded to Mariana's request, and resigned that office to become Archbishop of Toledo, but though the Primate of the Church in Spain was a high enough eminence for most people, he could never forgive the Queen Mother when he found that the man for whom he had made room at the head of the Inquisition was the hated upstart, Jesuit, foreigner, Father Nithard. From then on, Mariana could count on his opposition in everything.

He had remained at Court for some time and discharged his duties as member of the Junta, but one day the breaking-point was reached. It had always been agreed that the Caballerizo Mayor of the King along with the Queen's Caballerizo Mayor had the same right as the Papal Nuncio, the Royal Ambassadors and the Cardinals, to leave their coaches inside the Palace Square; but the new holder of that office had gone much further than this. He claimed that his coach must be parked immediately behind the Royal Coach and in front of the coaches of the Papal Nuncio, the Ambassadors and the Cardinals, since he needed, for the discharge of his official duties, to leave it in that position. Mariana supported him. Don Pascual considered this as a personal affront and an affront to the dignity of the Church. He therefore shook the dust of Madrid from his feet and retired to Toledo to sulk, perhaps to intrigue, and ostensibly to attend to the business of his archdiocese. He had now come back.

If Mariana had known why he had come, she would have been more surprised, more angry and more alarmed. Early in October Don Pascual had received a secret and official letter from the young King. He was told to hold himself in readiness for further orders. He replied that he would serve his King in all things, but reminded him that of all the ministers he was the one least pleasing to Mariana.

In reply there came a letter saying that on November 6th Carlos was going to take affairs into his own hands, and as Philip had singled out the Cardinal to help his son, his son proposed to use him in person. The official letter had a postscript in Carlos's own writing, though careful examination suggests that someone helped him form the letters: 'When you come,' it read, 'bring your household, because I require your service: Yo, el Rey.' We shall see in a moment who guided the hand.

Another rumour occupying the mentideros was that Don Juan was on the road from Aragon to Madrid. If this were true it would be bad enough, but the whole truth was a good deal worse. Carlos and the hand that guided him had written several letters to his bastard brother. He was acting without a word to his mother. The ventriloquist's doll was talking of its own volition; or had another ventriloquist taken it upon his knee? On the same day as Don Pascual's letter, one had gone to Don Juan which said:

> On the sixth I take oath and enter into the government of my estates. I need you at my side for this function and at my taking leave of the Queen, my lady and mother; so at a quarter to eleven on Wednesday you will be in my ante-chamber; and I order you to keep this secret.

There was a minor matter which escaped notice at the time, though it was significant: Carlos had requested that on his birthday the Conde de Medellín, his Mayordomo, and the Conde de Talhara, his Caballerizo, should be on duty, although it would be out of their turn. In a court where nothing was ever done out of turn, this must mean something unusual. These two were the leaders in a plot which remained a secret until the last, but, as we shall see, they could not have succeeded had not the most important matter, the conditioning of Carlos's mind, been carefully achieved by two others who were, perhaps, the last people to arouse Mariana's suspicions. She had supposed that the instilling of hatred for Don Juan which she had begun in Carlos's earliest years had been carefully fostered later by his teachers, both spiritual and secular. She was mistaken.

It was on the Tuesday when the royal party had returned from the bullfight that Carlos informed his mother that he had invited his half-brother to come to Court on the morrow. Mariana's reaction was delayed. For the moment, though her face showed disgust and anger, she did not speak. The world knew next morning why she had looked so upset: Don Juan, in preparation for the Day, had written and duplicated a manifesto announcing his coming, and that it was at the King's request; and a copy of this manifesto reached every grandee and minister on the Wednesday morning; and the contents were soon common property.

As the recipients of this document were reading it, three coaches, two empty, the other bearing Medellín alone, were observed leaving Madrid in the direction of a well-known water-course. In the water-course Don Juan was waiting. The coaches returned with windows closed and curtains drawn, but as they passed through the Plaza Mayor an inquisitive passer-by managed to peep inside and recognized a figure within. 'Señor Don Juan is within,' he cried, and very soon the whole city was in an uproar.

Crowds surrounded the coaches and as they entered the palace yard the hated 'Chamberg' guard had to push them back. In the audience room Carlos waited. Don Juan entered, and the brothers fell weeping into one another's arms; but, as it was time for church, political discussion was delayed. At the solemn Te Deum it is to be feared that the minds of the large congregation were not wholly concerned with religious matters. Moreover, there was a vacant place; Mariana had a sick headache.

After mass there was obviously nothing for it but that Carlos should visit his mother. What happened at the interview remains a secret between them and their God, but Carlos came out of his mother's room with red eyes. His first act was to tell the Duque de Medinaceli to order Don Juan to Italy. Don Juan not anaturally demanded that the order be given to him in writing, and Carlos sat down and wrote the first decree of his reign. Don Juan went, but not to Italy.

It was one of those occasions sometimes found in history where the cowardice of all the chief actors is responsible for a ridiculous anticlimax. Don Juan was only a theatrical blusterer; given a modicum of courage he could probably have won the day. He had great support, his enemies were loathed, yet he capitulated. He left Madrid literally by a back door.

Mariana was also a coward. In her anger she talked of banishing Don Juan to a remote island. If she had done so history would have been changed. Carlos would not have married a French wife, and her own many years of bitterness would have been less burdensome.

And what of Carlos? He had been living in a fantasy. All a child's resentment against the domination of a hard mother, stimulated by the flattery with which he was surrounded, had led him to imagine that he could be a king and a free individual. His mother had merely to mix anger with tears to show that the chains had not fallen from his limbs. But this does not altogether explain his behaviour, and we must look for the usurping ventriloquist.

There were two of them, and they were the men Mariana herself had chosen to turn Carlos into precisely the individual she desired. They were the King's Confessor and his teacher.

Father Pedro Álvarez de Montenegro had been the keeper of Carlos's conscience since he was less than six years old and had confessed him every week from the day of his confirmation. Chosen by Nithard for the task, he had established a perfect control over the child; and as Carlos had neither intelligence nor will, conscience was the only faculty of the soul which he ever revealed. He relied on his Confessor to keep him out of hell fire, and if any political matter was represented to him as leading him towards that misfortune, he was always anxious to oppose it. It followed that the man to be won over by fair means or foul by any ambitious politician, was always the King's Confessor. Carlos could easily be fooled, he could usually be relied upon to do nothing, but he could never be deflected one step from the strait and narrow path as mapped out for him by his Confessor. Don Juan knew all this.

Father Pedro had begun his Court career as a protégé of Father Nithard, but he had reached a stage of such genuine disgust at Valenzuela's misgovernment that he was prepared for any sort of change. It followed that he had gone into reverse as to the conditioning to which he was supposed to be subjecting his pupil. Carlos was not being urged into a half-conscious hatred of his brother, but into a belief that God wished him to save Spain from Valenzuela, using his brother as the instrument.

Second only to Father Pedro in influence was the very academic, not to say pedantic, sexagenarian who since 1667 had been the poor little boy's tutor. A man of law, not without merit in his own field, indeed with a reputation which spread beyond the borders of Spain, Don Francisco Ramos de Manzano had none of the qualities required in the teacher of a six-year-old boy. His surviving work on pedagogy suggests that his methods were bad. But he should not be blamed too much, for both the heredity and the environment of his royal pupil would have been enemies too strong even for a modern educationist with a child psychiatrist at his elbow.

He appears to have succeeded tolerably well in imparting a grim conspectus of Christian dogma, but to have failed almost completely to impart the rudiments of reading and writing. It can therefore be doubted whether any progress at all was made in Latin, French, Italian, geography, astronomy, fortification and history both sacred and profane, all of which were included in Don Francisco's marching orders.

Don Francisco was a bad teacher but, to do him justice, a good man. He was a puritan and had been the only councillor to vote against the reopening of the comic theatre. He had also been the chosen advocate to answer Louis XIV's legal claims to Flanders. His puritanism might well have put him against Valenzuela, whose only theory of political activity was *Panem et circenses* without the bread, and his legalistic training led him to detest the way in which the Valido and the Queen Mother carried on public affairs.

Thus, whenever Carlos was at his desk, his lessons confirmed what he was told when he was on his knees: the present government must be destroyed for the sake of Spaniard and God alike.

This psychological warfare, which concentrated on removing the Valido, was canalized in a direction favourable to Don Juan by Talhara and especially by Medellín.

Since children like Carlos and brought up like Carlos cannot by dint of a mere anniversary and a legal document free themselves from mothers like Mariana, the conspirators were all disgraced. Medellín was forbidden the palace, Talhara was dismissed, Don Francisco banished to Barajas, and Father Pedro was retired to a monastery. Carlos remained attached to Father Pedro and saw him once more, but all the dismissed Confessor asked was a promise that the King would never have any Confessor who was not a Dominican. As for Don Pascual, he dared to argue with Carlos, who thereupon lost his temper and told him to go away. He replied that nothing would please him better and returned to Toledo.

Mariana had triumphed, but the triumph was short-lived, for Don Juan, as we have seen, never went to Italy. Instead he went to Barcelona where he was popular, and refurbished his plans.

The events of the King's birthday had been exciting, but deplorable. It was as if the pretences had been torn off everybody. As far as Spain was concerned, it was now clear that no one, neither Mariana and Valenzuela on one side, nor Don Juan on the other, and least of all the boy-king, had that modicum of courage, that sufficiency of will to save the country from enemies without and chaos within. It could be affirmed that whoever made decisions and whatever decisions they made, the results would be lethal.

One might have thought that Mariana's position was now unassailable, so long as she possessed control over Carlos's body, and it might have been had she obeyed the rules prevailing in the world of fantasy. She could make every mistake in the real world of government – economic, political, ethical mistakes – and be unshaken; but her final undoing came because she was stupid enough to transgress the laws of etiquette.

She was already hated, but it was not because the people were starving; nor was it because her foreign policy was disastrous, nor because her favourite, Valenzuela, was amassing a fortune. She was said to share his bed, though there is no evidence of this, but even if she had admitted to doing so, it would probably not have ruined her. No, she was hated because she had continually crossed the threads in the network of fantasy. She had had a Jesuit Confessor instead of a Dominican. She had made him a naturalized Spaniard, as if any legal quibble could make that fantastic being, a Spaniard, out of one of the lesser breeds. She had made him Inquisitor General, she had put him in her Council, and each of these actions offended against protocol, injured somebody's obsessively held rights. To save the situation, Nithard had had to go. But Mariana had not learned her lesson. If you are a figure in the Spanish dream-world you must obey the rules which govern dreamers. She chose an upstart, not a bad man in himself, and one capable perhaps of useful work in the world of reality; but she threw him into the world of fantasy, she made him a grandee, gave him rights which he should not have had as to where he could sit, whose hand he could take, when he might keep on his hat. The hatred grew.

And now she took the final and fatal step. On July 8th, 1676, she put the pen in Carlos's clumsy hand and had him sign a decree making Valenzuela 'Gentleman of the Chamber of his Majesty with right of precedence over all his fellows, even the most senior'.

The nobility, too mean in spirit to work for their country's salvation, blind to embezzlement, deaf to the cries of the starving, indifferent to the defeats in unnecessary wars, united together to avenge and protect their dreams. Even in their vengeance fantasy remained uppermost. For one reason and another the Junta of Government was virtually extinct, it was impossible to get together a quorum, and common sense would have suggested that Don Pascual, the Cardinal-Archbishop of Toledo, Primate of the Church, distinguished, honest, even fairly intelligent, would have come forward and collected the fragments of decency still available to form a new government, to seek a new way out. But no, he was not willing even had he been asked. The disgruntled grandees turned once more to the man they had so disliked when he too was made to offend their dignities, the man whom nobody could still admire or trust, Don Juan, who had let everybody down only a few months before.

Why? Don Juan had no powerful military backing; he had shown himself a coward and weak of will. Perhaps his one claim to lead a new government was that he had royal blood in his veins; perhaps even bastards exercise that hypnotic effect which makes men see a divinity in most unlikely quarters.

Be that as it may, Don Juan was the rallying point of all those who hated Valenzuela and Mariana for what she had done for him. After months of anarchic vacillation, things were arranged. Valenzuela fled for sanctuary in the Escorial, whence later he was sacrilegiously torn, and now Don Juan stated his terms: Carlos and his mother must be separated, Valenzuela prosecuted, the Chamberg regiment disbanded.

On January 14th, 1677, Carlos saw a comedy, ate his supper, said good-night to his mother, and went to bed soon after nine, as usual. At eleven he got up, was helped to dress by Medinaceli, left the palace by the garden gate, got into a carriage in which Talhara awaited him, and drove to the Buen Retiro.

In the morning royal orders were sent to Mariana forbidding her to leave the Alcázar until she had further orders in writing. Don Pascual once more set off to deal with Don Juan, who was waiting with a rebel army at Hita. He persuaded him to come alone to receive the Prime Ministership from the King. Don Juan agreed on condition that the soldiers in Madrid should be disbanded before his arrival, Valenzuela arrested, the separation of mother and son made permanent by her banishment to Toledo.

All this was done to the accompaniment of religious exercises, bullfights, shouting in the illumined streets. But all that had happened was that Carlos Segundo now sat upon another ventriloquist's knee.

Of course Mariana stormed and raged, but in the end, when she saw that nothing could be saved from the wreck, human feeling peeped out from some hiding place within the amalgam of hatred, stupidity and injured pride.

> My son and my life [she wrote], as the hour of my departure has come, my love does not allow me to be parted from you in this way without telling you with how much sorrow and despair I part from you without seeing you, and I assure you, although this solace is denied me, that there can never lack in me a mother's duty, so great is the love I bear for you.

> I give you my blessing, praying God to grant all you desire, and hoping that you, for the love you have for me, will always mind those things which will bring me greater consolation.

As for Valenzuela, he spent the rest of his lengthy and wretched life an exile, first in the Philippines and then in Mexico, where he met his death from the kick of a horse. But his monument remains for ever in Madrid. It is the enormous Puente de Toledo over the exiguous Manzanares. Villars, the French ambassador, saying that it would have done very well over the Rhine, advised the Spaniards to sell the bridge or buy a river.

CHAPTER TWELVE

THE END OF DON JUAN

CARLOS's life had so far consisted in a struggle between contending political parties to obtain power over his body. Whoever found himself in a position to make him sign pieces of paper ruled Spain; more than that, he had a large say in the whole future of Europe. Was the great Spanish Empire to remain intact or to be divided up? And in either case was the Austrian Hapsburg or the French Bourbon to inherit all, or the greater part? The future of Europe depended on the answers to those two questions; and the answers depended on what power was guiding the hand of a youth with retarded development.

If Don Juan had not merely been another master of fantasy, his whole policy, once he had attained to power, would have been based on securing immediate peace. No country in Europe needed peace so much as Spain, and yet, under Don Juan, Spain remained the one country that made peace impossible. Defeated in every area of warfare, Spain still thought that she had a right to dictate terms. But the need for peace was far too real a thing to become a basis for policy; Don Juan's actions were guided by something quite different – the compelling need to thwart everything which Mariana of Austria had desired. In a Europe being moulded afresh by new forces, the twin guiding star of Spain's policy was the hate of a woman for her husband's bastard and the hate of a bastard for his father's legitimate wife. Don Juan's one obsessive fear was not Louis XIV, but that the mother and son should be reconciled.

It was at this point that Carlos began to show something almost positive in the make-up of his mind-body; he became conscious of a sensation other than fear of hell and pleasure in slaughtering wolves, wild boars and stags – in a manner which always included adequate precautions for his complete safety. The doctors reported that in view of certain physical manifestations it would be advisable that Carlos should marry.

When we consider his subsequent matrimonial history this medical warning is a little hard to interpret. We are not told what the doctors meant, but there is evidence that Carlos had shown an almost precocious interest in the choice of a wife. In childhood it had been the one subject which excited him. Indeed the explanation of the doctor's warning is probably that the idea of a wife excited him too much.

He had been brought up by his mother to believe that he would marry an Austrian princess. No other marriage was thinkable, and of course this involved maintaining the family habit of inbreeding, for the only Austrian princess he could marry was some unborn daughter of his sister, the Empress Margarita. When in October 1667, Carlos then being scarcely six years old, the news came that Margarita had given birth to a boy, he flew into a temper and said that his sister had promised to give him a queen. He was reassured, and told that the promise would soon be redeemed, whereupon he turned to his nurse, still chiefly preoccupied as to whether or not she should stand a yard in front of the Camarera Mayor, and said: 'When the news comes that my sister has given birth to a daughter, I and thou, without saying anything to anyone, will get into a coach and drive to Germany to bring back my fiancée.'

It was not to turn out like that, however, for Margarita had only one daughter, Maria Antonia, and she was eventually married to Maximilian Manuel of Bavaria, and in time gave birth to one of the three claimants for the reversion of the Spanish throne. Margarita, like a true Hapsburg, died at twenty-two, mourned for her perfections by a husband who candidly admitted that his second wife was a poor second best.

A year after Carlos's disappointment over the sex of his sister's child, Louis made a somewhat generous peace with Spain, and the two countries seemed less distant from one another than they had been for many years. From this time, there was a party in the Spanish Court which canvassed a possibility, hitherto far too heretical to be heard, of reinforcing these improved relations by marrying Carlos to a French princess. At first the suggested bride was his niece, the four-year-old daughter of Louis and his half-sister Maria Teresa, after whom she was named. Mariana of course opposed the very idea of such disloyalty to tradition, but when Carlos was shown her portrait, along with that of the Archduchess Maria Antonia, he seems to have preferred the French niece to the Austrian, and said: 'Let the French one come, and we'll talk of the other later.' However, death took the French one in 1672, and as Louis made war once more against the United Provinces, the French party was, for the time being, discouraged.

In 1674 the Austrian ambassador intervened with a long letter to Mariana in which he reminded her that the Emperor Charles V and the three last Philips had all married their sons to Austrian princesses and that the admirable cult of incest should now be continued. This was an opportunity not to be missed, since it would be a long time before the Spanish and Austrian branches of the Hapsburgs could again intermarry.

With Doña Mariana this was preaching to the converted, but when she put the proposal before the Council of State it was opposed by nearly all the Councillors, though not always for the same reasons. Peñaranda, the leading Francophil, opposed any alliance with the House of Austria, while most of the others wanted the princess brought to Madrid to be educated and the question of a marriage postponed until later. Some added that she must be brought at her father's expense.

It was the Duque de Alba who, as usual, talked common sense. What Spain wanted was an heir, he said, and the Austrian princess was only six years old. A marriage with her was bound to be fruitless for at least another eight years. He therefore rejected the proposed marriage, and suggested that someone must be found who could be relied upon to breed an heir in little more than nine months.

There were only three Councillors who were for an immediate betrothal, but, since this was what she wanted, Mariana accepted the minority opinion and announced the engagement forthwith. There were public illuminations and theatricals in the palace, but the opposition was strong. The public enjoyed the illuminations but refrained from cheering; Don Juan was loud in condemnation; but neither the public nor the bastard were responsible for the immediate collapse of the whole proposal. Carlos came to life so infrequently that it was always a surprise when he did, and he came to life on this occasion. He roundly refused to have anything to do with a child of six who was too young not merely as a wife but also as a playmate. Carlos was thirteen years old, and his usual mood of abject submission to his mother was from now on occasionally broken by spasms of rebellion. The Council and Mariana had to think again.

Mariana clung to her Hapsburg loyalties and proposed that her half-sister Maria Josefa might do for her son. This was the purest fantasy; the young lady was already twenty years old, and it would have been even more injudicious to keep her waiting for her thirteen-year-old nephew than to keep him waiting for his six-year-old niece. The Council resolved to carry out extensive research and to draw up a list of all the European princesses with any claim to eligibility.

As usual nothing came of the Council's deliberations. They rejected each and all, sometimes for reasons which history was to prove erroneous. Thus our future Queen Anne was thought unsuitable, as she was never expected to come to the English throne. In 1676 the Council was still debating and hearing the opinions of its members, and by then the voting was six for Maria Antonia and five against her, while two councillors came forward with other suggestions. The Duque de Medinaceli was still for the aunt, now twenty-two; Don Pascual, the Cardinal-Archbishop, produced a surprising novelty: if it had really proved impossible to find a princess in all Europe of the right age, religion, fertility, and temperament, the wisest thing would be for the King to marry a commoner from among his own subjects.

However, after all this talk the whole matter was dropped, since anything so practical as the marriage of their King was forgotten when the elevation of Valenzuela infringed the dignities of everyone. Then came the Valido's fall and the coming of Don Juan to power, and with that all the previous decisions went for nothing. The marriage was to be settled on quite other principles from those which had been present in people's minds hitherto. What was to select Carlos's bride was no longer Hapsburg dynasticism, still less was it patriotism, but solely hatred. Don Juan looked for support from a wife who would strengthen his position against Mariana. With a wife of his choice and out of the opposite camp he would be more secure. Either he or Mariana would have an ally in Carlos's Queen and there was no doubt in his mind which of them it should be.

He chose a French princess, but it was not until the beginning of 1679 that the Council agreed to his plans.

Don Juan was fortunate; not only did his needs coincide with those of Louis XIV but his choice captivated the heart of his King. For something occurred that nobody had ever expected; at one glance at the portrait of Marie Louise, daughter of the Duke d'Orléans, whom Louis and Don Juan had decided to use for their different purposes, Carlos fell deliriously in love. There was no fantasy about it. For the first time in his life and almost the last, Carlos knew what he wanted and that was a bedfellow. And so there was no difficulty in bringing about a marriage disastrous for Spain, for Carlos, and above all for Marie Louise, soon to be transmuted into Maria Luisa and to exchange Fontainebleau for the gridiron Escorial.

There were of course tedious transactions before the matter could be brought to a conclusion: the Emperor had to be told as tactfully as possible why his daughter had been jilted. The letter written for Carlos to sign explained that his inclinations were of course for the Archduchess Maria Antonia, but that as his subjects required an heir at the first possible moment it must be reluctantly admitted that she was too young. The Emperor took it rather well, only regretting that the choice had fallen on a French princess and mentioning several Germans of lesser rank than his own daughter who would have been a better choice than a Bourbon.

With France there were disappointments. Louis gave his consent, but disabused the Spanish diplomats of their fond hope that the marriage might result in Spain not having to give up quite so much in the unhappy peace that was being negotiated. Louis said that the marriage would be permitted but 'without any question whatever of fortresses or territory, as he would not give up as much as one garden for his niece's marriage, as it mattered very little to him whether she married into Spain or not'. The Spanish ambassador advised his government to proceed with the marriage nevertheless, as the princess was 'of remarkable artistry and physique, tall in proportions, graceful and well modelled, with dark eyes and hair, and, most to the point, apt for immediate fertilization, according to the information I have acquired'.

Don Juan, however, was not to enjoy the advantages of the marriage he had so carefully arranged for his own benefit. He was able to appoint people of his faction to surround the bride when she came, but before she came he was dead. He could not have served himself better. Spanish saviours have never before or since retained their popularity for more than a year or two and Don Juan was no exception. He had achieved nothing in the world of reality, the cost of bread went up, he had deliberately prolonged the war; in the world of fantasy he had inevitably offended almost everyone. Maria Luisa would not have given him enough weight to withstand another palace revolution, which would have treated him like a second, more hated, Valenzuela.

Don Juan had brought ruin, disappointment, misery to many, but in one thing he was on the side of the angels – he tried to give his half-brother some crumbs of education. He may not have tried harder than the banished man of law, but he certainly tried more sensibly. He even tried to teach Carlos to write, and for a whole summer persuaded him to copy out maxims. He got his attendant meninos to recite in chorus things he was supposed to learn by heart. But Carlos showed very little aptitude. Don Juan realized with genuine regret that a ventriloquist would always be necessary. Be it recorded to his credit that he never wished to play the part himself; he wanted a partner in government and not a doll. However, his preferences were of no importance, and he went out of the picture with nothing to show for his short months of power except a country some steps further on the way to total collapse, and a French marriage.

In one way his death was something of a misfortune for Carlos, since he clearly meant well of the marriage: but with the bastard out of the way mother and son could be reconciled, and Mariana's destructive hate would be turned on the unsuitable daughter-in-law even now on her way to meet her fate. As far as Mariana was concerned, she came with a double handicap; she was French and she was the bastard's choice.

Don Juan did not die without seeing the beginning of the end of his policies, or realizing how much more important in making up the King's mind a Confessor would always be than a Prime Minister. As Don Juan lay sick, the wives and relatives of nearly all the men he had banished came to the new Confessor and begged him to influence the King. This new Confessor was Fray Francisco Reluz who will turn up again at an exciting moment of this history and show himself a man of sense. Fray Francisco secured a number of acts of clemency out of Carlos and, when Don Juan on his sick-bed disapproved, Carlos astounded and delighted everyone by saying: 'What matters what Don Juan opposes, if I want it.' Carlos seldom felt like a man, but always felt like a king.

It was not long before Carlos consulted his Confessor as to whether it would be right for him to see his mother. Reluz replied that apart from possible political complications into which he did not wish to enter, there were no conscientious grounds for denying the meeting. Villars, the new French ambassador, saw that it would help Marie Louise with Mariana if he helped the Queen Mother to get what she so much desired, and lent his support to her. On September 17th, 1679, Don Juan died. Three days later Carlos was in his mother's arms.

CHAPTER THIRTEEN

THE FRENCH BRIDE

MARIE LOUISE was, unfortunately, the prettiest princess in Europe; even so, she was animated rather than beautiful, but nearly all the other princesses were plain and only half alive. Her temperament, assisted by her upbringing, was frivolous. So far as education was concerned, she experienced nothing but a perpetual finishing-school. She was expert at walking and curtsying, French style, she rode very well, she could follow a pack of hounds. She danced all French Court dances perfectly. She had every quality needed to make a husband enjoy life, provided that he had the capacity for doing so.

She was completely innocent of all knowledge of, or interest in, serious matters such as politics. Louis could hardly have hoped that he was planting a shrewd observer in the Court of Madrid. The granddaughter of England's martyred king, the daughter of Henrietta of England, who had almost certainly died by poison, and of Monsieur, the aesthetic, effeminate brother of Louis XIV, she was also the stepdaughter of Isabel Carlota del Palatinado, known as Madame, the greatest letter-writer, both qualitatively and quantitatively, of the day. She acquired from these neither aesthetic nor intellectual interests.

She had charm, grace, vivacity, the very qualities which counted for nothing south of the Pyrenees. Properly assisted she would have undoubtedly displayed the one attribute desired in the Court of Spain, fertility. She only wanted to enjoy herself, but she was quite capable of making others enjoy themselves in the process. Unfortunately her idea of how to be happy was not acceptable to Spanish etiquette.

She was not fitted to be a statesman, or to assume the responsibility which the King could not face because he was almost imbecile. She was not conspicuously religious, or afraid of God's vengeance. She was naturally orthodox, but not in the Spanish way. The Most Christian King's Court cultivated the deity in a very different manner from the Court of the Catholic King. Finally, she was not cut out to be the wife of an impotent husband.

Spanish historians are peevish about the legends which French and other writers have woven about her. The Duque de Maura proves conclusively that she was never 'in love' with the Dauphin, by asserting that nobody fell in love until the disease had been invented a century or so later, by people of a different political faith from the Duque. He is of course correct in so far as all seventeenth-century princesses regarded their marriages not as matters of personal preference but as diplomatic moves; nor had the fantasy of romantic hallucinatory fixation become fashionable so early. But he may be stretching a point when he deduces from this that Marie Louise was happy at the idea of becoming a Spanish Queen. There is no reason to doubt that she was a healthy animal with sexual appetites or that all she heard about her future husband filled her with dismay. Nobody yet knew the worst about him, but his looks, even in Carreño's portrait which came to her in a diamond-studded frame, did not suggest an ideal partner for a pleasure-loving, potentially sensual girl.

There is no sound evidence that Marie Louise, even without romantic feelings, had set her cap at the Dauphin. He was not particularly attractive either, and his betrothal had been announced some time before she was disposed of; and it is quite certain that, when Louis told her in public that she was to be Queen of Spain, and added that he could not have done more for his own daughter, she did not reply: 'For your daughter, no, but for your niece, yes.' She was not clever enough to think up such a *mot* on the spur of the moment, and if she had, she would not have been fool enough to say it. The French have a tendency to gild the lily of history with clevernesses which are seldom found in reality.

She lacked one emotional attribute which might have saved her. If only she could have hated. Mariana her mother-in-law, and many other queens of her time, were saved by the violence with which they concentrated on injuring someone they disliked. Marie Louise did not possess this capacity. All she wanted was to enjoy herself frivolously and this was quite impossible for a Queen of Spain.

Louis, of course, knew what his niece was going to find. He had no illusions about Carlos's physical condition. He knew that his jaw was so deformed that he was quite unable to masticate his food, which he swallowed in large lumps to the subsequent discomfort of his digestive system. He knew of his constantly recurring fevers, his attacks of giddiness, his discharges and his rashes. He knew that there was a mind appropriate to the body. 'This Prince,' he told his ambassador Harcourt, 'has passed his life in profound ignorance. Never have they explained to him his own interests, and the unique maxim in which they have endeavoured to instruct him is extreme aversion to France. His own inclination has kept him from business, and timidity makes him hate the world. His temperament is impulsive, choleric, and induces in him extreme melancholy. The sadness which possesses his spirit has the effect of stimulating the infirmities which afflict him.' This was not going to be a marriage of true minds.

So much for the bride and groom; the espousals and marriage by proxy took place at the end of August at Fontainebleau. There were weeks of festivities, enormous banquets, at one of which one thousand ortolans were served on gold and silver plate: Racine's last tragedy, *Phèdre*, was acted for the first time; the wedding presents were immensely rich; the bride's dress the most beautiful ever seen.

We are told that the French were surprised at the rich gifts and rich equipages of various Spanish nobles, as it was generally supposed that Spain was so impoverished that such things could not be expected even of her most wealthy. They little knew what was going on in Madrid in the effort to raise enough money to pay for necessities when the Queen arrived.

One thing which particularly worried the Council of State was that they had neither the money nor the material with which to build a state coach to bring the French princess from the frontier to Madrid. Even if they had been able to provide the coach, the roads were so bad that it was very doubtful whether it could have made the journey. There was Marie Louise riding gaily on horseback south from Paris, but she would not be allowed to ride once she had been handed over to her Spanish entourage, for

Queens of Spain must not ride. Though the Duque de Alba offered to defray the cost of a suitable state coach, it was felt that the roads could not be made up in time, and a litter was decided upon instead. From horseback to litter therefore was the first result of Marie Louise becoming Maria Luisa.

Even so the Spaniards found it impossible to make the minimum preparations in time, and secret messages were sent to the Spanish ambassador to delay Marie Louise's progress in every way possible. This met with no opposition from her, since she was feverishly enjoying riding on her Irish hacks and hunting with the pack of hounds she was bringing with her, while every town on the way was delighted to delay her still longer with festivities.

Two people were put out by the tardiness, however, Harcourt, who thought it was deliberately done by Marie Louise so as to put off seeing her unattractive husband as long as possible, and poor maundering Carlos himself who took her portrait to bed with him and covered it with kisses. Harcourt was quite wrong: the real reason was that Carlos's mayordomo and the Captain General of Guipúzcoa were quite incapable of making the necessary arrangements for the take-over at the frontier.

It is strange that the Spaniards, whose theatrical tradition is as fine as any nation's, have seldom been able to stage-manage their ceremonies efficiently, except in the case of an occasional bullfight or auto-de-fé. To this day things always go wrong with the timing, the stage props, the book of words. It was certainly so with the procedures at Marie Louise's coming. One would have hoped that people would enjoy themselves, for, after all, it was not a funeral; but one has only to read the contemporary accounts to realize that it was a pleasant experience for hardly anyone.

The river Bidasoa is not one of the largest rivers in the world but that is nothing to its discredit; for that matter nor is the Rubicon. But crossing them involved far more than crossing the Mississippi or the Amazon. Dividing the waters of the Bidasoa, half-way between France and Spain, is the minute Isle of Pheasants. Here Frenchman and Spaniard have tried more than once to see each other as human beings. On this occasion the French seem to have behaved as if they were on a visit to a zoo, the Spanish as if their guests were trying to catch them out by omitting one obsessional step in a ritual on which depended the continued existence of the universe. And apart from international distastes which were not always concealed, there were the usual fantasy-wars between one Spaniard and another. Who should sit where was disputed, who should keep his hat on, who should offer his hand.

Perhaps the worst shock for the French princess was her meeting with the formidable old dragon who had been selected by Don Juan de Austria for her Camarera Mayor. This lady, who was to rule her life for years, and to devote herself with the best intentions to making her miserable, was Juana, Duquesa de Terranova, of some sixty-five winters. Nobody liked the Duquesa, though Don Juan had occasionally found her useful.

Curiously enough for one whose life was devoted to the cause of etiquette, she was a murderess, or so the evidence seems to suggest, for of course the matter never came to court. She had been engaged in a furious quarrel with a cousin over some inheritance, and one night the cousin's body was found outside a Madrid convent with six wounds, all of them mortal. It is not suggested that hers was the hand that wielded the fateful poniard, but there was good reason to believe that hers was the inspiration. She found it wise to flee to Aragon and put herself under Don Juan's protection.

Having thus forcefully secured her inheritance, the Duquesa devoted her mind and faculties to mastering and implementing the most rigid and detailed code of etiquette. The sixth commandment she may not have much taken into account, but woe to the man who kept his hat on when he should have taken it off, or the lady who sat down on a chair with a back when she was only entitled to relax on a bench. This was the lady into whose hands Monsieur's daughter now fell. It involved a perpetual end to laughter, to riding, to dancing, even to eating in public: Queens of Spain could not do these things.

After much formality and feasting, and more muddle and breaches of etiquette, Marie Louise found herself ferried over the rest of the Bidasoa and inside Spain. The journey began with only a few of her French entourage accompanying her, and most of these leaving her at Burgos. In Madrid her companion was to be a certain Widow Quentin whom the Spaniards, with their habitual inability to pronounce foreign proper names, called La Cantina, and disliked intensely: another female companion, five ladies-in-waiting, a confessor, two doctors, a surgeon, a hairdresser, a cook, a groom and an Irishman to teach her Spanish.

Slowly the safari moved south-east, the roads were awful, the inns intolerably cold. Not only was Marie Louise in a litter instead of on the back of an understanding horse, but her sole companion within the litter was the formidable Terranova. The poor girl could not even look out of the window, for the curtains were drawn. The Duquesa explained that it would be very indecent for a Spanish Queen to be seen casually by ordinary passers-by.

When she got out of the litter to eat, Terranova told her that it would be just as indecent for anyone to see her eating except her serving girls. Indeed Terranova was impossible and Marie Louise protested. Her request for a certain amount of freedom was dispatched post-haste to Carlos waiting at Burgos, and he sent back permission to eat in public sometimes, and to ride when she could not bear Terranova and the litter any longer.

Meanwhile the King advanced from the south, taking a good deal of time over it, for although he felt himself physically more than ready to meet his bride, nothing else was ready at all; all the royal dwellings were being remodelled and redecorated and nothing could be finished on time. Wherever he went there were bullfights, but for once in his life they bored him, his fantasies being otherwise engaged. A number of courtiers had succeeded in avoiding this most tedious journey, made worse by incessant rain and intolerable cold. At one place it was freezing inside the inn as well as outside and there was no means of heating. Carlos had to go to bed for two days with a fever.

Apart from the physical discomfort and the worries about money, there were the usual offended feelings. Even Marie Louise's first mounting of a horse under her new charter of freedom caused trouble. Osuna was upset over a question of precedence and behaved rudely in front of her. He was banished to house arrest in Madrid until further notice. Next, Carlos decided that the marriage should be celebrated by the Patriarch of the Indies, an arrangement wrecked by the Archbishop of

Burgos who claimed the right for himself, as it was to take place in Burgos Cathedral. No sooner had this been agreed upon than the Archbishop gave unmistakable signs of being about to die. This would indeed have been a calamity had it occurred before the wedding, and it was resolved to hold the ceremony two days earlier at a wretched hamlet called Quintanapalla.

The French ambassador, Villars, was not told of the change of plans, and, observing that he was coldly received by the Spaniards when he visited Marie Louise, concluded that something was up. He found Harcourt, the French Ambassador Extraordinary, equally in the dark and hurried off to Burgos to observe the lie of the land. On the way he met the Patriarch of the Indies mysteriously driving in the direction of Quintanapalla. Villars felt that such a secret journey was odd, unless the object was to marry off the royal pair without letting the French know. This indeed was the intention, and it was only frustrated by Villars and Harcourt riding after the Patriarch of the Indies and, to the embarrassment of the Spanish plotters, arriving just in time.

Thus, in an atmosphere of senseless intrigue, and in a hamlet so ill-provided that a room for the wedding had to be improvised in the best farmhouse, Marie Louise finally became Maria Luisa. There was a delay while the French ambassador disputed as to who had the right to walk first behind the bride and bridegroom, but at last all was over; Carlos and Maria Luisa were joined and went off in one coach alone to Burgos. It is to be hoped that she preferred Carlos as travelling companion to Terranova, who followed on like destiny.

It were impertinent to speculate on how the young couple passed the hours in the coach and subsequently in the bridal suite, were it not that soon all Madrid, all Spain, all Europe were doing so. As they could not speak a word to one another, what could they do but make love? Carlos did not hide his delight in his bride and in the married state; Maria Luisa seemed content with that at least, though she hardly took to Spanish customs.

She was now dressed in Spanish style: no longer were the orbs of her breasts just contained at their middle line; her dress reached her larynx. She discovered that even the shape of the feminine buttocks was considered too alluringly intimate to be left undistorted by her skirt. Her hair was not allowed its natural curl but was smoothed and plastered down with water and other liquids. The unreliable Madame d'Aulnoy recounts that the dragon Terranova once flattened a recalcitrant curl with her saliva, but owing to Maria Luisa's protests did not repeat the method. It is safer to believe none of d'Aulnoy's facts, but they do sometimes bear an approximation to the truth.

Maria Luisa found Carlos less of a menace than she had expected, and certainly an improvement as travelling companion over Terranova since with him the curtains could be opened. Besides, she thoroughly enjoyed the unrestrained admiration of the Spanish crowds wherever she was seen. Fortunately she could not understand the remarks shouted at her, since it has always been a Spanish custom on such occasions to express their admiration a little too freely.

It is said that Terranova, being of the party of the dead Don Juan, had lost no opportunity of inspiring Maria Luisa with distaste and distrust for her mother-in-law, but, when the two queens met, Mariana went out of her way to be affectionate and conciliatory. It soon became clear that the French girl was going to be allowed more of her own way and of her own amusements than seemed likely at first – more indeed than was to prove good for her.

Beneath the surface things were not so satisfactory. The whole country was starving, and there was no functioning government. Carlos spent a quarter of an hour a day signing documents put before him by an obscure official; Mariana had never had any desire to transact the daily business of the state; and Maria Luisa was clearly not going to fulfil any public function.

The entire Spanish Court had convinced itself that there was only one solution to the country's problems and that was the speedy pregnancy of the new Queen. Clearly this would not solve the scarcity of bread, the breakdown of all public order to the extent that no road was safe from starving bandits, the stealing from the royal treasury, the melting away of tax receipts long before they reached their proper goal, the debasement of the currency, which left no one certain from one day to another what any coin was worth. Yet all this was submerged from conscious thought by the obsessive desire for an heir, and by a round of entertainments, presumably to honour and please the

Queen, though their effect was to bore her. We do not know what she thought of bullfights, but in these early days when her grasp of the language was virtually nil, the comedies must have been tedious in the extreme. It was partly to distract her, and partly to interest and soften a God who seemed to be put out with his own country, Spain, that it was now resolved to hold the greatest of all Spanish dramatic occasions. This was the function which, if all else failed, must surely induce the delighted deity to deal a little less hardly with his people: to lower the price of bread perhaps, and so ensure a closer sense of solidarity between the starving people and their stupid rulers. It was decided to hold an auto-de-fé, for who could tell? perhaps God, so signally honoured, would permit the now overdue pregnancy of Maria Luisa.

CHAPTER FOURTEEN

AUTO-DE-FÉ

THERE can be no denying that the show staged on June 30th, 1680, in the Plaza Mayor of Madrid, must have been one of the most dramatic, the most moving, conceived by the mind of man since the days when Christians and wild beasts fought one another for the amusement of decadent Rome. If we are to believe his contemporaries, it was Carlos himself who ordered the great spectacle.

It must also have been one of the most exhausting functions to which any king ever deliberately allowed himself to be subjected. From eight in the morning, all the fierce length of a Madrid summer day, until half past nine at night, Carlos and his Queen not merely took part in, but remained immobile and mask-like throughout a ceremony which was sometimes inaudible for hours at a time, amid a murmuring crowd in which religion, sadism and curiosity were combined. And to the same physical and mental stresses which their King and Queen bore so nobly, there were subjected nineteen men and women who would be burned at the end of the day. If they confessed their guilt they would be strangled first, and quite a number were to clutch at this small comfort. The fanatical remainder would be burned alive in a foretaste of eternal hell. The eighteen-year-old Carlos and all the crowds gathered with him were convinced that what they did was necessary and gratifying to God. Indeed, they got forty days, indulgence simply for their attendance.

Spain was not the only country to authorize cruelty in that cruel age, but no other country was so successful in combining pious cruelty with a nice sense of theatre. Throughout Europe, pious cruelty was burning thousands of witches, but crudely, with none of the dramatic genius of the Spaniard when he burned Jews and heretics. Nowhere else was the act of pious cruelty aesthetically turned into an act of mass ecstasy, a hypnotizing drama in which the passions of the mob were fanned into a mystical inebriation. It was not only the nineteen people destined for the *brasero* that were burned; something, one feels, must have been burned out on these occasions in the minds of everybody who was there. How could anyone remain the same, remain altogether human, after partaking in this act of holy sadism?

Fortunately the story can be told from purely Spanish accounts, for Spanish historians are to this day particularly sensitive to foreign comment on these festivals. Such autos-de-fé, they will tell you, saved religion in Spain from the devilries of a Luther or a Voltaire. Comment from a foreigner is inadvisable, and fortunately unnecessary, since Spaniards may be left to tell their own story unblushingly.

Carlos, we are told, had shown his love of the Holy Inquisition from the earliest days of his reign, that is, one must suppose, from the age of four; and he had more than once hinted that he would much enjoy taking part in an auto-de-fé where 'the living image of the majestic throne of Jesus Christ in Heaven' was made palpable. The Inquisitor General now told him that the prisons of the Inquisition at Toledo and elsewhere being full of condemned Jews, heretics and infidels, everything was ready for the celebration.

The whole of the month of June was spent in preparations. The labour of discovering and complying with correct etiquette was formidable, and money had to be raised in a country so afflicted with starvation and poverty that it had been impossible, a few months back, to equip a coach fit for a princess coming as a bride. An armed force had to be recruited, since there were no military units of Spanish nationality available.

The festival of St Paul was chosen because, as usual, a majority of the criminals against The Faith were relapsed Jews, and St Paul seemed highly suitable as patron of their discomfiture.

The first solemn episode took place a month before the culminating event. The thirtieth of May was deemed appropriate, for it was not only the Feast of the Ascension but of the sainted King Fernando, who had carried on his own shoulder a brand for the brasero where the Albigensian heretics were to be burned, 'thus leaving to posterity a heroic token of the fervid zeal for the Christian religion which burned in his breast'.

On that day the standard of the Holy Inquisition was unfurled over the Inquisitor General's balcony, while crimson damask adorned the whole façade of his mansion. Clarions and drums summoned the crowds. The familiars, officials and notaries of the Inquisition gathered at the windows. After two hours of this loud clangour, it was felt that enough time had been given for all to foregather. A cavalcade of a hundred and fifty people, all in the individual trappings of their office and bearing the sacred standards, followed by a crowd of lesser officials, perambulated through the city stopping at the traditional places to proclaim the coming Auto, and to call on all to attend. Attendance would be rewarded by the usual indulgences, and absence would be punished by loss of privileges. The crowds were so immense that the arrangements were several times interfered with and it was decided, therefore, that on the day itself carriages and horses must be prohibited from the streets of Madrid.

The preparations now went ahead full speed; everyone worked with a punctuality which seemed to the Spanish chronicler, Don José de Olmo, who was also chief organizer, quite superhuman; when more workmen were needed to build the 'teatro' they came forward without being ordered to, and they worked without taking a siesta. So great was their enthusiasm that they declared that if the supply of wood ran short they would pull down their houses to make good the deficit.

The Theatre in the Plaza Mayor was a hundred and ninety feet long by a hundred wide, with its second storey thirteen feet above ground level. A corridor was built through the structure so that the criminals could march under the balcony where sat the King and Queen, who would want to see at close hand every mark of ignominy borne by them. Altars, pulpits, thrones, benches and passages for the passing of participants to and fro, cells for the prisoners, robing rooms, refreshment rooms, all sprang up in a few days and, greatest marvel of all, a vast awning was stretched over the whole structure. Crimson damask and rich hangings adorned it and the balconies of one side of the square which was used for distinguished people. The rostrum from which the sentences were to be read was hung with purple. The balcony from which the royal party were to watch had been enlarged by breaking down the façade of which it was a part, and a rich carpet was laid for the Inquisitor General to walk over to receive the King's oath. The balconies immediately above had been removed, as no one must be accommodated immediately above the royal heads.

Meanwhile a special temporary army of two hundred and fifty officers and men were recruited and drilled. They were to defend the Inquisition, for the time being, from non-existent enemies, but their most moving duty was performed on June 28th, when they marched to a pile of faggots and thence to the Palace Square, each soldier bearing a faggot on his shoulder. Arrived at the palace, their captain climbed the stairs to the King's apartment 'carrying on a shield a faggot of brushwood, shaped and proportioned in the most decent way for presenting to the King, our master'. The Duque de Pastrana took it from the captain and handed it to Carlos, who carried it in his own hands to show the Queen. He then returned it to the Duque, ordering him to give it back to the captain and to tell him to have it thrown first on the brasero, in his name, thereby showing that he had inherited the piety of King Ferdinando III, though not the physical strength to carry the token of his piety himself. The soldiers marched to the brasero and deposited their faggots, but kept the King's faggot separate and under guard so that his wish could later be respected.

There were also enrolled for this occasion a supplementary host of familiars, that sinister body of men formed to carry out the orders of the judges and other high officers of the Inquisition. These familiars or members of the Inquisitorial family had been given many privileges by many popes, and especially by Pope Clement VII, who accorded them plenary indulgence and remission of all sins *in articulo mortis*, including those crimes and excesses normally reserved. Clement VII had gone further: any familiar who visited five altars in one church and said on his knees five Paternosters or five Ave Marias every day in the year was granted the same indulgences as would have been conceded if he had made a pilgrimage to Rome. Naturally, all who could, seized the golden opportunity; their numbers included twenty-five grandees and sixty nobles of lesser rank.

On the eve of the Day, the processions of the Green Cross and the White Cross wound through the streets with all solemnity. The Standard of the Green Cross symbolized hope; it bore on a black background, on either side of the Cross, an olive branch and a sword, the whole motif implying that there was clemency for those who repented. The Standard of the White Cross, which our commentator rightly says might with all propriety have been blood red, symbolized the severity of God's just judgment.

Chanting the Miserere, the processions visited the various churches and convents and the royal palace, and ended up late at night, the Green Cross at its place in the Teatro and the White Cross at the brasero on the outskirts of the city. All this was mere preliminary, a terrifying pomp to complete the psychological conditioning of the whole city for what was to follow.

'The crown of all these celebrations and the true function of the Auto-General-de-Fé, was the majestic pomp with which the Tribunal went forth, bringing with it the guilty to be judged at the most noble throne and magnificent theatre that human artistry has devised to arouse fear and veneration, since it can be properly compared to what will be seen on the fearful day of God's universal judgment; since on the one hand the ignominy of the unjust marked by symbols of their crimes and punishments will cause horror, and on the other joy will be caused by the glory of the just and the sovereign majesty of Christ and his Apostles, who, following the standard of the cross, attended by choirs of angels, will march to the valley of Josafat. There before the supreme judge on his throne, with those who followed him seated in their promised places, will be read in the presence of all the world our deserts and pleas, and, without any intercession being of use, sentences will be fulminated and executed.'

Nothing could sum up better the true meaning of the auto-de-fé. It was a dramatic simulation of the Judgment Day; partly a foretaste of that great pleasure which, according to Tertullian, was to be the reward of the good, namely, the contemplation of the tortures of the damned; partly a warning, by making the consequences of evil-doing most vivid, that it is wisest to be orthodox. Only by having real fire and torment for the lapsed could the psychological objective be achieved. Without them it would have been no Day of Judgment, for the whole thing would have remained on the level of a mundane theatrical performance—the crowds would have been spectators and not participants.

That evening, the criminals were removed from the private

houses of the familiars and incarcerated for greater security in secret dungeons. There, during the night, the oldest Inquisitor visited them, and his secretary read out their sentences. He said to those about to be burned:

> Brother, your case has been viewed and considered by persons learned in letters and science, and your crimes are so grave and so evil that for punishment and for an example to others it has been decided and adjudged that you must die tomorrow; prepare yourself therefore, and to help you make ready, two monks are remaining with you.

At each cell door two familiars were stationed, and the two monks set to work on each condemned person, to wrestle with him all night in an effort to make him repent. It was exhausting work for all concerned, and biscuits, chocolate, sweet cakes and drinks were liberally provided.

Throughout the night the monks painted the horrors in store for their charges, both in this world and the next, and made genuine efforts to get them to say the few words that would change death by fire into death by strangling and, by God's mercy, hell into purgatory and later even into heaven. It is astonishing that any held out, rather than that some gave in.

Most of them had been so exhausted by their previous experiences that they did not care what was going to happen to them, and perhaps did not even know what was going on about them. Most had been years in prisons, no better than prisons elsewhere in Europe in those days; most had probably been tortured to extract a confession.

It is quite untrue that the Spanish Inquisition made any subtle innovations in the art of torture: they followed the customs of secular courts elsewhere. It was essential for the accused person's own sake that a confession should be extracted, for, without one, eternal torment was certain. To help the penitent soul, which was assumed to inhabit the peccant flesh, the resistance of the flesh had to be broken down. Two methods were used: first, the accused had his wrists tied behind his back and a rope passed from them to the roof; with this he was gradually raised from the floor and let down with a jerk. Each time he was raised a little more. If that failed to break down his body's resistance to his soul's salvation, the water torture was tried: he was strapped head downwards by ropes that cut into his veins; his mouth and nostrils were stuffed with absorbent material, and he was slowly immersed until death by suffocation was only just avoided.

Confession was usually forthcoming; if it did not come, though it was illegal to torture a second time, it was quite legal to continue the first torture after an interval! Another humanitarian safeguard was that doctors examined the victim first, to see if he could withstand torture. Every effort was made to prevent the torture ending in death, but if a victim did die, the blame was not laid at the door of the officiating staff but at that of the victim, who had brought the accident upon himself by refusing to confess without torture. Moral theologians discussed the question whether a faithful Catholic might confess to heresy of which he was not guilty, so as to avoid torture. The majority opinion of moral theologians was that such a way out was not permissible.

It was all done for the best possible motives. What was an uncomfortable hour in a dungeon compared with an eternity of suffering at the hands of probably far more ingenious practitioners! But a confession did not necessarily save one from all this: if it was not considered complete, its completion was achieved by physical persuasion, and if a man confessed his own heresy but refused to implicate any of his neighbours, that too was regarded as insufficient.

On the same night, all roads leading into the route of the procession were barricaded, with ample holes in the woodwork for people to look through. At three o'clock in the morning the prisoners were clothed in their ritual garments, and two hours later they were given their last breakfast. The procession began to form at seven o'clock with the Soldiers of the Faith in the lead, followed by the Cross of the Parish of St Martin veiled in black and carried by twelve priests in surplices. After it, came the hundred and twenty criminals, each one with two monks at his side, first those to be most lightly punished and later those to be burned alive. Thirty-four of these were effigies, the real people having succeeded in escaping from Spain, or in dying in the secret prisons of the Inquisition. All these, save two, were also to be burned, and were therefore dressed in cone-shaped hats with flames painted round them, while the effigies of some who had died had their bones carried before them in caskets. The two effigies of criminals with lesser punishments wore *sanbenitos*, or penitent's cloaks, and they had their names written on placards on their chests. Next to the men carrying the effigies came eleven prisoners *con abjuración de levi*, prisoners who had renounced their heresies which were of a nature to deserve the lighter sort of punishment. These included bigamists and those guilty of 'hypocritical trickery', and superstitious observances. They wore conical hats, and halters round their necks with knots in them, one knot for every hundred lashes to which they had been sentenced. Next to them came fifty-four relapsed Jews in penitential cloaks. All these carried yellow unlighted candles. Last came the twenty-one to be burned, in cloaks and head-dresses painted with flames; those who still persisted in their heresies, with dragons as well among the flames. Twelve were gagged and manacled. Each of these was still accompanied by a monk who tried to persuade the impenitent and to comfort the penitent.

A great company of officials and familiars came next, and in their midst two caskets covered with gold cloth decorated with gold fringes in which lay the documents of each case and the sentences to be read out.

So far the procession was all on foot, but now followed a large gathering of people of importance all on richly caparisoned horses. After them came the officials of the Inquisition, two by two, dressed in black, on mules with black trappings, with the badges of their office on their chests. The contrast between the richly accoutred courtiers and these black figures, those on high stepping horses, these in whom the real power lay on humbler animals, particularly impressed the crowd.

All these preliminaries had raised the whole population of Madrid to the necessary pitch of excitement for everyone to share emotionally in what was to follow. There could have been very few who remained unaffected, for there were no sceptics, no free-thinkers – at least able to be vocal – no one protected from the general infection by an alien faith. And as on the Day of Judgment, there were no spectators; it was an interior experience for all alike.

The King, Queen and Queen Mother arrived at eight o'clock and took their seats in the twenty-ninth balcony on the lowest tier. It was familiar to them, for it was from there that they watched bullfights and other secular spectacles. All the other balconies on this side of the square, opposite the Teatro, about a hundred in number and four tiers high, had been allotted according to etiquette.

The ladies-of-honour were in the next balcony on the right, and the next eight balconies were filled by the ladies-in-waiting of the Queen and Queen Mother. On the left, the corresponding gentlemen of the King's Court had six balconies allotted to them. Don José is enthusiastic about the way the court ladies had 'sanctified their finery' by embroidering on their breasts the symbols of the Faith, while those who had had no time for needlework had bought symbols and fastened them on.

In the tier above were the grandees in three balconies, together with the most eminent head of the Church in Spain, the Cardinal-Archbishop of Toledo. Here also were the leading ambassadors; and the Duque de Medinaceli, as head of the Government, had two balconies to himself and family. The third and fourth tiers were occupied by officials only less glitteringly important than these. The whole was a sort of vertical Field of the Cloth of Gold.

Under the awning in front of this array of wealth, beauty, lineage, were many grim structural details. Below-stage were the criminals with their argumentative holy assistants. On the stage, officials occupied benches, while the Inquisitor General, the impersonator of the judging and avenging God, sat high on a throne. The pulpit was as yet empty, but ready to be occupied by a tedious Dominican. Stages were ready to receive each victim while his sentence was read out, while a stage higher than these was to be used for displaying the condemned men to universal ignominy and disgust.

And now the ceremonies begin. After prostrating himself in prayer beneath the Green Cross, the Inquisitor General robes himself. One priest brings the pontificals, one holds ready the mitre, a third the crozier, a fourth the Gospels. Don Francisco Reluz, the King's Confessor, carries the cross on which Carlos will swear allegiance to Christianity and the Inquisition, and promise to persecute all heretics and apostates. The procession moves across the rich carpet to the King's balcony; the Inquisitor reads the oath, Carlos listening intently, and eagerly replying:

'Thus do I swear and promise by my faith and royal word.' After the King, the whole Court and City of Madrid take the oath. They swear to persecute and bring to justice every heretic and everyone suspected of heresy, and they promise to help and give comfort to none.

Then the mass, and in due course the sermon. This rolled its periods beneath the tent in the gathering heat of the day. It began with Adam and touched on most of the chief characters in Holy Writ. It painted the horror of heresy. It is tedious to read, but we can visualize the gestures, the shaken fist, the hissing tones directed towards the prisoners; we cannot but marvel at the perfect faith in Spain's particular place in God's affection; the joyful certainty that in this smelling out of wickedness and this rewarding of it by a lingering death, the witch-doctors were doing the right thing. The soaring peroration likens the scene to the words used by the Holy Spirit to describe the whole Church: 'Beautiful art thou, my beloved, like a tabernacle of Cedar, and like the skins of Solomon.' Why did not the Holy Spirit, asks the preacher, compare the Church to the skies adorned by sun, moon, stars? Why not to a lovely garden? What praise is it to a delicate lady or a rare beauty to be compared to a cedar tent and the soiled skins of Solomon? St Jerome explains this difficult point: these people were so fond of hunting that they adorned their tents with the heads of wild beasts to show the valour of their arms, placing the dead skins on the ground, and the heads of a fierce lion, or horned stag, or striped tiger, against its posts. And it was to this that the Holy Spirit chose to liken the Church.

> And this is today the glory of the Inquisition: like a cedar tabernacle, like the skins of Solomon – To have killed these horrible fierce beasts, God's enemies, who we see in this Theatre, in some cases removing their errors before death, and by the recognition of their faults reconciling them to our holy faith, and in others, for their pertinacity, condemning them to the flames, whence on losing their corporeal existence, their obstinate souls will go at once to burn in the flames of hell, where God desires to be avenged on his worst enemies.

As he pronounced these words, the Dominican and the well-dressed box-holders opposite must have turned their eyes towards the victims. They did not look much like fierce wild beasts; they were in fact very tame by now. Hanging on posts were the effigies of the lucky ones missing or dead before the burning; those who had died in the prisons were represented by their rotting bones.

Next to them were those to be burned, in person, some of them gagged and manacled. Below them, on another stage, were those to suffer comparatively minor punishments, such as life imprisonment, five years in the galleys without pay, a few hundred lashes, public ignominy. Even these, one feels, if they were sufficiently conscious, were carried away by the eloquent preacher. Even these probably believed in a painful passage to hell. The reader must often have wondered what the mouse feels when the cat has played for a long time; nothing, we hope. Perhaps the mouse feels that a just God created him as a meal for the cat. Some such atonement must have existed in the pain-drugged minds of these 'wild beasts'.

After the two hours' sermon came the reading of the sentences, carried out with great efficiency so that no time should be wasted. While one secretary was reading one sentence, the next prisoner was ushered into place and his sentence found in the documents by the other secretary. In this way, not more than eight or nine hours were needed for the work of reading the sentences.

The lightest punishments, which were taken last, had been given to people like Leonor Diaz, widow of Nicolas Sanchez, born and living in Gibraltar, thirty-four years old, who went to the auto in penitential garb, with dunce cap and insignia of a superstitious witch. She was abjured *de levi*, admonished, reprehended and threatened, and on July 2nd was driven in shame through the public streets and banished for four years from the cities of Seville, Gibraltar, Madrid and eight leagues about. To have got off so lightly, her sins must have been minimal. Antonio Nieto and several others got five years in the galleys for bigamy. Inés Caldera, besides the other punishments, received two hundred lashes in the public streets. She had been three times married.

Several members of self-confessed Jewish families, who abjured their errors, got off with life imprisonment, but in most cases the crime and punishment were greater. Before these more fortunate ones, the cases of the nineteen prisoners who were to be relaxed were taken.

Now the Church is merciful and does not in any circumstances shed blood. The Holy Inquisition never executed its victims; instead they were handed over to the Secular Arm, that is, to the State, to be burned. Eighteen of these were relapsed Jews, the nineteenth was Lázaro Fernandez, alias Mostafa of Cadiz, a renegade who manned a privateer, twenty-eight years old, relaxed for pertinaciously remaining a Mahometan. He was not only clothed with the insignias of one destined to be burned alive, but he was kept gagged to the end.

It was already four o'clock in the afternoon when Mostafa's case had been concluded. The relaxed men and women, accompanied by a squadron of soldiers and still eagerly arguing ecclesiastics, marched out of the Plaza Mayor and through the streets to the Fuencarral Gate where the brasero awaited them.

Meanwhile another five hours were taken in completing the lighter cases. At nine o'clock the Inquisitor General could get into his pontificals again and take part in the abjurations and exorcisms with which the ceremony was concluded. The Green Cross which had hitherto been covered with the black veil was unveiled: the Veni Creator sung, the Absolution given, martial music and a salvo came from the military, the reconciled criminals were allowed to kiss the Inquisitor General's hand before being led off to the cells, and the Day was ended. Carlos, who must have been supported by some paranormal condition of mind and body through all these hours, asked if there was anything more to be done, and then went home.

Everybody was amazed and overjoyed at Carlos's endurance. He had been present from eight in the morning without allowing the heat, the crowds, the tedious length of the ceremonies, to affect him. He had not left his balcony for more than fifteen minutes even to eat. Others who felt the strain had only to turn their eyes towards the royal figures, immobile, absorbed, attentive, to be refreshed. It was felt that just as the matter of the heavens and stars suffered no corruption because there were no spheres higher, so God, by making Carlos independent of human influence, had conceded eternal life to the 'great planet of Spain'. It is not quite clear what Don José meant by this.

Nothing was left to do now but to burn the relaxed. The secretary of the Inquisition had advised the Secular Arm as to how many stakes would be required; so many for those to be strangled and so many for those to be burned alive. All was carried out with decency and clemency, save for the spitting and cursing of the exalted crowd. The Secular Arm had been enjoined on pain of Inquisitorial displeasure not to allow anything to be added to the punishment specified, for the Inquisition was nothing if not humane in these matters. By nine thirty next morning nothing remained but ashes; scattered to the winds, these flimsy remains could no longer do harm; the poison of heretical bodies had been purged away by fire. After his well-spent day, Carlos, surely exhausted at last, probably slept peacefully.

It is not difficult for those of us who are guilty, perhaps, of all the crimes of unbelief for which nineteen men and women were burned on that day, to visualize the spectacle; and it is easier still for us to abhor it and those who took part in it. But what is difficult and far more worth doing is to get inside the minds of the chief actors, to make their experience our own. What did Carlos think and feel all that long hot day, and again on his return to the palace when the distant sounds around the blazing pile were borne to him on the evening air?

A boy of eighteen, ill and almost deformed, ignorant to a degree hardly conceivable today, a subhuman person always treated as superhuman, above all the victim of fantasies most of which terrified him, he hoped that by whole-heartedly identifying himself with these horrors he would find favour with God and perhaps even cease to be impotent. He believed that almost anything he did, unless reported to his Confessor and absolved, might land him in such a scene as this on the last day, in such ignominious garments, in a hotter fire than that which his faggot helped to kindle. He was certain that his physical inability to produce an heir which for years to come he would stoutly deny, however well he knew his own defect, was both God's punishment and his own crime against God. That this weakling was able to remain in his balcony through more than fourteen hours without leaving it for longer than fifteen minutes, suggests that he must have been cast into an hypnotic trance by the psychological brilliance of the drama.

Indeed, one feels that many passed those hours in some half-conscious state induced by terror and exhaustion: sleeplessness, the sun, the nicely calculated sounds and sights, acting upon minds brought up to believe in the wrath rather than the love of God, must have acted as a euphoric drug on some, as merciful anaesthetic on others.

What did the criminals think and feel? Could they withstand the Inquisitional brain-washing? Did they go down to death convinced that it was the gateway to eternal torment? Certainly the crowds believed that these bodies, until reduced to ashes, were infectious. So long as they remained a part of the world and of Madrid, devils were near, danger of possession threatened every man, woman and child. Screams of genuine hatred burst out wherever the procession passed with its symbols of disgrace and dishonour.

The astounding sermon of the Dominican preacher carefully printed for all to read, since there was too much noise in the Plaza Mayor for even his strong voice to carry to everyone, contains statements of beliefs which we would do well to recognize as having been the common property of all that day. It is a silly sermon, but revelatory none the less.

We can see the preacher shaking his finger in the direction of the criminals as he described the torments to come, but we must not imagine that he is gloating, for his horror and his compassion are genuine. He is really sorry for their misery. He would help them if he could. And the monks sweating and thirsty in the heat were doing their best. If one of them induced a condemned man to say the few words which would bring him the mercy of the garrotte, we can imagine how that night, before falling asleep with exhaustion in his cell, he would fling himself on his knees before his crucifix and thank God for the privilege he had been vouchsafed, thank the Virgin and St Dominic for their intercession too, which had persuaded God to be so merciful. That this monk had a lively sense of the reward due to him for saving a soul, though not a body, does not detract from his fervour, does not introduce the least suspicion of hypocrisy.

Though the Inquisitor General must have derived some pleasure from acting the part of the avenging god all the long day, in the evening he would only be conscious that, old as he was, he had given all his strength to the greater glory of the Almighty. All those crowds went home after an exciting visit to the brasero, feeling that the Madrid air had been purged. Perhaps they were also strengthened in determination to keep out of the secret prisons and the ensuing dramatic finish by displaying their orthodoxy. They were more eager than ever, no doubt, to persecute their neighbours if they seemed tainted with heresy or partial to the laws and customs of the accursed Jews. Moreover, for a brief period their thoughts remained thus on higher things than the lack of bread and the insecurity of daily life. There was no haranguing voice in those days to ask how many loaves could be bought for the cost of these damask hangings, the gold fringes of the caskets, the Queen's jewels. There was no humanitarian voice to remind their friends that those bodies now reduced to ashes had lately felt and desired the same simple things as they. The Madrid air had been purged of demoniacal danger.

One enigmatic figure must excite our wonder: through these fourteen hours what were the thoughts of the Queen, so lately a French princess? Had Marie Louise d'Orléans become a different person now that she was Maria Luisa, a Spanish Queen, and Carlos's wife?

It is a subject which has irritated Spanish historians, since the French have attributed to this young girl a certain distaste for the auto-de-fé. They have a right to their annoyance, for no one, French, Spanish, or English, can have any idea of her thoughts and feelings. They have not been recorded. All we know is that she took a great deal of trouble with her dress for the occasion. We are told even by the Duque de Maura, however, that Maria Luisa found it hard to enjoy the interminable religious exercises which, after the slaughter of wild beasts — it could hardly be called hunting — were Carlos's chief entertainment. It is unlikely, therefore, that she got much pleasure out of this fourteen-hour simulation of the Last Judgment. This is not to say that she had any sympathy with the prisoners. Certainly she did not make a scene. But surely one is not propagating the Spanish *leyenda negra* if one suggests she would have felt more at home at some festivity at Versailles or Fontainebleau.

If one may hazard a guess, it is that when Maria Luisa was not half asleep or fully unconscious, she was thinking chiefly of how to get rid of the terrible Terranova. At least this tiresome manoeuvre, which had constantly occupied her attention, reached a successful conclusion shortly after the auto-de-fé. Carlos, as always, wished to please her, but nobody was dismissed from court-employment except for malpractice and with ignominy. The Duquesa de Terranova had done her job as she saw it, and her only fault was an excess of zeal. She might be suspected of murder, but that could not be counted against her in this matter and she had powerful friends. At last Carlos agreed to take action, but warned his wife to be careful whom she chose, as he could never take so serious a step a second time. Her going was dignified. Maria Luisa burst into tears at parting. Terranova told her that Spanish Queens must reserve their tears for far greater occasions; and she refused the offered compensation. Doña Armendariz y Ribera, Marquesa de Cadreita y Duquesa viuda de Alburquerque, served in her stead. Somewhat educated, less of the old school than Terranova, she interfered as little as she could and henceforth Maria Luisa could ride her horses when she liked, look out of the palace windows when she liked, and have the visitors she chose. As things turned out she might have done better by retaining Terranova, for her new liberty was too much for Spanish fantasy and led to her undoing.

Henceforth too, Maria Luisa stopped up until ten or eleven in the evening, and tiptoed to her room without waking Carlos who had usually gone to bed at seven. No wonder the courtiers, pondering as usual on the necessity for an heir, shook their heads.

CHAPTER FIFTEEN

STERILITY

CONSIDERING how incompatible they were, Carlos and Maria Luisa seemed to be settling down rather well. The first years had given Maria Luisa many shocks but some compensations. It was pleasant to have the admiration of crowds for her exotic beauty; it was pleasant to have a wardrobe of splendid and costly garments and jewels; she accepted what was inevitable in her Spanish surroundings; and profited as much as she could from any relaxation of etiquette in her favour. Thus she was allowed to have a French cook to prepare her meals, and food became one of her chief interests. She ate so much and so often that she became fat, and as she lay in bed for twelve hours out of every twenty-four and took little exercise, her figure deteriorated more rapidly than it should.

When she was not eating or sleeping, her occupations were riding and hunting, gossiping, watching comedies she could not understand, playing cards with Carlos for very small stakes, or the not too exciting game of spillikins for hours on end. There were of course as many religious occasions as she needed, and probably more. In a sense, these too were the occupations of her husband, but almost always with a difference which militated against true companionship. Thus, while she liked hunting small game with hounds, Carlos liked to go further afield and kill bears and wolves. She could not accompany him on these expeditions because they involved a night away from the palace, and nobody was prepared to face the appalling problems not merely of etiquette, but of decency and modesty that her presence would involve.

Her riding was a perpetual cause of palace disputes and intrigues. It is extraordinary how many people considered it their business to keep her off a horse, usually on grounds of etiquette, but later because, so it was rumoured, her equitation was the cause of her not doing her one duty of becoming pregnant.

Her gossiping was with the few French people who remained around her, and of course this made her unpopular with the court ladies. Moreover, she does not seem to have been very wise in some of her efforts to contact her countrymen. The French riff-raff of Madrid were in the habit of gathering under the walls of the palace to talk in finger-sign language to the French servants. Maria Luisa was foolish enough to join in this amusement and to be observed by those who were only too ready to think the worst of her.

It would seem that though the comedies were often a bore except as an occasion for showing off clothes, the King and Queen had some aesthetic interests in common. Everybody agrees that Carlos was genuinely devoted to music, and Maria Luisa was able to sing and play a few instruments. This devotion to music had been one of the few admirable traits of the Spanish Hapsburgs, and with Carlos music had almost a therapeutic value.

The gambling shows Maria Luisa in a good light; she had experienced, young as she was, the excitement of playing for high stakes at Fontainebleau, and to have shown interest hour after hour playing with Carlos for pennies must have been a strain, or at least a sign of a genuine desire to please. Playing with Carlos was like playing with a child, and with a child devoid of any attractive little ways. How she endured the spillikins it is impossible to understand.

In these ways the time went by. Medinaceli, who had been made Prime Minister, spared Carlos from having to do any work, and Carlos was in better health than at any other time in his life, and suffered nothing worse than an occasional fever, an attack of indigestion or a catarrh. It was a surface kind of life and few realized that beneath the surface, biding their time, were the terrors of poisoning, of witchcraft, of devils, and an overwhelming lava of hatred.

Her nostalgia for France was fairly well suppressed except when her stepmother, the Letter Writer, awakened it with her brilliant gossipy letters; but we cannot understand what happened later if we ignore the fact that below consciousness there raged a storm of regret which could only be calmed by the one thing that never happened.

Like many other women Maria Luisa compensated for her childlessness by lavishing care on a number of pet animals, a habit which caused the most spectacular of her contretemps with Terranova. Terranova did not like animals and regarded their presence in the palace as a breach of etiquette. In particular Terranova disliked the parrots because they talked French. One of them returned the sentiment and expressed it by a peculiarly irritating sound whenever the Duquesa appeared. One day this was too much for her, and she wrung its neck. Maria Luisa avenged the dying bird with a resounding smack on Terranova's cheek, which was received with unflinching dignity and reported in due course to the King.

Carlos ordered a mass slaughter of all the remaining parrots and this would have been carried out forthwith, had not Maria Luisa excused herself with an explanation – used now for the first time – which was to bedevil poor Carlos throughout two marriages almost to the last months of his life. She excused her lapse by saying that she was pregnant. Whether or not she believed it, we do not know.

The orgy of joy which this statement produced put an end to preoccupation with the parrot and the Duquesa, and not even the latter failed to be transported into the seventh heaven. Her mood of cold war turned into one of *Nunc dimittis*, and one is surprised that a Te Deum was not immediately ordered. A few days later, however, Maria Luisa had to admit that her state had already proved a Te Deum unsuitable.

Things now began to go wrong. Carlos, urged on by Terranova, took very badly indeed his Queen's descending to the use of finger-sign language with strangers, and, finding that the blame could easily be laid at the door of the French servants whom he hated already, sent them all packing. Maria Luisa was left with none of her countrymen except La Cantina, a clavichord player named Marguerite Lautier, her Jesuit Confessor, the cook, a groom, and a Madame Duperroy who was to prove the only limpet of the whole coterie.

Not only were there fewer French servants with whom to gossip but Maria Luisa began now to see very little of Carlos. He hunted all day, ate alone and went to bed without saying good-night. What had happened to his amorous inclinations? What was going to happen about an heir? When the royal pair met, it was usually to quarrel. Carlos began to display his deep irrational hatred of France and all things French. His early training was bearing fruit. He regarded Louis as the devil incarnate and Louis, it must be admitted, did nothing to disabuse him. Whenever Carlos was particularly enraged by some political manoeuvre which no doubt he only vaguely understood, he screamed at his wife, he abused France to her and she stood up to him, screamed and abused all things Spanish. These quarrels usually ended in a reconciliation during which the business of providing an heir was taken up again, but as always without the desired result.

We must now ask why this heir was not forthcoming, since it was the question all Europe was asking. Speculation at the time and in the pages of many historians has often been vitiated by a surprising ignorance of the facts of life.

It was certainly not because Carlos was frigid. On the contrary, he did not conceal an almost indecent enthusiasm for his wife's charms. Moreover, his doctors had long ago hinted that the sooner he was married the better, from which we infer that they were alarmed by an excess of what some people call autoerotic habits. It would seem that Maria Luisa was not at fault and that certain familiarities were concerted between them, since she told one French ambassador that she was no longer technically a virgin. From the various accounts, after incorrect biological notions have been eliminated, we can infer that Carlos suffered from that form of psycho-sexual impotence which causes *ejaculatio praecox*, that he could not achieve penetration, and that neither he nor his wife had sufficient knowledge to understand what was the matter.

Admittedly such ignorance is hard to understand, but only because in these matters we are very much the children of our own time and place. For the past two centuries or more, most Englishmen have been limited, by the ethical conditioning of their milieu, to a narrow path in their sexual practices, and we have come to regard this limited field as normal, and all deviation from it as perversion or individual idiosyncrasy. But a close study of the facts of history show how parochial this is.

We have come to suppose that any sexual licence between adults involves the completed act by which generation takes place.

Moreover, we know that at certain periods in history a very large proportion of women of one class or another, for example, the court ladies in seventeenth-century Spain, had lovers; and yet the number of bastards, though considerable, was nothing like what one might expect from universal promiscuity without contraceptive devices. How is this to be explained? It cannot be explained by assuming there existed any practice which involved the sacrifice of virginity, for to be a virgin was absolutely essential in an unmarried woman.

Readers of Balzac's *Contes Drolatiques* know the answer: ladies took their lovers on one or other of two understandings; they took them either for 'la grande oie' or 'la petite oie'. 'La petite oie' was an art which, well learned, gave sufficient satisfaction to both parties, while, if carefully executed, it did not involve any danger of unwanted pregnancies.

Of course the moral theologians fought against 'la petite oie' since it was a degradation of the sacrament of marriage and a flouting of natural law. The great casuists who wrote on the subject, for instance Thomas Sanchez de Córdoba, S.J., in his immense treatise *de Matrimonio*, describes in almost alarming detail the whole art of 'petite oie', and leave us in no doubt as to the universality with which it was practised. The Puritans were more successful in combating it, partly because, without the confessional, instruction in such things was harder to come by, and the English were convinced not merely that 'la grande oie' was the only form of sexual practice which was moral, but that it was the only form which gave adequate pleasure to the participants.

If we keep all this in mind, the situation between Carlos and his wife becomes clearer. The anxiety neurosis which Carlos suffered, owing to the dual burden of his inheritance and his environment, caused him to manifest the very depressing disability known as *ejaculatio praecox*; but his ardour, together with the ignorance of his wife, led them both to be content with the manoeuvres of 'la petite oie' save that they and the whole world were waiting for an heir. Moreover, this very ignorance may have led poor Maria Luisa to think that the fault lay with her rather than with her husband, a belief which throughout history, and in nearly all societies, has been reinforced by the assumption that sterility is almost always a female defect.

The result of such a situation was disastrous for both. Carlos would report his misfortune to his Confessor and be told that what he did was sinful; more than that, he would be told sooner or later that his unnatural disability might well be a sign that the devil had more power over him than was healthy for his body or his soul.

It must be remembered too, that Carlos was chaste. He is perhaps the only prince of those days of whom this can be said. He entered marriage as ignorant as his virgin wife and even if he knew where the deficiency lay, natural shame would prevent him discussing things with her. If so much ignorance and innocence seem out of place in such an uninhibited epoch, let us remember that it was regarded as part of a husband's rights that he should be the one to instruct his wife in the most elementary of sexual facts. Husbands enjoyed the assault on a person who theoretically at least did not know what was happening.

All that was wrong with this couple, one of whom, we should remember, was practically a mental defective, was that they had to be content with 'la petite oie' and were quite ignorant of what was needed for the transition to 'la grande'.

In view of other incompatibilities, these unnatural relations were quite sufficient to fray the nerves of both, and quarrels became more frequent. On one occasion Carlos shouted that he was going to ask his Confessor to give him permission to take a lover, and Maria Luisa could think of nothing better than to issue a similar threat. These quarrels were smoothed over by the French ambassador who succeeded Villars, the Comte de la Vauguyon, who seems to have possessed the high degree of tact common in those who do not lead a very moral life. He was able momentarily to support the unfortunate Queen from being gradually submerged in a tidal wave of popular hate.

She had come to Spain a beauty who would breed, she was now an adipose, sterile Frenchwoman. The Spanish crowds shouted abuse at her, and everyone quoted a clever quatrain, which needs no translation if we remember that *parís* is the second person singular of *parir*, to give birth, and *parid* is the imperative:

> Parid, bella flor de lis,
> que, en aflicción tan extraña,
> si parís, parís a España;
> si no parís, a París.

While the Spaniards to a man assumed that the trouble was caused by the French princess, Louis had his doubts. Just as some years back it was important to know if Carlos could survive, so now it was important to know if Carlos could beget. Louis used the same methods of coming to a decision; he sent ambassadors to ascertain the truth about the marriage bed.

Among these was an ingenious, rather opinionated and inexperienced young diplomat named Rébenac. His is the only contemporary account that goes into any detail about this intimate matter, but unfortunately what he has to say is virtually meaningless.

In a letter to Louis dated December 23rd, 1688, he writes:

> Finally, sire, she once told me that she was anxious to confide in me something she had never wanted to tell anyone, namely that she was not really a virgin any longer, but that as far as she could figure things, she believed she would never have children. Her modesty prevented her explaining any more fully, and my respect prevented me asking questions, but I gathered from what she said that there was a natural debility which was attributed to too much vivacity on the King's part, and finally, Sire, that the coction, as the doctor's call it, was not perfect.

Rébenac goes on to describe some researches of a very curious nature, indeed so curious that one begins to doubt his usefulness as a historical source:

> I have found the secret of how to get hold of some of the King's drawers, because, not to forget any detail, he does not wear his shirts longer than to his waist, and wears them with a very thick towel, which can rub him hard. I have had them examined by two surgeons. One believes that generation can follow: the other assures me, no.

As the result was so inconclusive, perhaps it does not matter that the procedure is incomprehensible. It does however impress one unfavourably with the value of certain other revelations of Rébenac which will be vital in the sequel. Louis himself seems to have been equally unimpressed.

In the same dispatch, Rébenac introduces for the first time the theme which will occupy almost the whole of the second half of this book. His words will be quoted here, but comment will be reserved until later.

> A Dominican monk, friend of the King's Confessor, received a revelation that the King and Queen were bewitched. I remark in passing, Sire, that the King of Spain has long since got it into his head that he is bewitched, and by Madame de Soissons. There was a question of breaking the spell, if it had been cast since the marriage. If it had been cast before the marriage there was no manner of remedy, so long as it lasted. The ceremony is horrible, Sire, the King and Queen must be undressed completely naked. The monk in vestments must perform the exorcisms, but in an infamous manner; following which, in the presence of the monk, they must see whether the spell has been well and truly broken. The Queen has been violently persecuted by the King to agree to this but has absolutely refused to consent. All this happened very secretly and I had no knowledge of it until I received an anonymous letter, advising me that if the Queen consented to the monk's proposal for procuring children for the King, she would be lost, and that it was a trap laid for her by the Conde de Oropesa. The scheme was to prove that the Queen was bewitched before marriage; and therefore that the marriage was void, or at least to make her hateful to the King and the people. We heard from the Queen herself what had happened.

All that need be said about this account is that it is pure fantasy. In no circumstances whatever would the Church even in those days countenance such indecency, and it is most unlikely that Oropesa or anyone else would have hatched such a plot on their own to get rid of the Queen. It would have landed everyone high and low in the hands of the Inquisition, charged with flagrant and manifest heretical practices. Rébenac must have been a fool; and the only mystery is why the astute Louis ever employed him.

The episode came in the last year of the young Queen's life and we must retrace our steps. Things had happened which almost explain how a sane ambassador could display such signs of persecution mania.

CHAPTER SIXTEEN

LA CANTINA'S ORDEAL

MARIA LUISA had been chosen from among all the princesses of Europe as being the most likely to produce an heir in little more than nine months. Now the years were mounting up, and there was no heir. This young woman, once the focus of admiration for her physical attributes, had become no more than an unloved animal, which, having been bought for breeding purposes, had proved a failure. The bringing of a French rather than an Austrian princess to their King's bed had given most Spaniards a sense of guilt, a self-accusation of treachery to the Spanish dream, which in turn now created a revulsion against the chosen victim proportionately intense. She became in their eyes a trap set by Louis to prevent Carlos from continuing his line.

As for Maria Luisa herself, she seemed to have retained her ascendancy over Carlos, but its texture changed; the sensuality and even affection which she had inspired at first, had given place to fear. Carlos was perpetually afraid of what she might do if she lost her temper, for again and again, having claimed to be pregnant to secure his good will, she threatened that unless some further whim was accepted the result would be a miscarriage.

The strength of these tactics did not lie only in inspiring joy with a pregnancy and fear with a hint of disaster and then exploiting this joy and this fear for all they were worth; there was also their effect on Carlos's self-respect and this, perhaps, was even more important. He could not have been so imbecile that he did not know there was something amiss in his performance of marital duties, and his wife's genial impostures gave him a hope that they were not as bad as they seemed. True, these very impostures gave Maria Luisa a hold over him, but that was only the price he willingly paid for the consequent reassurance. More even than this: if he were to believe in his own impotence, he would have had to assume that God was vexed with him at the very least; more likely that God had empowered the Devil to possess him as his own. That indeed was the *via crucis* his thoughts would have to travel in the end. Maria Luisa by pretending to be pregnant delayed the downhill progress to despair; and, in return, Carlos, almost alone among his people, in his stubborn though weak way, defended her from the pack of wolves which were now after her in full cry. For one incident after another showed plainly that she was being hunted by unscrupulous enemies.

The same bitter hatred that had caught up with Nithard, Valenzuela, Don Juan and many other saviours of Spain before and since, was now focused on her; a hatred born of dashed hopes. All these were to have saved Spain and, while there remained any hope of them achieving material results, their crimes against the rules of fantasy were forgiven, but when hopes faded, it was otherwise. Nithard, the foreigner, Valenzuela, the low-born upstart, Don Juan, the bastard, and now Maria Luisa the Frenchwoman, were suddenly remembered for what they were: insults to etiquette; by their very origin menaces to the world of fantasy, contradicting inviolable obsessions.

Maria Luisa, it was rumoured, was no more than a trap and a spy; Louis was using her to emasculate their King and to reveal their military weaknesses. Meanwhile the French personnel at the palace which, even if each individual had been a saint, could not have failed to attract hatred, behaved in a way bound to cause themselves and their Queen the greatest possible embarrassment.

Only in one way was Maria Luisa's lot at this time temporarily improved. The earliest French ambassadors, feeling as they did that it was their duty to protect a French princess against her uncongenial environment, had made matters worse; Villars, for instance, had no scruples against trampling upon Spanish feelings; but when he was succeeded by the Comte de la Vauguyon, Maria Luisa for once got better advice. He begged her to put up with the interminable religious exercises which the Spaniards considered the best remedy for her sterility; for hitherto, perhaps because she knew rather more than others of her husband's sexual habits, she had showed resentment at the number of specialist saints she was advised to call in to assist her. La Vauguyon was also able to improve her financial position, to get her personal debts paid and to help her avoid contracting more by arranging for her pocket money to be paid more regularly. He patched up the Queen's quarrel with the Prime Minister, Medinaceli, and he advised her to cultivate and rely upon whatever the emotional tie might be which bound her unsatisfactory husband to her.

Unfortunately, Louis XIV, having declared war once more, retired his ambassador from Madrid, and Maria Luisa lost her best friend at the very moment when her secret enemies struck.

It began with a trivial matter. She wanted to increase her stable of Irish hunters by importing several from Paris. Villars recommended a Frenchman named Viremont for the mission. Although he was at the moment exiled from France for having killed a man in a duel, he was given safe-conduct to complete his task in Paris. On his return he remained in the Queen's service and made enemies by exposing the chief of the royal stables, Vilanne, as a thief.

Vilanne had married the clavichord player, Marguerite Lautier, and the couple were united in their hatred, hitherto concealed, but now revealed, of La Cantina, the Queen's former wet-nurse and present favourite. When they were suddenly dismissed and ordered to leave Spain at once, the fat was in the fire. They went no further than Valencia where they waited for events to develop.

A judicial inquiry into certain rumours began – rumours even more ugly than usual. Doña Mariana de Aguirre, a court lady of good character and a friend of La Cantina, said she was at mass one day when she overheard two men discussing an alleged plot to poison the King with not only the knowledge but also the help of the Queen. The plotters were said to be some of the French staff. Vilanne gave evidence that this was true and swore that La Cantina was the criminal. He added that the order for his and his wife's expulsion from Spain was given by the Queen because she and La Cantina knew that they were aware of the plot's existence.

The accusation was so fantastic that, in spite of the howling of the wolves, La Cantina might have survived, had it not been discovered some time before that she was pregnant. Most people were surprised that she had not been saved from this predicament by her age and her obesity. This in itself was an offence against the laws of fantasy, as it was a breach of etiquette for anyone to become pregnant within the palace; but the Queen committed a worse breach by marrying the lady to her lover and then readmitting her to residence near her. Even though they were hardly expected to be vestal virgins in their single state, servants were never allowed to remain in the palace after their marriage. That this rule should be broken in the case of one of the hated French coterie was intolerable; it stirred up far more resentment than the scandal that had been its prelude. Vilanne and Lautier therefore were given an excellent chance for revenge.

Besides the plot already mentioned, Lautier accused La Cantina of other mysterious and criminal practices: she had given the Queen, unknown to Carlos, and under pretext of improving her health, a yellow drink and some dubious pills. She also made her take *triaca*, as the Spanish call theriac, as a precaution against poisoning.

Lautier further stated that she had tried the drink and the pills on herself and that the effect had been to bring on her periods, from which she concluded that they were given to the Queen to prevent conception. She added the rather contradictory statement that the Queen ardently desired a child and wept bitterly whenever the onset of menstruation put an end to her hopes. This must have been intended to show that La Cantina was acting contrary to Maria Luisa's wishes and fitted perfectly the rumours canvassed in the mentideros that Louis was plying his niece with abortifacients to ensure that there should be no heir to the Spanish throne. She also explained Viremont's safe conduct as a *quid pro quo* for his services through La Cantina in assuring this sterility.

Viremont and La Cantina were arrested, and the latter denied ever having given the Queen triaca except once in a drop of wine for her health's sake. She had also given her a medicine once in the King's presence. To this, Lautier replied that La Cantina used to signal to the Queen that she had the medicines and that the Queen would thereupon follow her out of the room and take the drink and pills secretly. Her evidence seemed to be corroborated by the discovery of a large store of pharmaceuticals in the Viremont apartment.

A committee of doctors and chemists was appointed to report

on this find, which included Water of the Queen of Hungary, triaca magna, quintessence of cloves and of hyacinth, and viper powder. The first was a very complicated prescription: essence of rosemary dissolved in alcohol was mixed with extracts of thyme, lavender, salvia, marjoram and other herbs. Taken internally it was considered remedy for palsy, lethargies, apoplexy and hysterical ills; but it was more commonly used externally, diluted with lily-water or bean flower water as a skin lotion.

Triaca was more interesting and looms large in the subsequent story, its chief virtue being that of a universal prophylactic against all poisons. As for viper powder: this was an ingredient of many medicines and did not entirely disappear from the pharmacopoeias of Europe until well on in the nineteenth century.

The committee reported on all this, much as a medical committee might today: most of the medicines had their uses and were likely to be beneficial if taken at the right time and in the right dosage with the advice of a qualified doctor. If they were wrongly administered much harm might result, triaca being very frigorific, and quintessence of cloves very heating. They considered that as the triaca caused stupor 'and other serious effects' it might very well act as an abortifacient.

La Cantina was re-examined and persisted in her denials, saying that the Water of the Queen of Hungary was for wounds and bruises, the quintessence of cloves for toothache and the triaca because it was much used in France.

As her evidence had resolved nothing, she was put to the torture. Before describing what happened, let us remember that at this time torture was commonly used in most civilized countries to extract confessions, for, as in Russia today, a confession was regarded as essential if a person was to be condemned. It is not to revive the Spanish *leyenda negra* that these hours in the life of an ex-wet-nurse should be recorded. However, when we realize that there is not a shred of evidence against La Cantina, that the charge of plotting to kill the King with the connivance of the Queen is absurd, that the procuring of abortion is even more absurd, as later events proved that the sterility was not Maria Luisa's fault, but the doleful inheritance of the wretched Carlos, we cannot but remark what hatred can achieve in a society where fantasy is more powerful than reality.

The Duque de Maura as usual is meticulous in giving us the facts, thereby making it easier for us to appreciate the sometimes peculiarly *castizo* or Spanish attitude to them which is possible even in this twentieth-century writer.

While the scene which I now recount was being enacted, the streets of Madrid were filled with a not very praiseworthy crowd. Maddened by the blows struck at them by Louis abroad, and by the rumours of horrible things at home, people went about crying 'Down with the *gabachas*', the pejorative word for French. They stopped anyone who by his features or his dress suggested that he was foreign, and made him pronounce the words *ajo* and *cebolla*; and if he failed with these shibboleths, they robbed and stripped him. Even a true Spaniard, bathing in the Manzanares, was ill treated when he got out of the water because the crowd found a French article of clothing among his garments on the bank.

On July 24th, 1685, Don Gaspar Bravo de Sobremonte faced La Cantina in the place of torment, and thrice called upon her to confess the truth. When she did not reply, he told her that if she died, or lost a leg or an arm as a result of what she was now to experience, it would be no fault of his, as all he wanted was to discover the truth.

She was told to undress. When she had done so Juan de Isla, the prison surgeon, examined her thoroughly limb by limb and solemnly swore that she had no lesion which should prevent her receiving torture.

She was tied to the rack.

'Holy Virgin help me,' she cried.

Her feet were now secured.

'Ah, God of my soul, if I cannot bear it,' and then louder, 'Ah God, my lord, let me die; ah, let me die; I cannot bear it.'

'Speak the truth,' Don Gaspar said.

'Ah, I am dying; I cannot move, I cannot say anything else! God help me. Ah, my Lady, why have they brought me here to suffer so! I cannot stand more.'

'Speak the truth,' Don Gaspar said.

'Though they put the rope round my throat, I seek my salvation; I can say nothing else.'

Don Gaspar ordered the first ligature to be tied to her arms, it being, he tells us, at twelve thirty by his watch.

'Mother of God, help me. What must I say to stop them doing this? I know nothing; that is the truth; if I knew anything I would say it and not have to suffer this.'

Don Gaspar ordered three more ligatures, and after a decent interval the next more severe torture. She begged him to tell her what to say.

'Speak the truth,' Don Gaspar said.

The torture was increased; she seemed to lose consciousness, so Juan de Isla, the surgeon, and a doctor were ordered to examine her again. The doctor felt her pulse, said it was safe to continue and the tortures went on. What had happened so far was mere playful teasing compared with what followed.

They continued until a quarter to four with ever more painful treatment; but at last they gave up. The most hideous pain had failed to extract the slightest admission of guilt. She must be innocent. She was allowed to recover slowly and when she could be moved, as nothing had been proved against her, nothing more could be inflicted by way of punishment; and so, for greater safety to the realm, she was exiled back to her native land.

The Duque de Maura is very critical of a French historian who, he says, exaggerates the permanent ill effects of La Cantina's ordeal.

> It is certain that the ex-wet-nurse took several months to recover from the traumatic consequences of the tortures with which by the hands of Spaniards, but through the fault of Frenchmen, she made easy expiation for so many sins committed in Spain and perhaps during the rest of her life; but it is not correct that either her left hand or her left foot was permanently injured.

In spite of La Cantina's steadfastness under torture, most Spaniards now believed in the wickedness of Maria Luisa and all Frenchmen. The Queen herself was sustained by Carlos's trust, for, we are told, Carlos always refused to believe that she had had any intention of murdering him. We know very little more about Carlos's attitude at this juncture; all his life he believed what he was told, all his life he hated all French people except his wife, and he was particularly apt to be swayed by the mass hysteria around him. Madrid was alive with the most outrageous rumours.

It was said that the accusations made by the player of the clavichord had been inspired by the Queen Mother, the Austrian ambassador and Oropesa, chief Francophobe. Their idea had been to accuse the Queen, shut her up in a convent, annul the marriage and marry Carlos off to a German princess.

It was said that an attempt had been made to get rid of La Cantina by giving her a pair of poisoned gloves, or by making her smell poisoned flowers. Others said there was a plot to poison both Carlos and his Queen if she refused to abdicate; still others, that Maria Luisa intended to escape over the frontier on horseback. It was also rumoured that the Duque de Oropesa was plotting to have himself made King of Portugal, and afterwards to unite the crowns of Portugal and Spain on his own head.

The elderly French ambassador of the moment, Feuquières, not only transmitted all these rumours to Louis but obviously believed some of them himself. In August 1685 he wrote to his King:

> The Queen of Spain is in very grave peril. She has been secretly tried for the crime of abortion, and her enemies have no difficulty in bringing for proof as many false witnesses as they need. Though the King continues his affection for her, I fear that because of his weakness he will sacrifice her to popular frenzy, which is being excited by the Queen Mother, the Almirante and the other conspirators in this rabid cabal whose head is Mansfeld [the Austrian ambassador]. Furthermore, Sire, to force the King of Spain they threaten to dethrone him.

This may have been nonsense, but there is no doubt that Maria Luisa had become terrified; nor, in the circumstances, was this surprising. The Duque de Maura has devoted a whole book to showing how ridiculous the French historians have been, and that there was really little to alarm her; but Maria Luisa had now been deprived of all her French household except one lady; she had only to go to the window to hear the mob cry 'Down with the *gabachas*'; she could not but remember the line, Si no parís, a París; she must have heard rumours of La Cantina's fate and of Lautier's accusations; she knew herself hated by the Queen Mother and, in fact, by everyone else, except Carlos; she knew

Carlos too well to hope for much from him; and all this, along with perpetual bickerings about her breaches of Spanish etiquette, must have been hard for her butterfly mind. If she became hysterical it is not surprising. She wrote to Louis:

> I cannot hide from Your Majesty that my life is in danger, since my enemies will snatch it away if their present designs fail. I trust only in God and in Your Majesty, who I hope will pity me in these circumstances by making it known to these people and to the Catholic King that Your Majesty is interested in my preservation and will regard the affronts of which I may be the object as if they were against himself...

and she begs him to send her a safe antidote against poison.

At this crisis Maria Luisa was to discover a compensating fact about mob hatred. She knew well enough by now that mob adulation could vanish very quickly, she discovered that mob hatred could also be evanescent. The feelings of the Spanish Court and of the Madrid populace were at all times based on such fantastical dreamings that there was little substantial about them. At this very difficult moment Maria Luisa played the one card she still possessed, the ace of trumps which for their various reasons no one could bring themselves to believe she did not possess. She announced that she was pregnant.

We cannot certainly know whether nature helped her to deceive herself and others, or whether it was merely her calculated cunning that lay behind this magical assertion; but in a trice all was changed. The mob hate vanished like a miasma breathed upon by a health-laden wind. The torture of La Cantina, followed by the expulsion of all the French, had for the time being lowered the pressure of neurotic hate against that nation, and by claiming pregnancy the Queen now withdrew the irritant chiefly responsible for the surrounding bitterness. But her real enemies hidden in the Court were little affected. There was only a short breathing space. Moreover, the deception could not be maintained for long.

Indeed her trials had only begun: a few months after the monstrous Lautier-Cantina affair, she received, through the ambassador Feuquières, a message from Louis which outraged her and increased her realization of underground and ruthless persecution.

When she had first come from France one of her accompanying guards was a vain coxcomb of a parade-ground subaltern named Saint-Chamand. This individual professed an undying, quixotic, platonic passion for his royal mistress and made an ass of himself in the process. Shortly after the La Cantina affair, someone – Maria Luisa very naturally assumed a Spaniard – forged two letters of a compromising tone which she was alleged to have sent him. These were sent to Louis, and Louis seems to have been deceived.

Louis ordered his ambassador to reprimand her and to point out that she had given her enemies a handle and that she would be lost when the King was told. Outraged and indignant she wrote so sincere a denial back to her uncle that he seems to have been convinced of her innocence; but the forgery, showing as it did that her enemies were determined on her ruin, undermined her morale still further.

It is useless for Spanish historians to argue that Maria Luisa should not have feared poison. As things were, it would have been a miracle of faith had she not. Her loneliness must have been extreme. Occasionally she sat by her husband's side at the comedy, but Carlos was usually killing bears and wolves or confessing his sins, after which he went early to bed. Riding continued to be her chief pleasure. It was an uneasy, twilight sort of existence and it is just possible that she now began to try and supplement it, in so far as her ill-equipped intellectual abilities permitted, by an interest in politics. For what it might be worth, Louis, no enthusiastic believer in her worldly wisdom, resolved on using her.

We have already met ambassador Feuquières's son and successor engaged in physiological researches into Carlos's sexual capacities; but that subject was by no means the only one about which Louis had given him instructions. Louis had already made up his mind that Carlos would have no heir of his body, and, indeed, expected him to die at any moment; in this he was wrong. For twelve years more this perennial moribund was to keep the nerves of all Europe on edge simply by remaining barely alive.

It was the middle of 1688, three years after the revocation of the Edict of Nantes. Just as Hitler's Anti-Semitism filled rival nations with the best scientists and technicians, so the persecution of French Protestants enriched England, Holland and other opponents of French imperialism. The hardening of anti-French feeling was seized upon by William of Orange to strengthen his coalitions against Louis, and Louis became more than ever preoccupied with controlling the way Spain would jump when the unfortunate Carlos died in earnest.

The new ambassador was given two sets of instructions, one of top secrecy, and both based on the assumption that Carlos's death was only a few months delayed. The instructions proved useless, since it was the wrong person who was going to die.

As so often, it was a matter of etiquette that was to occupy Rébenac's attention first. On arrival in Madrid he was to find out from some member of the embassy staff whether the late ambassador, his father, and the Emperor's ambassador, Count Mansfeld, were in the habit of visiting the Conde de Oropesa, President of the Council of Castille, Carlos's chief minister, in person and in his own house. The crux of the matter was that this haughty official claimed the right not to shake hands with grandees and ambassadors, if he received them at home. It was likely, therefore, that these important ambassadors, the French and the Imperial, rightly affronted at not being accorded *la main*, had refused to call on him, and had only communicated with him by letter. If, however, Rébenac found that the Emperor's ambassador had decided to put up with such treatment to avoid the inconvenience of a more indirect approach, then, and only then, was he to condescend to visit Oropesa.

Having settled the matter of *la main* he must ask the functionary known as the Introducer of Ambassadors, for a private audience with the King, so that he could deliver a letter Louis had written to him. This might be refused until he had got his staff and servants ready to take part in the official public audience, but in any case he was to tell Carlos as soon as possible many pleasant things, not in the least squaring with the instructions in the secret document.

After the King, he must have audience with the Queen, then with the Queen Mother. He must be particularly careful to assure the latter with '*expressions les plus honnêtes et les plus obligeantes*' that the French King continues to love and admire her. But in the secret instructions Louis clearly describes the Queen Mother as his greatest enemy, to be checkmated at the first and every subsequent opportunity.

Indeed the instructions go on to describe very precisely what Rébenac was to do about the Queen Mother. After telling him to repeat warnings already given, that Louis would regard it as an act of hostility if the Emperor's second son came to Madrid to be educated (which was at that time the Queen Mother's favourite plan) he is told to do all he can to prevent Maria Luisa from becoming friendly with her mother-in-law. The best person to warn her against any rapprochement would be her Confessor. She should be told that if the Queen Mother seemed to be offering a reconciliation it would only be a trap to win her over to the Austrian succession.

In all this Carlos himself was scarcely considered; the important business was all with the two women. Poor Carlos would never know what was going on in the women's quarters, nor even that the new French ambassador had come chiefly to give support to his wife against his mother in the cold war which never ceased between them, a war based on the assumption that the thing which could never be hinted to him, his impotence, was to be taken for granted.

Rébenac's three interviews went off very well. Carlos received him at the end of a gallery, with his back to a table on which burned a single candle. In this way the miserable King's deficiencies of feature and complexion were minimized. Near him on his knees was Don Manuel de Lira, secretary of the Despacho Universal, a man of great importance to Rébenac, since all letters and dispatches had to pass through his hands.

Carlos touched his hat with his hand, according to etiquette, and then bade Rébenac put his hat on, after which, Louis's gracious letter was presented. It was full of affection and bonhomie and Rébenac spoke at length of the importance of friendship between the Catholic and the Most Christian Kings so that the infidels might be the speedier discomfited. On this Carlos made no comment, and having asked after Louis's health dismissed the ambassador to present himself to the Queen.

Maria Luisa told him she had been impatient to have a French ambassador with whom to talk, and Rébenac, sticking to his brief, counselled her to gain the King's affections more and more.

What he really thought of this advice became clear in the sequel, and from his first sight of the Queen, and probably from an earlier period still, he seems to have become possessed of a romantic sentiment which was to obscure his objectivity and make it hard to distinguish between fact and fiction in his accounts of the deplorable events which followed. The value of a diplomat is lessened when he conceives himself to be a knight-errant.

As for the Queen Mother, in spite of her hatred of everything French, she was delighted with him because he was able to speak German – very badly it is true – but anything approaching her mother tongue was enough to enchant her.

Finally there was Oropesa. The difficulty about shaking hands was solved in a way which had now become that minister's customary solution: Oropesa remained in bed, for apparently the necessity for giving *la main* did not arise at all so long as he was recumbent. With Oropesa, Rébenac talked business.

He warned him that Louis would declare war unless Spain stopped inciting the Pope against France. He then visited other ministers to deliver the same warning, and having acquitted himself of these surface duties settled down to carry out the complicated intrigues involved in the secret instructions. These were, in short, to secure the immediate acceptance, directly Carlos should die, of the Dauphin as legitimate King of Spain. As usual Louis had up his sleeve a variation of his plans. If there was too much opposition throughout Europe to the succession of the Dauphin, Louis was prepared to nominate one of his two nephews instead. To prepare for this possibility the boys had already been given the names Charles and Philip, two names always identified with kingship in the Spanish mind.

Louis's instructions drip with piety. Should Carlos die it will be God's will that the Dauphin 'who is at present incontestably heir presumptive and the only legitimate heir' should be accepted by all God-fearing Spaniards. Louis was apt to equate fear of himself with fear of God, when it was convenient. 'There is,' he reiterates, 'no Spaniard who can with a clear conscience, and without being guilty of treason and rebellion against his prince, recognize any other master but Monseigneur. That those who are the first to recognize this will be the most esteemed by the

King, that tardiness will bring punishment,' must be made very clear in very good time. Promises and threats always help even the clearest conscience.

Directly news of Carlos's death reaches him, Louis will send a large supply of letters addressed to the grandees of Spain, to the members of the various Councils, to the Inquisitor General and other leading ecclesiastics and to various provincial officials, announcing the succession of the new and only legitimate King. Rébenac meanwhile must not wait idly for the regrettable demise, but must set to work to build up the French party. He should have least difficulty with members of the ecclesiastical estate, who will see that it is not only their legal duty to support the Dauphin, but their moral duty; since it will be obvious that God himself has planned his succession, first, by marrying his mother to Louis XIV, second, by contriving that her renunciation of all claims to the Spanish throne for herself and offspring should have been nullified by the non-payment of her dowry, third, by giving her such a son, endowed with such gifts, and, lastly, by recompensing Carlos with eternal glory, and not giving him, the Dauphin's uncle and cousin, any nearer heir than the Dauphin. Such deliberate planning by God obliges the ecclesiastical estate not only to set a good example to others, but even by their authority and remonstrances to prevent others from dissenting. To impress the ecclesiastics even more with their plain duty, Rébenac must speak to each individually, according to his 'individual talents, genius and inclinations' and promise whatever preferment for themselves and their relatives may particularly appeal to them.

Most important of all, Rébenac must get the Queen, 'or rather the King's Confessor' to prevent Carlos making a will in any other claimant's favour. The Confessor must be reminded of the ills such an act would bring down on Spain and for this purpose there is no bribe too great to promise him, for himself and any of his relatives. Rébenac must win over Manuel de Lira, secretary of the Despacho Universal, and he must try to get hold of the royal seals, but in case this proves too difficult, a new set will be made with the Dauphin's name, and with this new seal, notice must be sent to all chancelleries before there has been time even to bury Carlos, announcing that the Dauphin is King.

Rébenac must bribe the governors of San Sebastian, Pamplona

and Fuenterrabía to agree to admit French troops which will be massed in suitable places in the south of France for immediate invasion over the Pyrenees. The same must be done with the governors of Cadiz and the other principal ports.

With everything so well thought out it is almost regrettable that events, unexpected and sad, brought all to nought. For Carlos did not die, and Maria Luisa did.

CHAPTER SEVENTEEN

WAS IT POISON?

ON Tuesday, February 8th, 1689, Maria Luisa, accompanied by some of her ladies, took her habitual exercise on horseback. As she mounted, she was thrown against the saddle-tree, and, according to some accounts, fell to the ground. She forbade her ladies to mention the accident, as she feared it would be made an excuse for denying her one of her few pleasures. She went to bed and at six o'clock, ordered a light meal consisting of Chinese oranges, milk iced with snow, and 'a little of the badly fermented dough called *hojaldre* or puff paste'.

Her diet, like everything else about her, had for a long time caused unfavourable comment. For a month on end she would eat nothing but oysters, olives and cucumbers soused in vinegar. She was very fond of gooseberry fool. Besides these dishes she would eat almost anything that anybody told her would help her to become pregnant. Since menstruation was regarded as caused by superabundant heat she was partial to a diet of iced foods and drinks and she had many herbs and similar nostrums recommended to her by happy mothers in all parts of Europe.

Besides this preoccupation with her overdue maternity, there was another that influenced her diet almost as much, the fear of being poisoned. She was perpetually uneasy on this score. There is the evidence of her letter to Louis, there are the contents of the unfortunate La Cantina's medicine cabinet and the persistent use of triaca. As well as these, there is the more general evidence that almost everyone of importance was in those days heartily afraid of this hazard and apt to take precautions against it. The phobia and to some extent the practice were particularly prevalent in France whither it had been transported from Italy by the Medicis.

On Wednesday, the day after the slight accident, Maria Luisa again indulged her somewhat bizarre appetite. The main dish was one which, according to a contemptuous Spanish witness, 'is said to be eaten in France'. It consisted of broth made of veal gristle, chicken and meat frozen in four pounds of snow. She also ate oysters with lemon and a mug of cold milk, French olives and Chinese oranges to which she had always been partial and usually carried a few in her pocket to nibble.

This was at about six o'clock on the afternoon of February 9th. At five in the morning she awoke with stomach-ache, nausea, diarrhoea and a feeling of suffocation. Doctors arrived at once and diagnosed cholera morbus, a term which had nothing to do with the infectious and lethal complaint first recognized a century and a half later, but was used for the most severe grade of any intestinal upset. The doctors confidently attributed it to the mixture of salted, fiery, acid liquids accumulated in the pancreas and round the hypochondrium reacting with the bilious, flatulent, vitiated liquids from fermented food, to produce a violent expulsive reaction. Against such a grave misfortune a whole battery of remedies was discharged.

But the indisposition continued next day, the symptoms getting worse and the patient weaker. By midnight on February 11th all hope had been given up, though in desperation all imaginable treatment was continued. To stimulate her failing heart she was given, internally, emulsion of opium with cordial water, spirits of salt, pearl-salt, natural elixir with salt of absinthe, triacal water, and extract of egg yolk. Externally, they applied cordial unguent, elixir of life, various unguents and fomentations, plasters, coctions, along with cupping of the stomach and muscles.

Having exhausted their own armament, the doctors permitted at her request the administering of a favourite quack remedy. This was Agua de la Vida concocted and sold at a very high price by a charlatan, Luis Alderete, and very popular with wealthy self-medicators of the period. This, so she said, made her feel better, but at eight thirty on the morning of February 12th, Maria Luisa died.

She behaved oddly during these terrible days. At first she believed she had been poisoned. She asked the doctors, who replied that in so far as she was poisoned it was she herself who had administered it. They laid the blame entirely on her exotic diet. Rébenac maintained to the last that her suspicions were well founded, but, almost at the end of her agony, she called him to her expressly to say that, although she had at first suspected poison, she was now certain that she had been mistaken. But Rébenac, who had long ago made up his mind that his beloved Queen would one day be murdered, refused to change his opinion. It is a pity that he must have lost some of our confidence as a safe witness by his researches into Carlos's night-clothes and his fantastic account of an exorcism.

He demanded to see her directly he heard the news, but Carlos refused. Many French writers regard this as a suspicious circumstance, but the Spanish can point out that it was never their habit to expose their Queen *en déshabille.* After all there was at first no thought of anything but a bad attack of indigestion, and later when things looked more serious, Rébenac was admitted. He found Maria Luisa resigned to her fate.

It is not easy to accept the medical opinion on Maria Luisa's illness; after all, most of the items that they condemned are now considered healthy foods, particularly suitable for convalescents. We give our children gooseberry fool. It is impossible to imagine that such a diet could kill a person in these days, *unless* it had been contaminated by lethal bacteria or poison. It is late to hold an inquest on the poor woman, and the verdict will certainly have to be an open one; nevertheless the details throw much light on the society in which Maria Luisa had tried to be a wife to Carlos.

When events so unexpected as the death of Maria Luisa take people by surprise, masks are dropped. We have an excellent opportunity of studying character and divining motives which are usually kept hidden. It is particularly instructive when as here the cause of the event can never be certainly discovered.

All sorts of vested interests were affected by the life and death of this light-weight, superficial young woman. On February 9th she went to bed healthy and as happy as she ever expected to be, on February 12th she was dead. Why? And how were various people and interests affected?

What of her husband? Carlos had outgrown his sensual infatuation in the course of years of frustrated sexual desire. Fear and futility had taken its place. Count Mansfeld, the Emperor's ambassador, reported that he showed some sign of distress for precisely eight days and then he had, it would seem, forgotten all

facing: MARIA LUISA DE BOURBON

about it. Others reported differently, and we shall soon see that it is wise to look twice at anything Count Mansfeld says.

All Carlos wanted was to be left alone. His health was reasonably good. He enjoyed killing animals; and but for one thing he would never have dreamed of marrying again. That was the overwhelming demand for an heir. He had no need nor liking any longer for the art of begetting, but the duty remained; and like Philip, his father, however little he still wanted to sacrifice to Venus, he must continue to sacrifice to Spain. Between his wife's hour of death and his councillors' worrying him about beginning this sacrifice all over again, he was allowed only ten days.

So much for Carlos: if we turn to his mother we find that she surprised her contemporaries with a very genuine grief at Maria Luisa's death. Doña Mariana, Mansfeld reported, was so sad that one would have thought it was she who had been widowed: 'I do not know,' he adds, 'whether to weep with the Queen Mother or to give thanks to God for this blessing for the House of Austria.' When he went to say a prayer at the side of the dead Queen as she lay in state, he heard some heavily veiled women cry out half menacingly, half prayerfully, 'A German Queen, give us a German Queen.' And, indeed, as Count Mansfeld said, Maria Luisa's death must have been a miracle vouchsafed by God for the benefit of the House of Austria. If so he and God made one serious miscalculation.

Mansfeld naturally assumed that with the French wife out of the way, the Austrian mother would dominate politics, and as a faithful member of the Austrian family influence Carlos both to marry into it and to make one of them heir were he to die childless. What he seems to have forgotten was that the Emperor's first wife had been Margarita, Mariana's own daughter, and that her child had married the Elector of Bavaria. When in 1693 the Elector of Bavaria's son was born, it was Mariana's grandson and far closer to her heart than the Emperor's son by his third wife. This Archduke Charles was to be the choice of the Austrian party, but, after 1693, not of Mariana. All Mariana's influence during the rest of her life would be fruitlessly expended on trying to get Carlos to leave the kingdoms to her own grandson. She was finally to succeed, but posthumously.

At the time of Maria Luisa's death, however, it was the choice

facing: CARLOS SEGUNDO

of a second wife that was the central objective of all intrigue, and Mansfeld reports with self-satisfaction that he has already got his friends to tell Carlos that his marriage was a failure and not blessed by heaven, because he had chosen his wife at the orders of Don Juan and not on the advice of his mother. The fumbling mind of Carlos was sure to be feeling that Maria Luisa's death and, much more still, the childlessness of their marriage, was a punishment for sin. Any suggestion, therefore, that he ought to have consulted his mother would fall on well-prepared ground. Mansfeld and Mariana were at one over all this, and when Carlos had to marry it was they who chose the bride.

But before seeing how successful Mansfeld was to be in choosing the next Queen of Spain there is something to be recorded of his connection with the dead one. He reports more than once that a rumour is going about that Maria Luisa was poisoned at the instigation of Oropesa, as part of a plot aimed at a Portuguese marriage. Oropesa was related to the Portuguese royal family, and at various crises was whispered to be thinking of kingship for himself. Mansfeld mentions this, but is careful not to say that he himself is also named in some circles as the poisoner.

The Duque de Maura has devoted a book to the inaccuracies of French and other writers who have attributed sentiments and actions to Maria Luisa which contradict all we know of her on sound historical evidence; and he is particularly severe on anyone who claims that she was poisoned and even on those who regard it as an open question. But there are a few details which have either escaped his notice or have been regarded as too trivial for mention. One of these concerns Count Mansfeld.

There is a letter from the Emperor's third wife, the sister of Maria Ana[1] of Neuburg, soon to win Carlos's heart and bed, to her father the Elector Palatine in which we find the following very curious sentence:

> Mansfeld has repeatedly written advising delay in completing the marriages of my sisters with the Princes of Parma and Saxony Lauenberg, *because the Queen of Spain was consumptive,* although they tried to hide it. I did not lend much

[1] Both the Queen Mother and Carlos's second wife are called Mariana or Maria Anna and occasionally Maria Ana. To prevent confusion I have reserved Mariana for the Queen Mother and arbitrarily called the wife, Maria Ana.

credence to this hint, as no other correspondent corroborated the suspicion; but I now think I should consult you, father, on whether in fact these marriages should be proceeded with, or delayed.

Now this is a remarkable letter. Mansfeld, whose choice for Carlos was to be Maria Ana of Neuburg, writes to her sister hinting that lesser fry should not be accepted as husbands by the Neuburg sisters, as the Queen of Spain was consumptive, and therefore a poor life risk. Nobody would want to marry into Saxony Lauenberg or Parma, if Spain was likely to be open to them. But Maria Luisa was never consumptive, nor thought to be, nor was her health anything but robust. Why did Mansfeld hint at her early death? Had he any reason to suspect this healthy woman would die out of due time? Had Oropesa told him that he was about to poison her, or had he arranged to poison her himself?

In view of this letter it is not possible to agree with those who say that the Duque de Maura's study has ruled out the likelihood of poison altogether. A prosecuting counsel could have made it very awkward for a man who had written thus, before the death, and welcomed the death itself as a miracle vouchsafed by God for his party's benefit.

The prosecuting counsel would have derived little benefit, on the other hand, from the French witnesses, most of whom he would have been too wise to call. At the start he would have been embarrassed by Rébenac.

Rébenac may without injustice be said to have lost his head. Although he faithfully reported to Louis Maria Luisa's denial that she was poisoned, he acted as if certain that she had been. He demanded to be present at the autopsy and naturally was refused permission. He demanded to have her private papers sealed, and this also was refused. He made it perfectly clear that he suspected foul play; and, since he was one of those men who are always convinced that their enthusiasms are praiseworthy, he must have been sadly dashed at Louis's reply to his dispatches, though he should have known that Louis was never partial to dispatches charged with emotion.

Louis told him to keep quiet, and rebuked him for asking to be present at the autopsy. His reason was not that he did not believe in foul play – on that he made no comment either way – but that the request would have irritated the Spaniards and settled nothing. Louis, whatever his affection for Maria Luisa, and he claimed she had been a special favourite, knew that any discussion of poisoning would not help him in the political struggle with Spain. He hoped for neutrality still, and wished to avoid irritating Spanish opinion.

But at Versailles and in France generally, Louis was almost alone in showing apparent indifference. Open mention of poison was prohibited. The rumours proliferated the more. The Italian ambassador at the French Court wrote back that everybody assumed poison. Two weeks later it was stated that four grandees had died of the same poisoned dish. Madame, the dead Queen's letter-writing stepmother, enlarged on the matter:

> M. de Rébenac was not wrong in believing that the good queen of Spain was poisoned. They saw clearly when she was opened up ... that she had turned violet all over, which they say is strong evidence for poison. What makes me believe she was poisoned by oysters is that one of the queen's maids who also wanted to eat, was approached by a grandee who snatched the oyster from her hand, saying she would be ill if she ate it.

Madame de la Fayette wrote in her memoirs that she was poisoned with a cup of chocolate; Louville wrote in his the same story and so did Mlle de Montpensier.

None of this is evidence of poisoning, although it has great interest as an indication of the state of mind existing in France. The assumption there was that the Spaniards were capable of everything.

All this hearsay gossip is only of interest because what people think has happened is almost as important a part of the historical record as what really did happen. Legrelle unearthed and published documents of far greater interest, namely the medical reports of those who performed the autopsy on the dead Queen. No verdict could have been reached in 1689, since the symptoms of poisoning by man and by bacteria are alike. The authorities today would remove certain organs and make a chemical analysis of their contents; if they found poison they would seek evidence as to who was in a position to administer it and they would consider who would benefit from the death.

In the absence of all possibility of such an approach, we are likely to be prejudiced in favour of Legrelle's opinion and against the Duque de Maura's, for the Frenchman says that whereas nothing can ever be proved, the balance of probability is that Maria Luisa was poisoned; while the Spaniard in his quixotic tilting at the Leyenda Negra roundly asserts that in Spain such things did not happen, and attacks Legrelle as a professional detractor of all *cosas de España* and an incompetent historian. He goes so far as to say that Legrelle keeps an open mind about Maria Luisa's death because having been in the 1870 defeat at Sedan he hates Germans and therefore Spain – hard words about a painstaking documentary historian.

The dead woman's doctor, Francini, wrote a report which has some curious features; Legrelle publishes it in Latin and Maura in a loose Spanish translation.

Legrelle points out that it begins with so strong an emphasis on Maria Luisa's food habits that one feels that they are being used as a screen to hide some other factor. As has been said, all the items he mentions are now considered legitimate and even healthy for anyone enjoying normal well-being, and Maria Luisa seems to have eaten what she liked year after year with only a very occasional minor ill-effect. Why then did she die on this occasion?

If no more can be claimed than that the pathological details found at the autopsy fit poisoning and natural disease equally well, great suspicion must be aroused by the perfect timing of the death from the Austrian point of view; and this suspicion is reinforced by Mansfeld's letter. Nor can the defence rely at all on Maura's reiterated insistence that poisoning was not a Spanish characteristic.

Throughout seventeenth-century Europe there were numbers of suspected poisonings, and Spain cannot be excluded. Indeed a long list could be made of Spanish people whose untoward, and often timely, deaths were attributed by Spaniards to poison.

The excellent Dr Laguna, medical adviser to Pope Julius III, and closely associated with the Valencian school of herbalists, was the Spanish authority on pharmaceutical matters. He published in Castilian a commentary on Dioscorides, in which he gives excellent advice mingled with the errors inevitable in his day. A new edition of this treatise had been published in Valencia in 1636. The sixth book is devoted to poisons and their antidotes.

Dr Laguna says that it is particularly important for princes and rich men to study antidotes, as poisoning is a rich man's risk: the poor are seldom poisoned.

The first precaution is to stand well with God and to obey his instructions as to our duty to our neighbour. If a prince does not tyrannize over his subjects but treats them kindly like brothers, and with justice, the likelihood of his being poisoned is reduced. So also if fathers do not hang on to their possessions to their last breath, and do not irritate younger sons by too strict an interpretation of the law of primogeniture, parricide becomes far less common.

Next to good relations with God, the most important thing is a reliable cook. The two essentials are the cook's general character and his cleanliness. He must be so clean that there will be no danger of poisonous spiders in the kitchen. Dr Laguna tells us that in less than a day and a half a whole monastery of Franciscans in Florence died because a particularly poisonous spider was allowed by a careless cook to fall into their soup.

The butler's character is almost more important than the cook's as the majority of poisoners use wine, water and other potions for their purposes. Henry of Luxemburg was poisoned by Robert of Sicily with sacramental wine, a more than usually outrageous crime, since sacrilege was added to murder.

Dr Laguna says that practically all the great of Europe have their cooks and butlers taste the food and drink they serve, but that this has become mere ceremony as there are so many ways for a determined poisoner to get round such a test.

This might well be, but there is plenty of seventeenth-century evidence that the practice of having the food tasted by a servant was still continued. Louis XIII, writing to Richelieu in 1635, said: 'I send you some fruits from Versailles, which you will have tasted before eating, as with all that I send you.' And a few weeks later, 'I forgot to tell Nogent when he was bringing you the young wild boar ham, that I beg you to have it tried out on someone before you eat any.'

Dr Laguna further considers what can be done to guard against poison with specifics. Mithridates had immunized himself by taking a little poison every day, and so the first accepted antidote was later called in his honour, Mithridatic. It was modernized and improved by Galen and called *theriac*, or in Spain triaca; the word from which our innocent *treacle* is derived. Dr Laguna and his colleagues for hundreds of years afterwards firmly believed in *theriac*, though he admits that some of the traditional ingredients are vaguely described and the recipes often very obscure.

Dr Laguna considers the merits of various other specifics including oriental diamonds, emeralds and other stones in contact with the skin between elbow and shoulder. Dr Juan Portugués in charge of the Hospital of St John Lateran at Rome gave him a good tip: during a severe epidemic of plague Dr Portugués carried a piece of corrosive sublimate the size of a nut in his left armpit and not only survived the plague but lived to be ninety.

However, the best remedies for both plague and poison are unicorn's horn and a stone found in a stag's heart. Five grammes of the first or ten of the second, pulverized and drunk in wine, is proof against anything. For testing the genuineness of the unicorn's horn, Dr Laguna advises using the cook as laboratory animal.

After all this a modern reader might be excused from thinking that Dr Laguna was prepared to believe anything. This would be unfair to him. He admits doubt of some of his best stories. He refuses to accept the claim of some Arab doctors who recount that they fed a beautiful girl from childhood on aconite so that she could secretly poison with her breath a number of kings and princes whose enemies induced them to lie with her. Carlos and his courtiers as well as Dr Bravo, of respected memory, would have had no scruples about taking the Arab doctors at their word. The evidence is overwhelming that in Spain as in all other European countries poisoning was assumed to be very common. Whether it was so, is another matter: witches also were assumed to be common.

Maria Luisa, therefore, lived in an atmosphere of belief in poisoning, and in her own life she had had experience of it. Her own mother, Henrietta Maria, was almost certainly poisoned, and on several earlier occasions she herself had feared lest the digestive consequences of indiscreet diet were really due to the same cause.

Moreover, she knew that she was hated and that many people wanted her out of the way. What then are we to make of her curious denial of poisoning on her deathbed? Certainly not, as Maura would have us believe, that it is evidence against poisoning. There was nothing spontaneous about it. She suddenly recalled Rébenac and gave him a message. She could not have had any further evidence to make her change her mind. The most likely explanation is that she desired to die at peace with the world and to minimize any causes for further discord on her behalf.

And, whatever she said, Madrid maintained its opinion: many Austrian sympathizers thought it was poison, and something to be thankful for at that, while the French party redoubled their hate against the Austrians who were accused of the crime.

All night long the procession fought its way over the deplorable road to the Escorial, a spare hearse included in it, lest the one bearing the sumptuous coffin should break down. Her final destiny was not amid the tombs of kings and queens, but in the inferior quarters where Queens of Spain who had died childless were allowed to rest. Nobody thought much more of her after the prescribed ceremonies had been performed. The usual baroque sermons were preached, full of futile conceits. In Barcelona the preacher had a splendid opening, for Maria Luisa had died on the day of the Proto-martyr St Eulalia, much venerated in the Catalan capital; had she wanted to die because it was St Eulalia's day or was it not that St Eulalia herself had wanted her for herself and called her to a fuller life on her day? About the answer to this question we may be sure that Count Mansfeld did not much bother his head.

If it is true that Maria Luisa was poisoned, it only means that some determined persons having added a fifth line to the quatrain which had made her shudder, acted on it.

Si no parís, Paraíso.

CHAPTER EIGHTEEN

JOURNEY FROM THE END OF EUROPE

CARLOS, as widower, looked back on ten years of childless marriage. It had begun in a mood of sterile sensuality but it had dwindled into a mood of empty frustration. Perhaps at first it was the interfering image of his mother that distorted his reactions to his then pretty bride, perhaps it was mere physical debility, but in any case as time went on, nature and bad habits filched away all the glamour that Maria Luisa once possessed. The corpse carried all night to its rest among the other childless Queens of Spain had little power to make him weep; it had become too fat, and the spirit departed from it too irritable, too self-centred, to maintain a youthful ardour already tampered with by heredity and childhood upbringing.

With a sigh of relief, as if Maria Luisa dead was an obstacle out of the way, people took up the business of once more forcing an heir out of Carlos. But what did they really think? It seems almost impossible to believe that political necessity could blind them to biological fact, or at least biological probability. The rules they observed in their world of fantasy forbade more than a sideways glance at the almost certain truth.

It is significant to note that the attitudes towards this question, the most important in European politics, of France and Austria, of Louis and the Emperor belonged to two quite different frames of reference. Louis thought in terms of Carlos's health and put first the probability of his sterility and early death; the Emperor thought first of the divine rights of the House of Austria and inferred from them that God would give Carlos the strength needed to protect these rights. Louis did not concern himself with a new marriage and saw no advantage likely to come his way from whatever princess they might choose. The Austrian party concentrated on securing one of their number, and one who could be guaranteed under God to be fertile. They thought that God who, in his infinite mercy, had rendered the French marriage sterile, would contrive that many little German princes were produced when Carlos made a second attempt.

Mansfeld, who now became the most prominent and the most active statesman in Madrid, hinted that Carlos might need a little help if success in a second marriage was to be assured. Writing to the Emperor in April 1689 he says:

> As a matter of fact the King does not need too young a wife: the ideal would be a well-preserved widow with enough experience to assist the King's weak constitution. I suspect that the dead Queen would not allow His Majesty to enjoy marriage for fear of becoming pregnant; so that it would be of little use if the bride's inexperience was as great as the King's.

The suggestion that Maria Luisa herself tried to avoid conception is not the only distortion in a letter which aimed at proving the dead French Queen a criminal. It quotes a holy lady named Mother Mariana as saying that there are few devils on earth as bad as the dead Queen, and few martyrs in Heaven who have suffered as much as the King; and he says that the King himself has confessed that he does not know how he and his mother have been able to remain alive.

Finally we have this sentence: 'I regret that my ability was not enough to make my word believed, since you doubted my report that the throne would be soon vacant' – once more a reminder of his confident prophecy which can only be explained if we assume that Mansfeld knew she would be poisoned, and disguised his meaning by insinuating that she was tubercular.

Mansfeld was only one of the high-pressure salesmen working to get their merchandise preferred. A rival of importance was Oropesa, suspected of being the late queen's poisoner by almost as many as suspected the Emperor's ambassador. As we have seen, his choice was the Portuguese princess and his motive was his own aggrandisement as a member of the House of Braganza. The French party, discomforted and almost driven underground for the time being, favoured a Florentine claimant, who had the special attraction of being rich. Thus a complicated network of intrigue was the background against which the Council of State now initiated official investigations into which princess was best suited to be Carlos's bride.

Carlos had only been a widower ten days when the Council of State, having met and deliberated, sent him a respectfully worded order to remarry at once and procreate forthwith. It felt it its duty 'to put before your royal consideration how indispensable it is not to lose a single hour before giving these kingdoms the consolation so essential'. Some councillors went so far as to hope for an heir in about ten months, an objective quite out of the question, apart altogether from Carlos's possible incapacity, owing to the wretchedness of transportation at that time throughout Europe.

That was on February 22nd, and yet they only came to a conclusion about what candidates to recommend on May 8th. The single hour not to be lost was already lengthening, and the process was to continue.

Who were the candidates? Mansfeld enumerates them in a letter of February 22nd and, by the way, there was not a widow or experienced older princess among them. First, of course, there was the Emperor's daughter, but, alas, she was only nine years old. Carlos might well be less unwilling to wait for a nubile wife than he had been ten years before, but Spain could not wait for an heir. If only the child had been five years older she would have been a fitting sacrifice. Next there was the Empress's sister, indeed a choice of three sisters out of a family of seventeen. Two of them as we have seen were half promised to minor princes, but with one of them, Maria Ana, matters had fortunately not gone too far to be arrested without hard feelings; the disappointed prince could have one of the younger sisters growing up. These were the German candidates; the Infanta of Portugal and the Italian Princess completed the short list.

Mansfeld warned the Emperor that there would be opposition and that as Carlos was certain to do nothing, the necessary energetic action must come from him. The Queen Mother of course would be a great help, and on Mansfeld's advice she wrote for a full description of the three Neuburg girls. This letter must have been one of the few legible ones she wrote; usually, in spite of specialists employed precisely to decode them, they were indecipherable and were laid aside unread. This one was acted upon, and fortunately without delay since a barrage from a mysterious source was already being built up against Maria Ana.

At that time there were a number of ladies with equivocal histories, living on subventions from various governments, which doubtless got from them a *quid pro quo*. One such living in Madrid was Olimpia Mancini, Countess of Soissons. Originally sent by Louis to keep an eye on Maria Luisa, she was now suspected of perpetual intrigue on behalf of France against all that Mansfeld was trying to achieve.

The Countess had been implicated in the famous poison case when both she and her sister were supposed to have attempted the lives of their husbands – her sister with success. Shortly before Maria Luisa's death, Carlos, jealous of the intimacy between them, had attempted to expel her from Spain, but she seems to have resisted her enemies and continued to exercise considerable power in Madrid. It was from her, Mansfeld said, that a whispering campaign was being directed against Maria Ana of Neuburg. It was being said that she had red hair, which was particularly disliked by Spaniards; that she was covered with freckles in summer, that she was fat and as tall as a giant and that the Spanish Monarchy had not funds enough to support her numerous brothers and sisters, all as poor as herself. Another argument put up against the choice of Maria Ana was the extreme difficulty of bringing her across Europe now that France was at war with Spain.

Mansfeld admitted that personal appearance was important as a help to Carlos in doing his duty, but added that here in Spain they were rather easily pleased in this matter. As for the difficult journey, he was to come forward with a suggestion which was to cause him far more discomfort than he bargained for, and, in the end, no thanks.

The Council was virtually unanimous, though some very tactfully left the final choice to the uneager widower. The Duque de Alba, now over eighty and called by his impatient first-born, 'Eternal Father', gave the most pompous advice and talked of friendship based on good breeding, good intelligence and reasonable appearance as probably more lasting than a love-sick passion. The Almirante de Castilla said that in any marriage the first motive should be procreation, but in the case of Carlos this should be the only motive. Bearing in mind what was known of the Almirante it can be surmised that this rather unnecessary emphasis was meant to conceal the fact that his first and only motive in choosing a candidate was to make sure that she could be trusted to support his political views and personal interests.

Medinaceli, while backing Neuburg, advised Carlos to leave the decision to the Emperor and his mother. Even Portocarrero was for Neuburg, but he thought that the ultimate decision should be left to God who would certainly give good advice if sufficient prayer was offered to him. The simple Cardinal-Archbishop must sometimes in future days have marvelled at God's mysterious ways, if Maria Ana of Neuburg was indeed the answer to his prayers.

The upshot of their deliberations was that the Queen Mother's three closest allies, the Almirante, the Marqués de Mancera and the Inquisitor General, voted unequivocally for Maria Ana of Neuburg, while the rest left the choice open between her and the Italian princess. Carlos was given the two rivals' portraits, and after pronouncing the Italian princess 'pretty' said of Neuburg 'nobody could call her ugly.' The Italians offered more riches for dowry though less than had been hoped, but Carlos, after praying and thinking for eight days, decided in Neuburg's favour, because he considered she looked more fecund.

The difficulties were only beginning. On February 22nd it had been agreed that not 'a single hour' must be lost; and it was now May 16th and a princess had been chosen who must be in Vienna or some German town – nobody was sure where – at the other end of Europe. How was she to be brought to Spain and how could her journey be done on the cheap? Count Mansfeld came to the rescue. He agreed to get Maria Ana to a Spanish port for one hundred thousand pesos, and it was not long before his offer and advice were taken. Of the three routes, one overland through France was out of the question, as the countries were at war; another via the Mediterranean was hardly more practicable, since the enemies of Spain could be dangerous, or at least insulting to the bride, both on land and on sea. Moreover a problem of etiquette would arise, since the bride would pass in Italy through Spanish territory, which she could hardly do with propriety unless conducted by her husband. It was therefore the third route which was chosen, by way of the English Channel and the Atlantic Ocean; and Mansfeld went off to England to ask for the English fleet to protect the bridal party from any attempted interception by the French.

Meanwhile there were great difficulties to be surmounted at the other end. The Neuburgs were connected with all the best families, but they were poor. If all their distinguished relatives and powerful associates decided to come to this very important wedding, there would be neither room, nor furniture, nor food available to put on an adequate show.

Philip William, Elector Palatine, already the proud father of the Empress and soon to be proud father of the Queen of Spain, moved heaven and earth to make preparations for the inevitable guests. The Emperor was to leave Vienna on July 27th, bringing with him a third part of the Imperial Court, the secret Councillors, 'all the necessary staff' of the Chancelleries, three troops of halberdiers. And this was not all, the King of Hungary and his retinue were coming with him. Philip William quailed before this invading army: the furniture promised from Düsseldorf had not arrived; the Elector of Trèves had not sent the promised wine; the poet had not supplied the words for the numerous cantatas ordered from the composers for the ceremony; a cook had to be borrowed from the Grand Master at Heidelberg; the Bishop of Breslau had to be persuaded to bring as small a retinue as possible and to find his own lodgings as there was no room at the palace – even Philip William and his wife were having to turn out to make room for easily offended guests.

When Philip William read the list of the Emperor's party in the official Gazette his strained nerves very nearly gave way: human beings in droves were not the only menace; there were two hundred and ninety-seven Imperial horses as well as the sixty-one belonging to the Archduke Joseph and the grand total of four-footed beasts seemed likely to exceed nine hundred.

The most terrifying thing was that nobody knew how long the friendly invaders would have to be entertained, for nobody knew when the marriage by proxy could take place; Count Mansfeld seemed to have disappeared. He had not arrived in England, and it seemed likely that he had been drowned or at least detained by bad weather, or perhaps captured by the French. Until he sent news there was no point in making plans for the journey, since only he could tell them whether King William had agreed to lend the English fleet.

Meanwhile, bad news was accumulating. One of the bride's brothers was killed in battle. Pope Innocent XI died, and a pro-Bourbon, anti-Hapsburg successor reigned in his stead. By August 14th everybody had arrived for the wedding, and everyone was eating and drinking and lodging at poor Philip William's expense.

Four days earlier, however, good news came at last from Mansfeld himself; the King of England was disposed to lend his fleet, and would like to know when they would wish to leave the Hague. There was fresh delay until Mansfeld could reach Neuburg in person, and every evening there had to be entertainments, music, banquets, all at a crippling cost. Perhaps when later we are outraged at the wholesale plundering of her new realm by the future Queen of Spain, we should remember that all this cost far more than could be found by an impecunious German prince without borrowing on the security of future plunder.

At last on August 24th Maria Ana of Neuburg was married by proxy to Carlos Segundo, King of Spain and its vast empire. The 'single hour' on no account to be lost had been substantially lengthened; but the worst was yet to be. Ten days after her wedding, the Queen of Spain was ready to start on her journey. And what a journey it was! It led in its first stage from the banks of the Danube to Düsseldorf, where she arrived in mid-September and remained for several weeks, since the English fleet, though it had been promised, had not yet been prepared.

It was not only in Neuburg that the delays had proved depressingly costly; the Spanish Court, where there was only a vague idea of European travelling conditions, had imagined that if the King went to Valladolid he would meet his Queen there on October 15th and the Marqués de los Balbases had already arrived by then at Santander with a staff of seventy to greet Maria Ana when she landed. He had a long and debilitating wait before him. Maria Ana was still at Düsseldorf on November 6th, her distant husband's birthday. But a week later she was afloat, though only on the Rhine, down which she cruised amid fireworks and salvoes of musketry, the local princelings doing her honour. At Dordrecht they took on six barrels of butter, twenty of ham and twenty-four of smoked tongue as well as many other provisions to be exhausted long before the main voyage had begun. The lower Rhine was already icing up.

Until December 15th the poor Queen had to remain on board, cold, damp and seasick, but then she was allowed to rent a house on land for three weeks, and at last on Christmas Eve came the news that the English fleet had arrived. She hurried on board; the ice was broken for them in the harbour itself, but, lower down, horses had to tow the ship through the frozen river. Cannon boomed out from Willemstad, through a fog of zero visibility, at Steenbergen the tide was so low that they could not make the open sea. On New Year's Day there was so fearful a storm that many dikes were washed away, and when day broke, Maria Ana saw boats blown on land, great trees uprooted, houses destroyed. It is no wonder that she took to her bed and vowed to go on pilgrimage to Santiago de Compostela if she ever got to Spain at all. It must have been one of the worst winters on record and, as might be expected, the Spanish Court now began to lay the blame for everything that was happening on Count Mansfeld.

> The Spaniards denigrate him [wrote Lancier], and say that if a Spaniard had taken on the obligation, he would have known how to bring the Queen by the promised date. What most upsets the ministers is that the Queen's household left for Coruña four months ago and is costing three thousand florins a day, a great loss for the royal exchequer.

Mansfeld himself must long ago have regretted his bargain; heaven knows how much more it was costing him than his one hundred thousand pesos, and no thanks at all came his way.

At long last on January 28th Maria Ana was transferred to the noble English man-of-war, *Duke*, ninety paces long, twenty-three wide and with a twenty-two-foot draught. It had ninety-two cannon, its anchors weighed five thousand pounds and it had a complement of three hundred and eighty. Maria Ana's cabin was protected by two files of cannon. There was an audience chamber with an armchair for the Queen, backless benches and hassocks for courtiers, so that seating arrangements throughout

facing: MARIA ANA DE NEUBURG

CARLOS SEGUNDO WORSHIPPING THE SACRED FORM

the voyage could be strictly according to Spanish etiquette. But Maria Ana took to her bed at once; she was seasick and there is some ground for believing that she made matters worse for herself by taking aphrodisiacs and fertilizers in a laudable effort to be fully prepared for the duties which awaited her in Spain.

It were tedious to describe the rest of her journey in detail: it was at least as luckless as the journey hitherto. More than once the fleet was driven back into Portsmouth or Tor Bay, where they were still sheltering on March 4th. It was now over a year since the Council of Spain had begged Carlos to lose not a single hour. Mansfeld was down with fever, the Baron de Novelli, the Duke of Neuburg's ambassador given up by the doctors, Dr Geleen, Maria Ana's private doctor, and her barber-surgeon seasick, many of the ladies feverish, the sailors much concerned about the possible consequences of an eclipse, the French fleet reported in the offing. But Maria Ana at last began to feel less ill, and as the weather improved she was able to lie above her bedcover.

On March 18th *Duke*'s mainsail was carried away; two days later the French coast was reached and passed with the fleet in battle order. But nothing was seen of the French, and the only narrow escape Maria Ana had to suffer was that *Duke*'s powder magazine was almost blown up by accident.

Soon all danger from the French was over, but not the danger from the elements. On March 26th, in sight of their destination, Coruña, a fearful gale blew away two of *Duke*'s sails, and there was nothing for it but to ride it out off the neighbouring anchorage of El Ferrol, where she dragged her anchor, grounded and remained six hours on her side until floated off by the tide and brought to safety in the little bay of Mugardos. This ill wind blew the inhabitants of that village some considerable good, since Carlos was so delighted with their services to his long-suffering Queen that he exempted them perpetually from service in the Army and Navy.

Maria Ana was not at the end of her troubles, far from it. Hitherto she had had to contend with the elements; now she encountered the menaces of Spanish etiquette. It was of course not distasteful to her that she must go on shore in Spanish costume, and the arrival of tailors and dressmakers on board must have been a diversion; but after that her unpleasant experiences began.

The Marqués de la Laguna and the Duquesa de Alburquerque had been appointed chiefs of Maria Ana's household, and they had awaited her for many long weeks at La Coruña; and now, instead of arriving at La Coruña she had been forced to arrive at El Ferrol, only a few miles, it is true, from the expected destination.

There are certain solitary wasps which, having placed their egg in a hole in the ground, seal it up with a paperlike substance. In due course the matured offspring eat through this lid and fly away; but if an experimental entomologist places a second cover a fraction of an inch away, the offspring, on encountering it, does not know what to do and gives up the struggle for existence. This is an exact parallel to the action or rather inaction of the Marqués de la Laguna and the Duquesa de Alburquerque.

They had been told to receive the Queen at La Coruña, and when she arrived at El Ferrol, a few miles away, they refused to budge. They would not send her 'so much as an egg for breakfast, or a bed to sleep on'. She had to wait on board several days while fresh instructions were requested from Madrid. Laguna seemed to think she must come to La Coruña by sea, at the risk of being blown back to England, but in the end she was permitted to make the short journey by land.

Another difficulty arose: the documents handing over Maria Ana officially had been drawn up in the name of the Emperor, but the Spanish officials said that they should have been made in her father's name. They had asked her of her father, and therefore it was her father and not the Emperor who should give her. It seemed likely that they would insist on sending to Neuburg for confirmation that Maria Ana's father really approved the marriage and this would have meant a delay of perhaps many months. The difficulty was overcome by Mansfeld's saying he had had verbal instructions from Philip William to hand over his daughter in his name, so that the documents could be adjusted in this sense without more delay.

There was a week of festivities at La Coruña, then Maria Ana went off to fulfil her vow at Santiago de Compostela, where she pleased her new subjects by praying for a full hour before the saint's tomb; Carlos having sent her a particularly beautiful rosary for this purpose.

Those familiar with the glorious Cathedral of Santiago will wonder whether Maria Ana performed one ceremony which was as likely perhaps as the medicines she had been taking to ensure an heir. If so we are not told. Behind the Portico de Gloria – a stucco facsimile of which is to be seen in our Victoria and Albert Museum – there is a small statue of the inspired sculptor. With an obscure reverence for the creative power of such a genius, the childless women of Santiago to this day rub themselves against it, in the belief that the creative power will help them to have children.

On May 4th, 1690, the marriage was confirmed at Valladolid. On July 26th, Novelli, who had survived the sea voyage after all, wrote to Maria Ana's father announcing signs of pregnancy. It was the first occasion on which wishful thinking, combined with wilful deception on at least one person's part, sought to score a political success. It was only the first of many such occasions.

CHAPTER NINETEEN

THE NEW QUEEN

MARIA ANA of Neuburg must have been an unpleasant woman; but counsel for the defence could have said much in mitigation. Had she married a potent husband, as most of her sisters did, she would have reared a large family and devoted herself to forwarding their interests by marrying them into all available European courts. She soon found that that was not to be her fortune and concentrated on what would always have in any case concerned her almost as much as the welfare of sons and daughters, namely the welfare of brothers and sisters. Her background was quite different from that of Maria Luisa, who certainly could not have had any sense of inferiority about the station she was leaving. Maria Ana on the other hand was daughter of a minor German prince and brought up in a rather comfortless castle bursting with children and poor relations. She had to work hard not to admit to herself that it was a step up to become Queen of Spain, and she regarded her good fortune as something to be shared with all the members of her family.

At the very beginning she blundered. She had come of course to breed, but she had a second duty: over there in Neuburg there was a nest of fledgelings with wide open beaks waiting for her to provide them with fat worms. No sooner had her wedded destiny been confirmed than her first assignment was clearly given her: on her way through Düsseldorf she agreed to have her brother, John William Palatine, made Governor of the Low Countries. What was her dismay, her pained surprise on arrival in Madrid, to find that her mother-in-law had views of her own. She was intent on getting this honour for Maximilian Manuel of Bavaria. The importance of this contest between the two queens far outweighs the not very palatable bone which caused the contention. It is hard to see why anyone should have wanted to be governor of the Low Countries at that very difficult moment of their history, but it is easy to see how vital the decision was for the rival queens.

Maria Ana regarded her marriage with the King of Spain as primarily an opportunity to exalt a stodgy, impecunious minor German family, and this was to be her first step. She had set her heart on it, she regarded success here as the cornerstone on which her family's fortune would be built. But Mariana had even deeper reasons. Maximilian Manuel of Bavaria was the husband of Maria Antonia, and Maria Antonia was the daughter of that Empress Margarita, whom Velazquez had painted in her *guardainfante, her* only daughter. Now Doña Mariana could have had few illusions about her son Carlos's ability to continue their line. Therefore the Bavarian son-in-law was the only source from which might proceed the flesh and blood immortality which all Hapsburgs desired more than life itself. Not on this would Mariana give way to her stolid, impertinent new daughter-in-law.

Nor would rivalry between the two queens stop at the governorship of the Low Countries. The Emperor's first wife had been Mariana's daughter, but his third wife was Maria Ana's sister, whose son, the Archduke Charles, was plainly the choice for heir which would be closest to the hearts of the Neuburg clan. Thus even at the beginning of her reign, Maria Ana could see clearly that it would be a fight to the death between herself and her mother-in-law, to set their respective family on the Spanish throne. Carlos was doomed to an eternal tussle between the two, his wife wanting him to make a will in favour of the Archduke Charles, his mother in favour of the son soon to be born to Maximilian. In December 1691 Maximilian was appointed to the coveted post, ten months later he was a father.

Now the battlefield was set. Carlos as usual was hardly considered. Nobody said openly that no heir was expected of his body and, when it suited them, everyone, including his wife, pretended that one was on the way. But in fact, though it still was kept underground, there was from now on a Bavarian party led by the Queen Mother, an Austrian party led by the Queen Regnant, and a French party at present disintegrated and weak, but for ever ready to take advantage of dissension and disunity. There was no party that pinned its faith on a child of the royal marriage.

Yet no party could hope to be successful unless the do-nothing nonentity in the centre of things could be induced to sign his name to a piece of paper. And that nonentity did not take kindly to discussions which implied that he himself was incapable of creating a future monarch who would keep the seamless garment intact.

It was not merely a battle between two women to induce the wretched crowned victim to vote their way, the whole future history of Europe was involved. That future depended on whether an ingrown mother-son relationship or a wife's fairy tales of false pregnancies should prove the deciding factor. From 1690 to 1696, when his mother's death initiated a period of new miseries, Carlos was torn and lacerated almost daily by the opposed pleadings of the two women, both fighting for the continuity of their germ-plasm, both realizing that the direct means of achieving such continuity had come to a stop.

Meanwhile we should say farewell to a figure of importance. Mansfeld's popularity did not long survive the service he had performed for Spain. He found it fatal, as others have, to do a favour for the Spanish aristocracy. When wind and weather prolonged Maria Ana's voyage, extending the 'day not to be lost' to over a year, voices were quickly raised to say that this was because a foreigner had been allowed the privilege of bringing home the Spanish Queen. If a grandee had gone, they said, things would have been very different. A Spaniard would no doubt have ruled the waves and flouted the anger of Neptune.

It was only a step from this to accusations that Mansfeld sat up too late at nights talking to the Queen. A commission was appointed to consider whether he should be recalled. It found that he had been indiscreet. So Mansfeld went, and the Emperor lost his best adviser who might have counteracted the growingly disastrous behaviour of the Queen's bosom friend Berlips and her crew. The two men who decided Mansfeld's fate gave ear to a rumour of quite another sort. Evidently during these nocturnal discussions Maria Ana had alluded to her husband's disappointing sexual behaviour, for Mansfeld had raised the question as to whether Carlos was bewitched. Some such confidences on the Queen's part seem more likely to have suggested witchcraft than the reason given, namely that Mansfeld had heard Carlos in a screaming fit address his wife in terms which did not square with the great love he professed for her. Irritability alone would hardly have suggested witchcraft. Possibly Mansfeld had gone so far as to hint that in his opinion the fault for the royal sterility lay with Carlos rather than Maria Ana. This would have been quite enough to make Carlos glad to see the last of him, although out of gratitude he had so lately made him a grandee. In any case, Carlos could not for long feel gratitude to anyone for transporting Maria Ana.

At the end of June 1690 Maria Ana wrote to her father that she had been bled in the foot by her German barber for headache, lack of appetite and insomnia. It was the first sign of what was soon to be an unquestionably neurotic decline. She was to suffer all the discomfort, physical and mental, of a healthy animal denied the exercise of its normal functions; with Maria Ana's type, lack of children and the physical and mental frustration involved can only be compensated by 'organ jargon', the crying out of an unused body.

By September false rumours of a pregnancy became insistent. On October 18th the rumours were shattered. Six weeks later another rumour of pregnancy was set in motion but no more is heard of it, nor indeed of the Queen's health, for another ten months.

Then the first of many desperate crises came. Carlos had been ill, and that had worried her, for even thus early she must have found herself wondering what would happen to her if she was widowed. She must have resigned herself to never becoming a mother, and she must in spite of her national thick skin have observed that she was already, to say the least, not loved by her adopted countrymen. Novelli wrote to the Elector Palatine, her brother – for her father had died in October 1690 – that for several months she had been depressed, and that now she had gone to bed with a sick headache and violent indigestion. Eight days after her illness began, she had such violent pain that she was two hours unconscious, and only came to after she had twice been bled.

Having regained her sensibility she resigned herself to death and concentrated on spiritual consolations.

Next day she fainted again and for longer than before, Carlos and Mariana standing by, tears coursing down their cheeks; the palace was crowded with people waiting to hear of her death, but fortunately the corpse of San Isidro was brought, and in an instant she began to throw off her illness. In a few days she was convalescent, but what according to Berlips seems to have completed her recovery was that a Carmelite Father who occupied a couch near her, presumably to ward off evil influences, went into an ecstatic trance. Berlips notes a more material detail where doctors differed: 'Spanish treatment is unlike the German; here the doctors give the patient a drink of iced water before and after the purge, instead of hot liquid. The German doctor reserves his opinion on this.' The cold drink and the ecstasy were, on this occasion at least, successful.

Having got over her illness, Maria Ana and her doctors concentrated once more on means to make her conceive. It was suggested she should take the water of Puertollano which had cured the Countess Oropesa after thirteen years of sterility; but once more the German doctor, Dr Geleen, and his Spanish colleagues could not see eye to eye, and the matter was for the time being dropped. Almost at once it was publicly announced that the Queen had symptoms which might mean pregnancy, but more probably they were the result of mere weakness; however, the people began to hope at once, and the King to redouble his prayers. Dr Geleen reserved judgment, and advised a visit to Valladolid 'as it is essential to correct by a change of air the disequilibrium between their majesties' temperaments, for otherwise they will never have heirs'. The Spanish doctors disagreed with the travel cure, and the Queen began the water cure instead. How many of the people concerned really believed in their treatments or that Maria Ana was the person who needed treating?

Maria Ana had brought with her an entourage which included a gang of superior pickpockets. Of those who remained with her in Madrid only one showed respectable qualities. This was Dr Geleen. Rather pedantic, he always brought in a Latin tag in his letters, but was clearly above the average in intelligence and medical knowledge. The rest so far as we know them were worthy of their most conspicuous leader, Maria Josefa Gertrudis Bohl von Gutenberg, Condesa viuda de Berlepsch, called by Spaniards, with their understandable contempt for such foreign names, La Berlips or even La Perlis, and finally La Perdiz, the partridge. Her chief colleague in evil-doing was the son of a Neuburg court official lately expelled by Maria Ana's sister from Portugal, and known as Limping Wiser. A friend who lost no time in attracting universal hatred was a musical castrato named Galli. This gang knew how to get what they wanted by playing the old game that had once served poor Maria Luisa, namely the announcement of false pregnancies.

By 1695, matters had reached such a pass that the Council of State, presided over by Carlos himself, concerned itself with the need to expel the whole gang. Cardinal Portocarrero told the King that unless they were all sent packing at once, his subjects could not continue to give him advice or help. Another councillor said that even if these people were Infantes of Spain it would be essential to get rid of them so as to calm public clamour. Monterrey said that the expulsion was as necessary for the service of God and the King as the expulsion of the Moriscos. The chief defender was, as one would expect, the Almirante de Castilla, ever faithful to Maria Ana.

Carlos went straight from the Council meeting to tell his Queen all about it. She took very efficient steps. On Holy Innocents' Day she announced an abortion, and made it quite clear that it had been caused by the attack on her friends. Carlos was immediately shaken, and refused to act. This gave rise to a popular *seguidilla*

La Perdiz, poderosa
Más que el monarca,
Cuando quiere, a la reina
La hace preñada

The Partridge, more potent than the King,
whenever she wants to, makes the queen pregnant.

Limping Wiser wrote a full and indignant account to the Elector Palatine. He said it was all a plot to depose the King, shut up the Queen in a convent and call to the throne the young Bavarian prince under the regency of the Queen Mother. 'When the King told Montalbo,' he added, 'that the Queen had had three miscarriages in fourteen months, Montalbo replied that nobody believed it, and added other insolent remarks which he was careful to repeat to the rest of the Councillors.' He describes the counter plot which he claims to have devised with the help of the Almirante de Castilla. He was certainly exaggerating his own importance; however, for the time being, the Queen's pretended misadventure saved her friends.

Maria Ana, the Partridge and Limping Wiser settled down to perfecting a technique for extracting money, jewels, furniture, works of art, antiques, tapestries from the royal palaces and the homes of the grandees, all to be salted away in Germany against a rainy day. Even now it is usual in Spain, a relic perhaps of Moorish custom, to assure a guest that your house is his. Maria Ana took the sentiment at face value. Her gracious visits to aristocratic houses were financial disasters for their owners, as we know from the malicious correspondence of another of those ladies whose mode of living cannot fail to make us lift an eyebrow. Judith Angelica Le Coutelier, veuve Le Jumel, Marquesa de Gudannes lived in Madrid and ran a salon which everybody of importance attended. Spanish historians do not like her as a historical source, but what she wrote was for a purpose where truth, though not necessarily the whole truth or nothing but the truth, was necessary. It was her task to keep the French Court informed of what was happening in Spain and not merely, like her daughter Madame d'Aulnoy, to entertain the general public with second-hand stories.

Gudannes had had an interesting life of which only fragments are known. In 1669 she had been forced to leave France because she was implicated in a case of blackmail. In 1676 she was in Rome having an affair with a secretary of the French embassy, and during a tender passage with him she put her hand in his pocket and extracted a file of top-secret importance. This she later presented to a Spanish lover who passed it over to the Madrid government. The Spaniards were so delighted that they gave her a handsome present and the right to live in Madrid. She established herself there in a house, strategically well-placed, with a garden contiguous to that of the Almirante de Castilla, and gave all her energies to spying in the interest of France. She became remarkably well informed and quite ruthless in what she repeated about the guests at her garden parties. Thus though she was on the most friendly terms with the unspeakable Berlips – she always hoped to buy her for the French interest – she had no scruples about describing her activities. We shall review them later.

Another shady character was Maria Ana's Confessor, usually called Father Chiusa after his birthplace. It may be counted in his favour that it was not his own nest that he wished to feather. He passionately desired to found a church and monastery in his native Tyrolese village and for this holy purpose plundered as ruthlessly as the ladies. As he was a Capuchin every Jesuit was his enemy, for it was regarded as a perquisite for Jesuits to mediate between the Queen and her God. Father Chiusa, or Father Gabriel, was indefatigable in shady transactions and soon came to be hated by the Madrid mob.

Maria Ana must have understood from the start that the cause of sterility lay in Carlos and not in herself, because though not a widow she was better equipped than Maria Luisa with information about the facts of life, and had evidently had previous instruction. Indeed it is possible that she had been warned beforehand not to expect too much marital activity from Carlos. Her assumed pregnancies were cold-blooded acts of deception designed to achieve her ends, but also perhaps to disguise a certain guilty secret. It seems almost certain that she was epileptic, though another explanation of her illnesses is possible. It may be of significance that she became unwell at moments of especial emotional stress – when she discovered the facts about her husband, when her father died, and when she was forced by public opinion to resume fictitious intimacy with Carlos. On the other hand she never had any attack remotely resembling epilepsy when she was separated from his bed or during her long widowhood.

Once more therefore we find the same equivocal situation: neither wife nor husband really expected children, but both denied the impossibility, he for reasons of personal shame, she because it would have robbed her of any excuse, in the eyes of Spaniards, for being in Spain, where she found such excellent opportunities for amassing wealth. She had to risk being blamed for what was not her fault, so as to reap advantage from time to time from claiming that things were quite otherwise. While she had to pretend that her chief function was to provide an heir, all her private scheming had to be to secure the succession for one of her own party and family by coaxing Carlos to make an appropriate will. And this she must do without him sensing the implied insult to his virility. It was a situation calling for more subtlety than was likely to come out of Neuburg and, true to type, Maria Ana never learned how not to put people's backs up.

There were other signs that nerves were becoming frayed. Maria Ana had been married just two years, and there was nothing to show for it except some very dubious pregnancies of which no more was ever heard after a month or so. The populace was not yet wound up enough to show its hatred of the Queen, but Berlips, Limping Wiser and Galli were left in no doubt as to their unpopularity. It was none of these three but the Queen's German tailor who first got into serious trouble. In April 1692 along with Berlips and Limping Wiser he was accused of a witchcraft plot against the King and Queen and found himself in the prisons of the Inquisition. The chief, in fact the only, evidence against him was that he was found to have sewn little pieces of lead into the corners of some garments made for them. These were believed to be a malign charm, though of course this was the normal practice of tailors then and now when a weight is required at some point, such as a long sleeve, or skirt. He was soon released, but Maria Ana was so distraught with anger, and justifiably so, that she had to stop in bed a whole day to recover her breath. Others were arrested as accomplices in this sinister plot but were discovered not to be witches but bigamists. Bigamy being an insult to the sacrament of marriage was considered heresy, and therefore within the jurisdiction of the Inquisition. Hardly had this scandal died down than a rumour was spread of a prophesy that the Queen would be barren so long as there was no image of Santa Inés in the palace. Orders were hastily given for its construction, and the royal pair, who must have been in need of a holiday from all this, wisely went off for a few weeks rest at Aranjuez.

For the next year or two the emphasis seems to have been on the need to force a decision about making a will, rather than on ways of producing an heir of the body. The wife and the mother both did all they could to separate Carlos from the other, for he was inclined to listen to whichever was the nearer. The ministers and courtiers and even the doctors took part in this game, ordering or advising the King to spend a few days at some royal palace where his mother could find him alone, or arranging a visit of the King and Queen together in a way which would exclude the mother. On these occasions Carlos would be teased and prodded towards making a will in favour of the Bavarian or the Austrian as the case might be. Always he refused, and usually he was put in a rage at the innuendo against his virility.

The scenes with Maria Ana had become more and more indecorous. 'I'll starve myself to death. I'll stop my breath,' she would cry, and then if Carlos was still unmoved: 'If you don't grant them this, they will cast the evil eye on you,' and that threat was usually enough. Some thought Maria Ana was coming within an ace of madness.

The Almirante de Castilla tried other tactics; he had artists paint the three little boys who shared the honour of claimant to the Spanish succession: the Bavarian, the Austrian and the Bourbon. But when Carlos glanced at them, he could only say that all three were pretty. Maria Ana's nerves became more jangled daily, for she was well aware of how many were intriguing against her choice. She filled the Alcázar with spies; whatever mother and son said to one another supposedly in private was at once told abroad; and at last they had to plan a secret meeting at a convent so as to talk seriously and avoid Maria Ana's eaves-droppers. Mariana seized her chance; going straight to the point she had in half an hour persuaded Carlos to send at once for the little Bavarian, when the door opened and Maria Ana, Berlips and a bevy of court ladies, richly dressed, sailed into the room. Maria Ana did not trouble to make pretences or to suggest that the meeting was a chance one; with fury in her eye she seated herself in silence and not a word was spoken by anyone for an hour. Not a word was spoken even by the King or the two Queens. At last Carlos made the ritual motions to break up the party and with all the prescribed curtsies and bowings the three retired in separate directions. Maria Ana had won a victory.

From now on there were two fishwives in the palace. They cared not at all what they said, nor who heard them, and among others Gudannes listened at keyholes and repeated the best of what she heard.

If we are to believe her, the infuriated Queen Mother flounced off to Carlos and advised him to get rid of his wife on the ground that she was sterile and the marriage therefore null. The Church, she said, would permit him to do so on this sufficient reason, then he would be free to marry some one more attractive and therefore more easily made a mother. She saw the Papal Nuncio about this plan and also Carlos's Confessor. She could not have believed it possible; she must have either been mad with rage or merely saying whatever would be most likely to infuriate her daughter-in-law when, as was certain to happen, it was passed on to her. Carlos refused to listen to her and gradually she seems to have calmed down.

It was now Maria Ana's turn to show how far uncontrolled hatred can possess a person. She staged a scene in which she flung the grossest insults at her mother-in-law and threatened to support the French claimant unless she changed her tune. Mariana countered in the same coin and taunted her with her shameless pretences of being pregnant. She should no longer tempt God's vengeance by the sacrilege of giving thanks for a grace she had never received, even publicly worshipping the Consecrated Wafer and begging it for a happy delivery of her non-existent child. Not only were Maria Ana's claims a sacrilege and a fraud, but they were a grotesque absurdity, for everybody knew she would never be a mother.

And so the noisy quarrelling went on: 'Let me tell you, madam, that people far higher than you have humbled themselves before me, people over whom you have only one advantage, that you are my son's wife, an honour which you owe to me alone.'

'Ah,' replied Maria Ana, 'it is that which makes me hate you so.'

When things get as far as this there is only one solution to the dilemma, the *Deus ex machina* so often at hand at the essential moment in Spanish history – death.

CHAPTER TWENTY

DEATH OF THE QUEEN MOTHER

THOUGH March is seldom a pleasant month in Madrid, as it goes out there is a general feeling that spring is in the air; and in the seventeenth century this gave rise to a ritual for getting rid of the evil humours accumulated during the winter. These humours were real enough, but as usual they were attacked in a mood of fantasy. Instead of cleaning their streets, the inhabitants of Madrid, from Carlos down, cleaned themselves through purging and bloodletting; and there was more liquid in the barbers' receptacles than in the Manzanares.

The state of the public streets can hardly be imagined today. At eleven o'clock every night, to the cries of 'agua va', household slops of every description were thrown from upper windows, and every corner was a heap of ordure. What few efforts were made towards sanitary control were more mystical than practical. To prevent the use of dark corners as latrines, crosses were erected with the sign 'Do not defecate where there are crosses' and Quevedo, when he found these words at his favourite place of easement, is said to have scrawled 'Do not put up crosses where I defecate.'

Spanish writers of the period tell us that the air of Madrid was so wonderful that the dead dogs, cats and even mules, left rotting in the streets, had no evil smell. They made a virtue of the prevailing foulness and asserted that decaying ordure was very good for the health. It is true that from time to time the Madrid local government imposed heavy penalties on those who threw out *inmundicia* before eleven at night in summer and ten in winter – four years' exile from the city for the house owners and a hundred lashes for the servant – but it is not recorded that these measures had more effect than the crosses.

As for the health-giving air of Madrid, it is obvious that a very large proportion of the population, including the royal family, suffered from malaria and other fevers. Indeed one of the chief factors in the astonishing decline from Spain's Golden Century must have been the gradual eating away of strength, moral, intellectual and physical, by debilitating disease of this type. Quinine was beginning to be used, in spite of considerable opposition, but the chief therapeutic methods remained purging and bleeding, processes which must have completed the damage started by the ubiquitous mosquito.

The spring cleaning was far more than a medical attack on winter, it was a social function controlled by a strict etiquette which included the ceremonial giving of expensive presents. We may be sure that Maria Ana insisted on everyone conforming to this; and we find that ambassadors included in their expense accounts the cost of obligatory gifts to the Queen on the occasion of her official purgings and bleedings.

In March 1696 preparations were well advanced at the palace, and the barbers ready to perform on all the Royal family, when a sad piece of news came to dampen the ardour for the normal ritual. The Queen Mother admitted to her doctors that many months ago she had noticed a lump in her breast, which modesty had kept hidden even from them; but now the tumour was the size of a new born baby's head and perhaps, said Queen Mariana, the usual bloodletting was contra-indicated.

The doctors were at last permitted to examine her, and on April 5th reported in Latin that there could be no doubt that the Queen Mother was suffering from what Galen calls a cancer, and Cornelius Celsus a carcinoma. The Venerable Royal Council of Doctors and Surgeons in full consultative assembly agreed that cure must be attempted by the preservative and palliative method, and that, as an operation was out of the question, the tumour must be prevented from growing by using attenuant and evacuant medicines. The document ends by praying that God, who is the best doctor, might restore the patient to health and give her many years of life.

Sentences of death of this sort – for no one expected any other end unless a miracle was vouchsafed by God – produce strange effects in those most closely concerned. What effect did it have on Carlos? As usual the records are scanty. He was already in the first stages of the severest illness he had so far suffered; a commission about to sit to consider his chances of having a child was postponed by his mother's illness and death; his Queen was simulating pregnancy once more; his dying mother continually begged him to make a will in favour of the Bavarian prince; he redoubled his religious exercises; and this is all we know. But within his unconscious mind there was a ferment, which six months later produced its delayed action, as we shall see.

It was Maria Ana who showed the greatest immediate concern. She was so much moved by the horrible torments which her mother-in-law, with her habitual stubbornness, tried in vain to conceal, that even her habitual hate was diminished. 'When I saw it for the first time,' she wrote home to Neuburg, 'I thought I would die of fright.' She had no faith in the Venerable Royal Council of Doctors and Surgeons, nor in any of the Court doctors. She begged them to send the best German specialist available, and also wrote to the Emperor for one she had heard well spoken of in Cologne. These foreign reinforcements set out for Spain, but it was inevitable, as Maria Ana must have known from her own experiences, that they would all arrive too late.

Lancier, the Bavarian ambassador, wrote to his Elector that Mariana could live some time longer, provided the doctors did not complicate her illness with their treatment, which, alas, they were already doing. Their dosings had made her vomit and increased her fever and had had no good effect whatever. Towards the end of April, perhaps because the doctors knew that they could do nothing by its means, orthodox medical treatment was supplanted by the summoning of a typical Shaman or medicine-man from La Mancha where he had a great reputation as a faith-healer. He was an ignorant peasant who owed his supernatural abilities to being the seventh son of a daughterless marriage. Such a man was widely believed to possess a gift for healing, and experience seemed to confirm this belief. *Santiguadores*, as they were called, certainly had their successes.

It was necessary for them to be somewhat more than a seventh son, however; as Stanhope wrote home, unsympathetically enough, about this specimen: 'a seventh son, a holy man of the strictest celibacy; who by certain charms or prayers he uses, is said to have done wonderful cures. The Holy Office has approved him,' and 'her holy man, who is an idiot that can neither write nor read'.

The Santiguador was harmless enough from the religious point of view, provided he did not complicate his art with plainly heretical embellishments, and from the medical point of view he certainly did less harm than the *Sangrados* who bled and purged away their patients' remaining strength. And what was his art? The treatment consisted of holding a crucifix over Mariana and saying three times: 'I cross thee, God heal thee'. This was repeated twice a day for nine days, but, in spite of all other medical treatment being suspended during that period, Mariana got no better. Nor could Carlos help, though he remained in almost continuous prayer before a specially miraculous image of Christ kept in the Pardo.

Another powerful force was employed to bring aid to the stricken Queen; the Imperial College in Madrid of the Society of Jesus had always been particularly close to her heart, and on hearing that their benefactor was in need of all the help men could muster, the Jesuits mobilized their manpower to wage spiritual warfare against the intruder, the pagan carcinoma.

Every Jesuit was ordered to supplicate for the restoration of her health in all their orations, masses and other exercises agreeable to God, an order easy to implement, as almost all of them had already begun to carry it out spontaneously. Many solemn masses were said at her favourite altar of Buen Consejo, in which the genius loci was reminded of how much time she had spent on her knees there and was begged to intercede with God to prevent the loss of these pleasant visits. The five Jesuit colleges joined in procession and visited the Body of the Glorious San Francisco de Borja, who had comforted Juana la Loca in her last days. As usual the Virgin of Atocha was carried to the Convent of the Barefoot Nuns and was placed in their famous oratory, full of 'living and dead relics'. The Jesuits proceeded to the Almudena where they celebrated mass, 'with prayers on their lips and tears in their eyes'. They had great hopes of help from this shrine, for it was the resting place of the body of San Isidro Labrador, who had a special reason for intervening for the stricken Queen. When her malady had become known, some of her household begged her to have a relic taken from his body and brought to her bed, but she had repulsed the suggestion vehemently: 'Don't take anything at all from him,' she had said, perhaps partly influenced by the memory that a like act of pious impiety had on an earlier occasion been punished.

St Francis Xavier was implored to add one more to his many miracles. He was told that for her services she deserved to be adopted as their sister by the Jesuits; let him say what Rebecca's brothers said: 'She is our sister, may she have increment of thousands of millions.' God then may be persuaded to allow her, their sister, to live thousands of years. But none of it was availing; the tumour was now as big as the head of a seven-year-old child. All that the prayers could do was to give her an almost miraculous patience in her terrible suffering. Nobody heard her so much as sigh even at the most intolerable moments; and at the end, so those near her reported, she turned to them with the utmost calmness, saying: 'Is this dying?' This calmness was not natural to her character, nor to her mode of life and could only be explained by her life-long habit of devoting three hours daily to mental prayer.

The *Llantos Imperiales de Melpomene Regia* published in 1696 by a Madrid priest supplements these details with a list of the innumerable acts of piety, the heroic virtues, the liberal donations to the Society of Jesus that had marked all her life. Indeed it is quite clear that even as she lay dying an image was being created which took no account of the facts of her secular life, but rather displayed her as a saint in all but official sanctification. Nor was this mere superficial adulation; there was much more to it than the nothing-but-good-of-the-dead philosophy, so easily accepted by almost all human beings. Once more we are confronted by the fact that the Spain of Carlos Segundo had capitulated to a dream. Spain's past history had created a national soul which could find no food in the world of reality. Thus in the palace of the real world there was nothing but an imbecile King and two bickering and hating Queens. How could this support faith in their divinity? But that the Catholic King was more than rather than less than a reasonable being, was an essential belief; and whatever went on around him must conform to ideals which did not exist. Nor must we overlook a crucial fact hard for those brought up in a Protestant community to appreciate: Spain was not only a theocracy, but a *civitas dei*, a heaven on earth, not in the sense in which that phrase is generally understood, namely, a paradise on earth – for that Fantasy itself could not have imagined – but a kingdom of God wherein men were bound together by a granite faith which in theory and practice controlled everything except what Protestants tend to identify with religion, namely ethics.

There was no hypocrisy involved in considering Philip IV, for example, as a model son of the Catholic Faith. He more than conformed in everything that mattered, in ritual and rogation, in zeal against heresy, in charity to all ecclesiastical causes, and the fact that he plunged daily into sexual immorality meant nothing, because he tried as consistently to reform, and above all threw himself upon the mercy of God's Church in the hope of a reconciliation with God. In this frame of reference Mariana was a perfect woman. It mattered not at all that her neglect and ignorance had contributed much to the ruin of the Spanish people, or that womanly hates and all too human evil characteristics dominated her political activities; in ritual and rogations, in Christian zeal and charity, especially charity towards the Jesuits, she excelled; she was therefore the perfect Christian, as far as perfection is to be expected, whatever she was as a woman or a Queen.

Mariana clung to life with the same tenacity she had shown in all its crises, but on May 10th she was clearly near the end. The familiar ritual of royal deathbeds began to be performed. She received the Viaticum in the presence of Carlos and the whole Court. She said farewell to the King and Queen and showed scarcely less affection to her enemy Maria Ana than to her son Carlos. She sent her Confessor into the crowded antechamber to ask forgiveness of any that she had offended. She wrote a will and signed it with her own hand, with seven grandees as witnesses. The body of San Isidro arrived, still intact thanks to her, and the miraculous image of Our Lady of Atocha set off as usual to the Convent of the Descalzas Reales. The crucifix of Pope Pius V was put in her hand and she waited serenely for death. But death did not come even then for another six days.

On May 16th, 1696, she surrendered. It was at the moment when a total eclipse of the moon reached its maximum.

When her will was opened, her private income was found to be three hundred and fifty thousand escudos, but she left behind debts and obligations for her heirs. Her entire staff had to be sheltered and fed in the palace until they could be pensioned off. Berlips says that their number was even greater than the figure of two hundred and fifty given by Dr Geleen, and that Maria Ana, who inherited them, now found herself with nearly seven hundred female attendants, as well as a largely increased male staff. Thus, the King was saddled with having to find five thousand rations daily for his Queen's establishment and his own.

'This evening,' wrote Berlips to the Elector Palatine on July 16th, 'the Queen Mother's family entered the Palace; nobody had any idea it was so numerous. It was frightening to see them gathered together, but there is no way out of the business. The whole Alcázar has had to be turned upside down to accommodate them. The Queen's legacy is a diamond studded holy water stoup, the King's a diamond jewel. The unique inheritance of the King is therefore extra expenses.'

Mariana had ordered fifty thousand masses to be said for the repose of her soul and they had to be paid for. Seven altars were built in the chief state room of the palace, and mass was said or sung continuously for three mornings while the afternoons were devoted to the Office for the Dead.

After the will, the lying-in-state; and then the journey to the Escorial which lasted all night and was held up for nearly an hour by an accident to the hearse. The most elaborate precautions were taken to make sure that the body at last made over to the Prior was the same as had started on the journey, and that it was in fact the Queen Mother's.

The official charged with proceedings queried his instructions rather unnecessarily, pretending that he was not certain whether Carlos wished his mother deposited in her final resting place at once, or put first in the *podridero* as laid down by Philip IV, until what time the unpleasant consequences of death and corruption were no longer offensive to the participants in the last rites. The matter was soon cleared up however, and to the *podridero* she went.

Long before the end of the journey, fantasy had regained momentum. Miracles had begun to be reported. No sooner had the coffin left the *capilla ardiente*, in which the crowds had said their farewells, than a dove was discerned flying about it, a white dove which finally disappeared into the heavens. Everyone understood the omen. The crowds gaped and believed. A nun who had attended the Queen at the palace had begged a garment for remembrance. She slept in it and next morning awoke cured of a life-long paralysis.

From time to time in this story we have the advantage of comments from a man who, while an honest and sincere witness, stood outside the universal Spanish dream – Stanhope, the beef-and-beer Englishman. They are always terse and usually quite objective, some would say cynical. On this occasion he wrote:

> There is now great noise of a miracle, done by a piece of waistcoat she died in, on an old lame nun, who in great faith earnestly desired it, and so sooner applied it to her lips, but she was perfectly well, and immediately threw away her crutches. This, with some other stories, which will not be wanting, may in time grow up to a canonization.

A different attitude was adopted by Berlips, by now heartily sickened of everything Spanish, except the loot:

> The miracles attributed to her after her death are not yet proved. One knows how easily such things are made up and attributed to people who have been calumniated while alive. There is no doubt that the dead Queen was a saint, because of her irreproachable conduct all her life, but the Spaniards don't deserve miracles from her, since they embittered her existence.

In view of her own treatment of Mariana, this was surely outrageous of the Partridge. Meanwhile, artists and poets were composing their indifferent tributes, used to embellish the final memorial services.

The Jesuits excelled in these tributes and published sonnets, poems in many classical metres, acrostics and a peculiar exercise called a Labyrinth, in which ingenuity reached new heights of folly. Other poets and providers of sermons found two splendid themes to hand: first, what could have been more fortunate for these creative artists than that she had died at the very moment of the moon's eclipse? And, second, there was the nature of her fatal illness. Barcelona's mourners made particularly good use of these.

> What signified that fatal eclipse; with which heaven and earth were clothed in deepest black on May 16th? ... What fate placed in the heavens themselves the sign of Cancer? ... Ah, cruel Cancer what hast thou done? Didst think perchance only to execute thy malice in that royal breast, the deposit, the sovereign archive of most heroic virtues? Thou wast deceived. For no one has been less harmed than this Crowned Eagle. Two worlds were spheres too narrow for her winged flight: she had to be transported to the immense spaces of these heavens. Alas! thy cruelty has executed the fiercest blow in our hearts. Samson's column, Rachel's child-bearing, David's sling, Sisera's nail, Haman's gallows, Saul's sword, Absalom's oak, Jezebel's dogs, all Egypt's plagues together – all these fatal instruments killed not so many; for thy malice has wounded infinite hearts with mortal sorrow. The sun when it is eclipsed robs everything of its natural colours, says St Anthony of Padua, plants, beasts, men, the very elements. There was eclipsed by thy malevolent influx, oh perverse Cancer, the sun of the heavens of Spain in our Queen Mother Doña Mariana of Austria. Even the moon swooned with grief, in a sudden fit, that lasted three hours.

Thus far Dr Francisco Garrigo from the pulpit of Barcelona Cathedral.

The sermon, typical of many, was published with some notable poetry. Two poems are to the 'Cancer Ennobled in the Breast of the Defunct Queen of Spain'. The first refers to the happy Cancer, which was transformed into a constellation by Juno.

> Happy indeed, but not so happy as that which has killed our august Queen, since this found in the Royal Breast, which it tormented, not only a shining sphere in which to live but nutriment of its very life.

The second described the womanly fury of the captive queen and gipsy, Cleopatra, and the asp with which in her despair she poisoned her breast and how 'our great Mariana' made amends and gave an example of Christian suffering 'seeing that a pestiferous cancer had taken refuge in her breast, she did not refuse the poison, but protected an enemy, to be a witness that her modesty and innocence were equal to her unconquered patience'.

With all this, one element in the Spanish dream doggedly persisted, one illusion refused to face reality, one hope the Spanish people could not abandon.

Dr Geleen, writing to the Elector Palatine, eleven days after this death says: 'The anxiety to see the succession secured is so great here that it is taken as certain that the Queen is pregnant, although she has had no period missing, and only because the inflictions of these last days have brought on vomiting and great depression of spirit. The Court and People are persuaded that God is in duty bound to compensate for the recent loss by the sending of an heir. Would that it were certain.'

CHAPTER TWENTY-ONE

CARLOS WITHOUT HIS MOTHER

IT might be thought that the death of Mariana would change Carlos's life fundamentally. Instead of being tugged in two opposite directions, he would now have only one woman, his wife, dragging him where she wished; and now there would be nothing to oppose her efforts to get the Archduke Charles made heir to the Spains. It was not so simple as this. The Carlos-Mariana type of mother-son relationship is usually strengthened by death. Mariana, the mother, had taken with her the key to his prison cell; Maria Ana, the wife, never succeeded therefore in unlocking that prison and placing him in one of her own choosing.

The death of the mother was by no means the death of the Bavarian cause. In less than four months, Carlos had done what she, while living, had begged of him in vain: he had made a will in favour of the Bavarian child, Mariana's great-grandchild, the rival to Maria Ana's nephew. It was the one thing that Maria Ana had determined to prevent. How then did it come about?

The immediate event was a severe illness which overcame the Queen Regnant, and marked a new phase in their emotional life. Carlos hated and feared her, but even when illness weakened her grip, he could not act on his own initiative; he sought guidance from the hand of a dead mother. If Maria Ana was available to interfere, the equal and opposite pulls on his will from the living and the dead cancelled out. He could neither withstand the living woman's technique, her pretended pregnancies, her threatened abortions, her bad temper, nor could he detach himself from the dead woman's apron strings. There is no more powerful spirit for good or for ill, than a dead mother – and none so hard to exorcize.

The contending European rulers assumed that all power would be in the hands of Maria Ana, while Carlos of course would be nothing; yet a nothing upon which ultimately all depended, and moreover a nothing unapproachable except through his wife. Two psychological factors escaped the politicians of the seventeenth century: first, they did not realize the power which dead hands can retain; second, something which only a Spaniard could appreciate, the obsessional hold over Carlos of the mythos of the seamless garment.

On the surface Maria Ana was in a very strong position, and she must have felt capable of surmounting all obstacles. True, she was hated by almost all Spaniards, but against this hate within Spain, she could place the adulations, the bribery, the flattery of crowned heads and their diplomats. She could know that the Emperor, Louis, Maximilian Manuel, the Elector Palatine, in their various ways and for opposed reasons, all found it essential to cultivate her.

Beneath the surface, her personality, her unity, was torn asunder. First there was the continual dissimulation about her marital life, an impotent husband but a political urge to pretend pregnancies; second, the task of persuading her husband to appoint her candidate heir, without offending him by hinting at his impotence; third, her desire for a minimum of good will from Spaniards, if only to accomplish her political ends, hopelessly defeated by her quite uncontrollable greed. There were poisonous growths proceeding from a ground conditioned by the frustrated animal needs of sex and maternity. She came of prolific stock, and yet was barren; the fumbling and clumsy service of Carlos's bed must have been more exasperating than unmarried virginity would have been. How tragic for a woman whose ambitions could only have been satisfied by means of offspring, daughters to be laboriously pushed up into eighth squares, sons to carry on the traditions of family dynasticism.

With a child every twelve months she would have become one more stolid, unattractive, pushing, greedy mother; as it was she became a neurotic.

As we saw, Dr Geleen was writing to Maria Ana's brother only eleven days after her mother-in-law's death that the whole Court believed her pregnant, on the one hand simply because she had vomited and felt depressed and on the other because their need of an heir was so great. Towards the end of June he wrote again, enumerating the signs and symptoms on which this belief, which he did not share, was based.

> Shivering throughout her body, sick headache, vertigo, frequent nausea, vomiting, prostration, weak pulse, hard, turgid, painful breasts with very red nipples; cold extremities, cramps, perverse appetite, aversion to normal food, pain in stomach and back, malaise, insomnia, tendency to bad temper, discontent, sluggish kidneys, and a protuberance on the right side of the stomach near the navel ... If only these symptoms included the most usual indication of pregnancy there would be no doubt, but unfortunately there was no suspension of her periodicity. However one must remember that there was no such suspension when the Empress was carrying the King of the Romans.

At any rate, the midwives were satisfied that the desired condition had begun. But on July 5th Dr Geleen had to write that all hope was now dashed, and the Queen's enemies were saying that the story was a fabrication of Berlips intended to influence the ministers into awarding a large income, until recently enjoyed by the late Queen Mother, to her daughter-in-law. Others, however, persisted in their hopes, and on July 19th Father William, a German ecclesiastic, wrote that no one doubted that God had blessed Spain in this way.

The Elector Palatine went so far as to write congratulating his sister and warning her against the doctors. She was to be moderate in drinking asses' milk, in purging and bleeding, and to refuse medicines; but even he seemed to feel the symptoms were those of a disease rather than of a pregnancy. And so they were, the psychosomatic consequences of her ill-starred emotional life; and, to make matters worse, in mid-August she became feverish after eating an eel pie which Berlips, a maid, and a dwarf also ate with similar bad results. At once the cry of poison was raised and soon taken up in France where the queen of letter writers, Maria Luisa's stepmother, wrote from Versailles early in September to the Duchess of Hanover:

> Yesterday evening we received some news which distressed me greatly and made me shudder. I mean the announcement of the lamentable death of the Queen of Spain. They opened

> her and took away a baby which was still living, in order to have it baptized. It was a boy. This is a terrible tragedy for the country. A German lady called Berlips, and two of the poor queen's chambermaids also ate the same poisoned eel pie and they died at the same moment that she did. It is a horrible affair and any Princess who is doomed to become Queen of Spain is much to be pitied ... I cannot forgive the Spaniards for poisoning all their queens in this fashion ... They poisoned our queen [Maria Luisa, her stepdaughter] because she had no children, and now this one because she was going to have one.

Even among Madame's letters it is not common to find a document like this with not one word of truth in it.

There is another letter dated October 10th, 1696, inspired by the Queen of Spain's illness, less picturesque but far more informative. Its writer is Berlips, and it is an account written for the Elector Palatine, the Queen's brother, and for him alone.

> The Queen is free of fever these two weeks, thanks to quinine; she is up eight hours a day, eats well, sleeps more, and has a less bad complexion than was to be expected after what has passed. The rumour which ran, coming from France, of my having been poisoned along with her, was baseless. Spanish gravity does not consent to the use of powders and other venoms; it prefers to distil calumny each day, causing one to suffer slowly, as it does with Your Majesty's German servants and the Queen herself, thereby producing attacks such as the one she has suffered.
>
> The King too was more than six hours in a faint, and in such danger that the Council of State met three times that night, although the Cardinal [Portocarrero] made his colleagues swear to divulge nothing of what passed there. His Eminence counselled the King to designate an heir by a testament, and His Majesty answered that if he had to designate a French heir he would rather not do so. The Council of State met again and, as it seems, the Prince of Bavaria was accepted as heir. The Almirante and three more members voted for the Archduke of Austria, but the Cardinal carried the majority for the Bavarian.

So the will was signed, and undoubtedly the King forgot the Queen when he thus excluded the House of Austria. Really what is intended is not that the House of Bavaria should succeed, but the French, and it is no use talking much of superior claims since after all the older of the two sisters of the King, was the French and not the Empress. Renunciations do not mean much as Your Highness has experienced in the Palatinate.

If the Catholic King abandons the House of Austria, claiming the right to elect, it is very probable that the Most Christian King will say that he also will exercise the right himself. What looks most probable is that the Counsellors of State were minded to act as a Regency until the Bavarian Prince came of age, availing themselves of the royal income and meanwhile secretly encouraging the French, so that in due course France could exclude both Electoral Prince and the Archduke Charles by force.

Some three months back, before Their Majesties fell ill, the Council was discussing the question of the succession and a reunion of the cortes was considered, a suggestion which the Queen thwarted by getting the King to veto it. These same persons have now profited by the King's illness; but the Queen, with her great intelligence, will devote herself to frustrating their plans, though the King is very irresolute and fears the Council of State greatly, and listens to the rubbish they talk.

The worst was that the public demonstrated and not even the Queen's illness stopped them. When the King fell ill the people were led to believe that he had caught a contagion from the Queen, and the Spaniards were so rabid that that night four thousand gathered before the Alcázar shouting against the Queen and all her servants and threatening to stone them to death if the King died. The storm subsided, thank God, but there is no security against its return, considering the sick complexion of the King who is made ill by the least breath of air ... I beg you to burn this letter when you have read it.

The letter goes on to say that the Almirante de Castilla is their best friend, that the Prince of Hesse, the Queen's cousin, must come to Madrid (he was commanding in Catalonia) with six thousand soldiers to protect her, that the Council had recalled Oropesa, the Queen's greatest enemy, but that when Carlos recovered, knowing the chagrin this would cause his wife, he had countermanded it.

Here we have in one letter a full epitome of Spanish politics, at least as seen through the highly prejudiced eyes of Berlips. Everything hinged on the succession. Nothing else mattered. We need not believe that the choice of the Bavarian claimant was merely a ruse to further the eventual coming of the French; it is more likely that Portocarrero regarded this solution as most capable of preserving the seamless garment, and as for Carlos, believed dying once more, his choice was his dead mother's.

Berlips was as little capable of understanding what was in Portocarrero's mind as Macaulay (to whose strange misjudgment we shall return), for neither of them was a Spaniard, neither of them lived inside the Spanish dream in which succession was not a matter of family destinies but of a mystical need to keep the seamless garment intact. At different times Portocarrero favoured all the rival claimants, but this is not to be accounted vacillation, for he always favoured the candidate who seemed most capable of keeping Spain inviolate.

Dr Geleen also wrote next day to the Elector Palatine and underlined the gloomy situation painted by Berlips.

> Of the calumnies that have run about these last months I will only refer to two: when the King became ill shortly after the Queen, the foul rumour went about that she was rotten with disease and had infected him with a secret infirmity. The second is that the Queen feigned her pregnancy intending to palm off as her own the son of a German woman. I say no more lest I make the paper blush. Enough has been said of a country where the Divine Redeemer would be ill treated if he came in the shape of a foreigner.

Not until the end of August was all hope of a pregnancy given over, and the diagnosis of disease accepted. But what disease? All the doctors differed, but the final conclusion was that her not having been bled early enough was the cause. The doctors explained that they had believed her pregnant and therefore in need of all the blood she possessed. The result was that she had too much blood as was proved by haemorrhages from ears, eyes and mouth and all the other systems. It was rare for Dr Sangrado to be consulted too late, and here was proof of what happened if he was. Our Lady of Atocha and the body of San Isidro had to be called upon as usual.

Finally we have Stanhope's grim comment:

> by all accounts I have of her she can scarcely live out this night [August 22nd]. The Court has provided his Catholic Majesty a third wife, the Emperor's daughter, being about fifteen years old. Poor lady! if it be her fortune, I most heartily pity her.

Meanwhile, as we have learned from Berlips's letter, by September Carlos had malaria and his life was given up.

The Council of State met to draw up a will for him to sign; at three in the morning he confessed, at four received the Viaticum, and at five a purge, so successful that he began to recover at once, and at seven he signed the will. This and the seriousness of his illness were to be kept secret from the Queen whose convalescence may have been helped by a box of 'unguentium linarium' sent by her brother the Elector with strict injunctions that Dr Geleen should test it for poison before dosing her, since it had to pass through France. Bitterly disappointed in their hope of an heir, the Spanish people looked around for victims. The Italian doctor who had treated her for threatened abortion had to take refuge in a ducal palace, but the Queen had to bear the chief blame; and it was widely said, as Dr Geleen reported, that it was she from whom Carlos had caught his fever; only it is clear from him that she was accused of giving him syphilis, a curious reaction to the fact that she had disappointed them all so deeply.

However, both the royal invalids were free from fever by mid-September, although Carlos could not get up for a fortnight more because the application of cantharides had left such painful sores.

These letters crossed one from the Elector Palatine which is concerned with a very different matter: in one of the rooms of the Alcázar there is Paul Veronese's picture of 'Our Lord disputing in the Temple'; the Grand Duke of Tuscany would very much like to possess this painting. Could his angelical sister the Queen arrange this? It would make this easier if she got the court painter, Jordán (that is, Luca Giordano), to make an exact copy to replace the original, and if she assured the King that the copy was even better than the original. Father Gabriel, the Queen's Confessor, to whom the request was made, replied that he was afraid the same would happen as when the Queen asked to have Rubens's 'Adoration of the Magi' to give her brother the Elector. Carlos said it was part of the patrimony of the Crown and therefore inalienable. However, he would do what he could.

Five months later Father Gabriel asked the Elector to send an orchestra to help divert the melancholic Carlos, and the Elector replied: Yes, but what about the Paul Veronese?

Indeed, no sooner had Maria Ana got on her feet again than she proceeded to the feathering of her own nest with added vigour. Her chief preoccupation, after the matter of the succession, was to alienate as much as she could of what remained of Spanish treasure, for the benefit of her family and herself. Perhaps her plundering expeditions to the houses of prominent grandees were neurotic manifestations of her interior conflicts, a sort of kleptomania without the need for concealment; she could not get Carlos to change his will, which, by the way, was supposed to be a secret between the King, Portocarrero and the official responsible for drawing it up, but which everyone knew was in favour of the Bavarian princeling. Not only this, but from the beginning of 1697 the doctors had ordered the royal pair to refrain from whatever sexual activities Carlos was by then in the habit of carrying out. Carlos was at this time little more than an animated corpse, and it was feared that any deviation from total continence would be the death of him, and, therefore, the letting loose of the international inferno. But as the summer of 1697 reached its height the whole situation was changed. In the second week of August, Barcelona fell to the French, and the war which Spain had brought upon herself by her own folly in refusing to remain neutral in 1689 became more futile than ever. Louis was exhausted, but Spain was utterly defenceless. There was nothing to prevent French armies marching to Madrid, and there was virtually no government to organize further resistance. Fortunately for Spain it suited Louis not only to make peace, but to demand very lenient terms. Intelligent observers who had no illusions about the French King's generosity could have understood his real motive without much difficulty. When, on October 10th, 1697, the Treaty of Ryswick was finally ratified and published in Madrid, Louis had decided that Spain was going to fall into his hands without the loss of another French soldier. As usual he had miscalculated the power of resilience still possessed by the royal moribund. Carlos had been very weak and ill throughout the last months of the war, and the peace acted as a sort of shock therapy. After the fall of Barcelona, a fantastic whisper suggested that Carlos would take the field at the head of an avenging army (which did not exist), but the common sense of the 'traitors', as the Austrian party called them, prevailed, peace was made and Carlos did not have to pretend to a military career.

It was hardly possible to recognize him; only a year ago Stanhope had told the Duke of Shrewsbury that

> his constitution is so very weak and broken much beyond his age [35] that it is generally feared what may be the success of such another attack. They cut his hair off in his sickness, which the decay of nature had almost done before, all his crown being bald. He has a ravenous stomach, and swallows all he eats whole, for his nether jaw stands so much out, that his two rows of teeth cannot meet; to compensate which, he has a prodigious wide throat, so that a gizzard or liver of a hen passes down whole, and his weak stomach not being able to digest it, he voids in the same manner. The King's life being of such importance in this conjuncture as to all the affairs of Europe, I thought might excuse these particulars, which otherwise might seem impertinent.

And now, a year later, Carlos was almost enjoying life. Dr Geleen notes that he laughs more in one day than he did in a whole year before the peace. He went to Alcalá to visit the body of San Diego; he went to Toledo where he was received 'with extraordinary joy' and bullfights, horseback masques, fireworks. Moreover, the general joy made even the Queen popular: 'She hears nothing but vivas and applause, and cries of "angel" and "seraph",' which must have been a great change; and as always when people were happy, the crowd became certain she would soon be pregnant.

And now we have come to the very verge of the final drama of this unhappy life; though for the moment Carlos seems better than usual it is only six months until he enters the final depths; the devil himself is about to occupy the centre of the stage. What is the balance of forces?

By consenting to a reasonable peace, Louis had almost won the day, for he had begun to make his position impregnable by conciliating Spanish public opinion. So long as he was waging war he could scarcely hope to be popular, but at the coming of peace he had the great advantage of being the least hated of the contending powers. Maria Ana and the Austrians became loathed as the war party; everybody knew that peace would have come years sooner but for them. The German coterie had so shamelessly robbed the country that nothing but a successfully concluded pregnancy could have saved them from universal hatred.

All this was the deliberate intention of Louis. He cared not at all that his own countrymen were disgusted that so long a war should apparently have ended with such miserable gains, or rather without the annexation of territory won by the sword:

> Les trois Ministres habiles
> En un seul jour
> Ont rendu trente deux villes
> Et Luxembourg.
> A peine ont-ils sauvé Paris
> Charivari.

If Louis had been in the habit of answering lampoons he would have said that such lenience would end in gaining all Spain itself.

Maria Ana began to realize she was fighting a losing battle. Although the Cardinal Archbishop of Toledo, Portocarrero, had been an excellent host during Their Majesties' visit to Toledo, he was determined that the King's will should neither be rescinded nor, as the Austrian party hoped, stolen and burned by the Queen. Her only hope of success, she felt, was to do something before Louis's new ambassador arrived, for once a popular representative came from France, the Francophils would be dominant, and Carlos himself likely to be seduced.

At this juncture we must mention another figure whose brief moment of glory in Madrid is more important as an indicator of how people thought than for anything it achieved. This is George, Landgrave of Hesse, the thirty-year-old cousin of the Queen, who was one of the few people to come out of the Barcelona campaign with a reputation for courage and intelligence.

From his arrival in 1696 he had never had illusions about Spain; he calls the ministers 'bedevilled' because they do not want Catalonia overrun with Imperial troops, he tells Aloysius Harrach, the Emperor's ambassador, that he is glad of his arrival, as it means there is at least one honourable man in Madrid; had he known what an accursed country Spain was he would not have sacrificed a single German soldier to Spanish indolence; he regards even the Almirante de Castilla as treacherous to the Queen; his sole policy is to fill Spain with Imperial troops so as to keep the French party submerged.

It is no wonder that this young man made enemies, nor need we be surprised at the forms which the attacks on him took. The Marquise de Gudannes noted the honours poured on him, Grandee of Spain, Knight of the Golden Fleece, Viceroy of Catalonia, and had her own explanation – he was allowed to enter the Queen's room without so much as a lady-in-waiting present. 'If he were eighty years old, one would think less of it, but he is only twenty-eight or thirty.' Saint-Simon, as usual, wrote more bluntly: he had been made a grandee solely to give him easy access to the palace so that eventually he might 'give the Queen a child'. Cynical Spaniards said that if God would only vouchsafe the miracle of an heir it did not much matter by what vehicle the miracle was achieved; and when, shortly after the Landgrave had returned to Barcelona, the Queen arranged for the Almirante de Castilla to reside in the palace, he was supposed to have taken his place. But evidence is lacking, and the balance of probability being against any such dangerous intrigue, we may agree with Maura that French love of scandal invented the stories; we notice, however, that the pretence that Carlos would eventually have children seems to be growing thin. From now, an increasing number of people will ask: 'What is wrong with Carlos?' rather than 'What is wrong with Maria Ana?'

CHAPTER TWENTY-TWO

IS IT WITCHCRAFT?

IN March 1698, while all Madrid purged away the ill-humours of the dying winter, two events, superficially of very unequal importance, ushered in the final agony of Carlos's life. William of Orange, intent on his policy of balance of power in Europe and worried that all Spain might fall into Louis's hand when Carlos died, began negotiations with the rival European powers for a Treaty of Partition; and in Madrid, Carlos, at the end of his tether, sent for the Cardinal-Archbishop Portocarrero. Until the problems were temporarily settled, William of Orange and Portocarrero were to be the headpieces of two rival parties with rival solutions for the Spanish succession: William worked for a solution which would save the European balance of power, Portocarrero for one which would not destroy the mystique of the seamless garment.

There is a curious result of this confrontation of two such different men: Macaulay, whose hero was of course the William who could do no wrong, is guilty of a remarkable libel on the Spaniard. The English historian's superb prose was probably never used to distort facts more completely than in this context.

Portocarrero was not very intelligent, but he was honest to a degree not at all usual in Spain, or for that matter in all Europe, at that time. An unkind lampooner in Madrid wrote a much-quoted quatrain:

> Three virgins there are in Madrid,
> The Cardinal's Library,
> Medina Sidonia's sword
> And the Queen, our lady.

His reading never went beyond his breviary and a few small religious books which he found useful in preparing sermons; but, according to his contemporaries, he was a good man. Lorenzo Folch de Cardona, from whom we are about to hear a great deal, was of the Queen's party, and therefore opposed to the Cardinal, yet he writes:

> He was adorned with a holy fear of God, which made him reverent, zealous for the divine cult, most pious in disposition, always prompt to satisfy the needs of his flock with public and secret acts of charity. Were the number of poor widows and ministers, which he supported, known, it would be thought incredible; he only had to be told that some distinguished man was in difficulties for him to offer help, without troubling much as to the man's moral worth.

He looked after his archdiocese and insisted on a modicum of education in his parish priests and, though a poor scholar himself, he was always on the look out for promising young men at the University of Alcalá and ready to give any such student a first step in a career.

That he was inconsistent in the support he gave to candidates for the succession can be explained easily and to his credit, for all his changes were motivated by his consistent faithfulness to the idea of keeping the Spanish Empire whole.

It is unfortunate, therefore, that Macaulay, influenced by his hero-worship of William and by his realization that Portocarrero was the champion of that obsolete attitude towards life and politics doomed by William and the march of events, should have chosen him as the supreme example of the venial practitioner of political priestcraft. These are Macaulay's words:

> Portocarrero was one of a race of men of whom we, happily for us, have seen very little, but whose influence has been the curse of Roman Catholic countries. He was ... a politician made out of an impious priest. Such politicians are generally worse than the worst of the laity, more merciless than any ruffian that can be found in camps, more dishonest than any pettifogger who haunts the tribunals. The sanctity of their profession has an unsanctifying influence on them. The lessons of the nursery, the habits of boyhood and of early youth, leave in the minds of the great majority of avowed infidels

> some traces of religion ... But it is scarcely possible that any such trace should remain in the mind of the hypocrite who, during many years, is constantly going through what he considers as the mummery of preaching, saying mass, baptizing, shriving. When an ecclesiastic of this sort mixes in the contests of men of the world, he is indeed much to be dreaded as an enemy, but still more to be dreaded as an ally ... There are two feelings which often prevent an unprincipled layman from becoming utterly depraved and despicable, domestic feeling and chivalrous feeling. His heart may be softened by the endearments of a family. His pride may revolt from the thought of doing what does not become a gentleman. But neither with the domestic feeling nor with the chivalrous feeling has the wicked priest any sympathy ...
>
> Such a priest was Portocarrero; and he seems to have been a consummate master of his craft ... To reanimate a paralysed and torpid monarchy, to introduce order and economy into a bankrupt treasury ... were achievements beyond the power, beyond even the ambition, of that ignoble nature. But there was one task for which the new minister was admirably qualified, that of establishing by means of superstitious terror, an absolute dominion over a feeble mind; and the feeblest of all minds was that of his unhappy sovereign.

There is not one shred of evidence for this view of the Cardinal's character.

It was, of course, in complete ignorance of William of Orange's negotiations for a partition of his Empire that Carlos sent for Portocarrero, also it was for a personal and not a political reason. His illnesses, though they had a firm basis in inherited lesions, always contained a prominent psychological element; when after his mother's death he did what she wanted and signed a will in favour of the Bavarian child, there had been an immediate improvement in his condition; but this improvement was undermined very rapidly by the nagging of his wife, who never ceased in her efforts to have the will rescinded or stolen and burned. In this her adversary was Portocarrero.

By 1698 Carlos was again prostrate. Stanhope wrote that March:

> The King is in a languishing condition ... He fancies the devils are very busy in tempting him ... [and] The King is so very weak, he can scarcely lift his hand to his head to feed himself; and so extremely melancholy that neither his buffoons, dwarfs nor puppet shows can in the least divert him from fancying everything that is said or done to be a temptation of the devil, and never thinking himself safe but with his Confessor, and two friars by his side, whom he makes lie in his chamber all night.

And now not even his Confessor gave him confidence; and this was why he sent for Portocarrero. He could not go to his mother, and so he sent for his mother's most trusted friend.

By this time Maria Ana and the Confessor, Father Motilla, had got Carlos in a strangle-hold. If ever he wished to go against his wife's requests, Father Motilla was able to impute sin to him, for if he crossed her, she would be less likely to share his bed; so that to thwart the Queen was tantamount to neglecting his chief duty, that of producing an heir. And yet his wife's incessant desire was that he should revoke the will which embodied his mother's darling wish. Thus crucified between a living and a dead woman he stretched out his arms to Portocarrero.

There was an even more agonizing cause of his prostration, something which wounded deeper than the blows of contending parties bent on his choosing their candidate for heir. Carlos had begun to face the fact which he had so long tried to ignore: that it was not Maria Ana's fault, as it had not been Maria Luisa's fault, that Spain was left without a prince of her own; his was the fault; he was impotent. Wives, doctors, the world in general, all usually arrive at such a truth before the man himself.

But why was he impotent? Doctors today distinguish between two causes; organic malformation or physical lack, and psycho-sexual impotence which comes out of some mental quirk, some emotional mishap. In the seventeenth century also, two types were described but very differently.

Carlos now began to accept the fact of his inability to procreate, but he did not regard it as a permanent lack forced upon him by a defective body; rather he supposed that it was a condition imposed by God's will, which could at any time be removed if God changed his mind; and since believers of Carlos's temperament always have a lively opinion of God's capriciousness, this removal, he thought, might take place at any moment, perhaps without a warning. And if God had without warning changed his mind so that Maria Ana was indeed very pregnant, and if, after that, by some thwarting of her will he had annoyed her to the extent of bringing on a miscarriage, was he not virtually a criminal abortionist? No wonder he longed to bury his head in his mother's skirts; no wonder he sent for Portocarrero.

This is the explanation of Stanhope's comment, 'He fancies that the devils are very busy tempting him,' for in these matters it was thought that God worked through the devil who in his turn worked through a witch. Carlos was not a great reader, but we can be fairly certain that so sick a hypochondriac, so superstitious a valetudinarian, would have consulted some of the innumerable books dealing with such things. Today there are many neurotically disposed people who, reading a 'Family Doctor', discover in themselves every disease contained therein; and in the same way it would have been only too easy for poor Carlos to find in himself the replica of descriptions of something far worse than a sick body. For impotence could be either of two sorts: a natural frigidity, or the result of witchcraft. Carlos began to ask himself whether he was bewitched. It is more than likely that in his parlous condition, in his preoccupation with the devil and all his works, he would have his Confessor or some more than willing friar translate — his own Latin being unequal to the task — pages describing such witchcraft, as well as demonic possession, and its cure through exorcism. And what would he hear? A clinical picture of himself.

It might have been in the admired Mengus, whose works on exorcizing the demon are enough to terrify any nervous man, or it might have been the handbook written by Zacharias Vicecomes, the *Complementum Artis Exorcisticae* where he would have found the following 'signs of being bewitched':

> First: bewitched people crave for the worst kinds of food and are vexed by solid foods. They cannot retain the food they take and are molested by continuous vomiting. Others always have indigestion and feel a heavy weight on their

> stomach. Some feel a bolus frequently ascending from stomach to throat, which they seem to vomit, and nevertheless it descends to its original position. With others there is a gnawing at the mouth of the belly. Others feel a frequent throbbing in their neck, or pain in their kidneys. With some, faintings are frequent, often at the same hour of each day. With others there is a continuous unnatural pain in the head, or brain, with which they are seen to be weighed down, shattered and transfixed. The heart of a bewitched person is afflicted in such a way that he feels torn by dogs or serpents or pierced by nail or steel, or suffocated. With some the viscera are tortured, and the stomach intensely and frequently inflated. Many bewitched people are loaded down by a melancholic humour which makes some so infirm that they are not willing to speak or hold converse with men. A very notable sign of bewitchment is when medicines administered do not help the sufferers.

In this, Carlos could not help seeing his own living image. How could he doubt any longer that all his troubles were due to witchcraft? There was only one alternative: if he was not bewitched, then something worse had befallen him – he must be possessed of a devil, and perhaps of a legion of devils. Carlos had only to turn back a page or two in Zacharias Vicecomes's book to read the 'signs of possession':

> Often possessed people have swollen and blackened tongues protruding from their mouth in an unnatural manner or their throat is inflated or constricted. They weep without knowing why. They reply angrily when asked questions. Even when forced to talk, they do not want to. They clench their teeth and refuse to eat. They pursue men with hatred. They talk much with little meaning. They are oppressed with heavy stupor. They remain senseless from time to time. They persecute themselves, tearing their clothes and their hair. They have terrible, horrible eyes. They are afflicted with sudden terrors which quickly disappear. They imitate the sounds of various animals, roarings of lions, bleatings of sheep, lowings of oxen, barkings of dogs, gruntings of pigs, and the like. They grind their teeth, foam at the mouth, and show

other similarities to a mad dog. Fire courses through their bodies, or an icy vapour. They feel as if ants were moving in their bodies, or frogs jumping, or vipers and serpents, or fish swimming, flies flying and the like. They see and hear various things contrary to nature ...

Yes, Zacharias Vicecomes could not have described poor Carlos better. Almost every one of these horrible sensations, these unnatural gestures, had been his experience for years. He was indeed possessed and therefore doomed, not only here but hereafter. There was only one hope, and that a very slight one; Zacharias Vicecomes admitted that many of these symptoms of possession occurred also in those who were merely bewitched.

Carlos would have been tormented by such fears if it had only been his general health that pointed to a malign condition; but the impotence made the whole thing doubly certain.

A reading of the medical authors, the demonologists and the moral theologians of the times, suggests that no misfortune was so common or so feared as what today we call psycho-sexual impotence. The Antwerp Canon Eynatten, a universally accepted authority on how to fight the devil, says that impotence is very common, owing to human lack of faith, hope and charity in God, which God justly punishes in this way. Pastors, therefore, must admonish those about to marry, and married couples also, to harbour no fears, but to trust in God to help them perform properly the sacrament of marriage.

On the other hand the Church had to carry on an unceasing fight with those who used pagan methods to combat the evil. There were frequent complaints that betrothed couples went to Church with salt in their pockets or coins in their shoes; and that bridegrooms urinated through the wedding ring three times before giving it to the bride. Frequently church provincial councils had to forbid the widespread habit of forestalling the marriage ceremony with premarital coitus, allegedly to avoid witchcraft.

A provincial council at Rheims in 1583 pointed out that married couples might feel capable of avoiding the danger by concentrating on fear of God and longing for children, rather than on lust for copulation. Synodal Statutes in 1606 state that

> Human malice has reached such a stage that to help themselves against sorcery and other diabolical inventions for hindering the marital act some Christians, through being too weak in faith, find themselves so timid and disturbed as to look for secret places, unfrequented by people, to marry in, and even marry at night time and secretly: the which the Church has at all times prohibited and abhorred. Wherefore we prohibit all ecclesiastics from celebrating the Sacrament of Marriage except in full daylight, in the face of the congregation and in the presence of three or at least two witnesses.

Again and again throughout the seventeenth century the prohibitions were repeated, and the object of these forbidden nocturnal marriages was always said to be the avoidance of impotence.

All this Carlos would have known, even if he never read a book, for it was common knowledge; and in the secrecy of the Confessional he must have discussed the possibilities again and again. He also consulted high ecclesiastical authorities. In 1696 he sent for the Inquisitor General, Valladares, and they considered at great length the likelihood of his being bewitched. Valladares was apparently convinced that there was something in it, but he could not carry the Council of the Inquisition with him, and the matter had to be dropped. Once more in January of this fatal 1698, Carlos had summoned the new Inquisitor General, Don Juan Tomás Rocaberti. Once more the matter was referred to the Council who expressed a very wise sentiment:

> This Senate so holy, so wise, so politic, replied that it would be very difficult to enter such a labyrinth without the clue of some notice, indication, or suspicion, however remote, about a particular person on whom they could start to work; for without this, and acting blindly, how could it be discussed and what could be done which would not start scandal and fill the Court with perturbation?

Yes, indeed, subsequent events were to show how true this was. First, catch your witch, then torture her, and so reach the truth — this was the normal and sensible procedure. If the King had been bewitched, who was the witch? The possibilities here were altogether too dangerous. One could never be certain who might be accused; politics could hardly be kept out of such matters.

Now, Rocaberti was a very different type of man from his predecessor. A fanatical ascetic, he never wore linen or silk, he only ate vegetables and fish, his bed was more like a martyr's rack than a high ecclesiastic's resting place; ingenuous though well-educated, he was addicted to supernatural explanations and seems to have left Carlos more agitated than ever, without giving him any comfort or help.

And under the strain, Carlos broke down. He regressed into childhood. His mother was dead and therefore he sent for Portocarrero.

Portocarrero, hearing Carlos's cry, hurried to the palace, for here indeed was an unexpected opportunity. He listened to his King, and all he could say by way of comfort – his vocabulary being notoriously limited – was that once the fault had been found the remedy could be applied; a sentiment that could be understood in many ways and which was certainly not understood by the poor King in the same way as the simple but crafty Cardinal. Certainly, too, the Cardinal was not thinking of witchcraft.

He hurried back to his lodgings and summoned the leaders of his secret party. Now at last they might hope to get rid of the unspeakable Berlips and all her crew.

CHAPTER TWENTY-THREE

ENTER THE DEVIL

PORTOCARRERO saw that his hour had come. With Carlos in his present mood he could strike at the Queen and her hated Germans. He hurried back to his palace and talked matters over with Urraca, his chief adviser, and they agreed that that very night their cabal should be summoned to a council of action – the Conde de Monterrey, the Marqués de Leganés, Don Sebastian de Cotes, and Don Francisco Ronquillo.

Directly the group were seated, Urraca, without preliminaries, blurted out what had happened, and Monterrey, as the senior member, was asked for his opinion. He was not for heroic action. He reminded them of the fate of several others who had rashly crossed swords with the Queen. Now that Portocarrero was admitted once more to the King's private thoughts, the best thing would be a gentle but persistent pressure to wean him away from his wife's political interests – a ticklish business, not to be done in a day. Monterrey had had many ups and downs, dismissals, banishments, as well as high offices, and had long ago developed a habit of not giving his opinion if he could help it and of leaving to others the equivocal tasks of designing intrigues.

The swashbuckling Marqués de Leganés, a very different type of man, spoke next. He had no use for this dilatoriness. He counselled that they should strike at the root of the trouble, at the King's evil angel, the Almirante de Castilla. Let him be banished and everything else would follow. And the Almirante was in no position to resist, as his bodyguard consisted of a quartet of picaresque poets and some buffoons, whereas he, Leganés, kept in his establishment two hundred well-armed and well-trained trusties ready to move off in any direction at a word.

Ronquillo now interrupted out of turn: even this was not

enough. It was the Queen that mattered and she must follow the Almirante into exile at las Huelgas de Burgos.

This was too much for Monterrey who roundly characterized such schemes as worthless, brainless and called on Cotes for wiser counsel. Cotes, according to our informant, made a speech worthy of Cicero, and a speech, one feels, constructed like Cicero's after the fact by our informant himself, for it is more than doubtful that any kind of shorthand report was taken. Nevertheless, whatever his words, Cotes gave excellent advice.

Of course it would be a good thing to have the Almirante banished, but not if the Queen were free to get the order cancelled next day. It would be better still to banish the Queen, and best of all if, with the philosopher's stone, they could induce the King to do it himself. However, the wisest thing of all would be to strike not at the Almirante de Castilla but at the King's conscience which was plaguing him, and that meant to strike at the keeper of the King's conscience. It was Father Motilla who must be removed.

That was the essential first step, and one which could be taken, since Carlos himself was turning, in so far as a worm can turn, against this formidable character. Since he dimly realized that Motilla was the mainspring of the machinery which enabled Maria Ana of Neuburg and the unspeakable Berlips and all their crew — 'this army of vermin,' says Cotes, 'or better, swarm of devils' — to plunder the country, it would undoubtedly be possible to get rid of Motilla.

But who was to succeed him? Not a single holy man in Madrid seemed to stand the tests spiritual and political which the cabal felt inclined to impose. Monterrey, as might have been expected from his habitual attitude, did not know a suitable candidate, and Leganés said, 'I know nothing and understand less about Friars, but only about soldiers; I leave it to your Eminence.' Ronquillo, who always wanted to put a finger in every pie, mentioned a possible candidate in Córdoba, a very holy man as well as learned, but it would take too long to transport him, even if he were willing to change his contemplative cell for the worldliness of the Court. At last, Cotes thought of a professor at the neighbouring university of Alcalá de Henares, 'a learned man, sincere, virtuous and charitable too'. This was a great relief to them all. The Cardinal went off to get the King's consent and, that gained, the Conde de Benavente's coach was sent to collect the astonished professor – or rather the professor who would have been astonished had not Ronquillo, anxious to have the credit with this Father Froylan Diaz who would soon be so powerful, rushed off the previous day and told him that he had himself been the man to recommend him.

Father Froylan stepped out of the carriage at the palace and was taken without ceremony into the King's private room: in the anteroom Father Motilla was chatting to the King's doctor and at once realized what was happening. Changing colour a little he exclaimed: 'A Dios, my friend, this begins where it ought to end,' and with this not very clear remark rushed off to his Monastery of the Rosary. And there a month later he died, it is said of disappointment, though of course there were not wanting those who hinted at poison.

At the palace there was the greatest confusion. It was assumed that the new Confessor had not come without a briefcase full of unpleasant decrees, of names of new candidates for the patronage which went with the post. The Queen herself learned of the change when she came according to the normal etiquette to watch Carlos eat his dinner. Father Motilla had for some time, he explained, not dealt honestly with him and, instead of clearing his conscience, he had added to its burdens. Not without some difficulty the Queen hid her feelings, but she succeeded in saying that as nothing was dearer to her than the peace of mind of her husband, she shared equally in his satisfaction, always provided that the choice was his own and not one imposed on him from outside. On this point Carlos quickly set her mind at rest. It was entirely his idea that Father Froylan had taken Father Motilla's place. And he probably thought so.

But once the Queen was free to withdraw she went to her room and summoned the Almirante de Castilla. There were bound to be other changes, and they must work quickly to frustrate those which were likely to be unpleasant. Father Froylan was surrounded with spies who watched to see with whom he associated, and the Queen's party busily made its defensive dispositions. Chance, however, was preparing a surprise little dreamed of by anyone concerned in this tense situation.

The Queen and her party misjudged Father Froylan, although they were of course quite right in supposing that the French party had sought for political reasons to introduce a Confessor whom they could control. But Father Froylan was not Father Motilla reversed; he was not a politically-minded Confessor, although he owed his promotion to party politics. He was more interested in theology, and his field of operations was the supernatural rather than the chancelleries of Europe. He was far more concerned to fight the powers of darkness, than Louis XIV or the Emperor or even Berlips.

It was natural that many of Froylan's old friends would come to congratulate him on his preferment, and among them one day came a college friend and brother Dominican, Father Juan Rodriguez. The old friends had not met for years, and they had many questions to put to one another about their university days. Where is good old Antonio? Froylan presently asked Juan.

He had had bad luck, was the reply, an illness had forced him to give up his studies. He was now a preacher and Confessor in a Dominican convent in Cangas of Asturias. Ah, poor fellow. And he was so promising. What a wretched job!

Well, yes, but the devil assures him that he is being reserved for an important service.

Jesus, a thousand times! Do you mean to tell me he talks to the devil?

Yes, in the course of his duties. You see, we are cursed with two or three nuns who are possessed, and of course he has to talk to the devil when exorcizing them. The devil has repeated the hint several times, he tells me. Ah! What he has had to suffer in those exorcisms!

This bit of news was like a spark falling on dry tinder in the mind of the excellent Father Froylan. Here was a chance indeed. If Father Antonio Arguelles was in a position to discuss things with the devil, why shouldn't he find out once and for all what was puzzling everybody? Why shouldn't he ask so good an authority whether the King's impotence was due to natural causes or to bewitchment?

It was a bold and indeed a rash idea. Father Froylan was well enough instructed in the Canon Law to know that he was treading on dangerous ground. It has always been understood by the

Catholic Church that exorcisms and converse with demons were not to be undertaken lightly. The exorcist was in any case subjected to the very gravest dangers, since demons were constantly transferring their residence from the original victim to the exorcist himself. Unless the exorcist had prepared himself with prayer, fasting and absolution beforehand, he was only too likely to be vulnerable to their attack. Moreover, in talking to the devil he was in danger of falling into heresy of the gravest kind, for it was strictly prohibited to ask a favour of any demon or to discuss anything with the devil in a friendly spirit.

Could the devil be asked for advice and if so in what circumstances? It was one of those problems which could be argued either way by those whose knowledge was sufficiently subtle; therefore it was certainly wise for an ordinary priest, even though he was or rather, especially if he was, the King's Confessor, to get very good backing indeed, before taking any risk.

Consequently, Father Froylan wrote at once to the Inquisitor General telling him the news and guaranteeing his old friend Father Antonio's discretion should he be asked to ascertain from the devil or any lesser demons, which might be inconveniencing the nuns, what they all so earnestly desired to know about the King.

And what was the precise question which troubled these learned ecclesiastics so much? It was certainly not whether Carlos was impotent; for whatever the King with his sense of shame or the Queen with her use of fake pregnancies might wish them to think, they knew perfectly well how that question should be answered.

What they wanted to know, for on the answer depended the proper course of treatment, was whether the impotence was natural or the result of witchcraft. Had he been disarmed by natural or by supernatural forces?

The Inquisitor General and the King's Confessor had, no doubt, consulted the authorities, as it was their duty to do. They would have read both the medical and the theological scholars. To begin with, as we have seen, there was the long-winded Dr Bravo who had included in the third edition of his Folio a *consultatio* on impotence caused by witchcraft. He quotes several authorities who have distinguished between this and cases due to natural causes. There is Rodrigo de Castro who gives as the legal definition that those unable to have sexual connection with any women are called *frigidus*, while those whose incapability extends to one woman or some women only are *bewitched*. Capella of Toulouse uses *frigidus* for those unable to have an erection, and *bewitched* for those who, while able to function thus far, cannot achieve penetration; other equally learned authorities prefer to use *frigidus* for those without semen and *bewitched* for those inconvenienced by premature ejaculation. Dr Bravo himself seems to play for safety and to achieve bathos, for he uses *frigidus* for those impotent from a natural cause, and *bewitched* for those interfered with by a devil, thereby begging the question.

Dr Bravo mentions a number of cures by 'natural magic', that is, by natural science, including fumigation with a fish skin as the couple are about to go to bed, theriac mixed with hypericum juice, anointing the male member with hypericum juice, wine and honey, and the use of various herbs in conjunction with unpleasant substances, but he is sceptical enough to regard all these as contrary to the laws of scientific medicine, and, since supernatural magic, involving a pact with the devil, must be ruled out, falls back on exorcism as the only hope.

Thus far the late royal medical adviser and most authorities likely to have been consulted by the Inquisitor General agreed with him. There had been written innumerable treatises on these matters, but one of the blessings of enforced orthodoxy is that it is seldom necessary to read more than one or two of such treatises, especially if an opinion on the question in which one is interested has already been given by Galen or St Thomas Aquinas. St Thomas had long ago shown that it can be taken for granted that the devil can produce impotence by witchcraft, and therefore most of the masters waste no time in further argument.

Moreover, general agreement had been reached long ago as to the various ways in which the devil went about achieving this malice. The five methods generally described were first stated by Peter de Palude the Dominican (1384) and these are repeated in the *Malleus Maleficarum* (*circa* 1486) and later in the textbook which superseded it, Martinus Delrio, *Disquisitiones Magici. Libri Sex* (1599-1601). Then again Thomas Sánchez de Córdoba in his great treatise *de Matrimonio* (vol. 2, Liber VII, Disputatio XCIV) describes the five ways whereby the devil devises impotence with the help of a witch and with the permission of Almighty God; but as this is not a practical treatise on the physiological behaviour of the human male, we can safely leave the reader to consult the authorities and content ourselves with mentioning one of the many characteristics of impotence which can be used to distinguish between the two causes, the natural and the supernatural.

It is a certain sign of the machinations of a witch if a man while potent with other women is impotent with his wife – that is if any contributory physical impediment on her part has been ruled out.

The Spanish doctors of theology studying Delrio and Sánchez and even Augustine and Aquinas in order to form an opinion on the King's sexual disabilities were here faced with a difficulty, and a very rare one. Carlos was one of the few men recorded of his age and place who was entirely faithful to his wife. There was no escapade of the King's from which a comparison of his sexual conduct with others could be made; nor was he willing to provide such evidence in the interests of science. It was not clear whether the fact that he had been equally unsuccessful in two marriages was to be regarded as strengthening or weakening the suspicion of witchcraft. Indeed the learned men were puzzled and could not come to a decision either way.

Besides, there was always the possibility that Louis XIV or the Emperor had more to do with the King's defect than the devil. There were many reasons why foreigners as unscrupulous as these might be glad of a sterile marriage. It was commonly whispered therefore that abortifacients and frigorifics were sent to the innocent pair, probably disguised or mislabelled as fertility drugs or aphrodisiacs, from a number of interested sources.

For years 'natural magic', always canonically permissible, had been all that was openly tried to relieve the situation. Of course there was no doubt whatever that on no account could recourse be taken to witchcraft to untie the ligament, because that involved intrinsically invoking the devil's help through witchcraft, and, long ago, St Thomas Aquinas had forbidden this, his veto being a direct consequence of Leviticus XIX and XX; but there was also secret resort to that borderline sort of magic, the legitimacy of which was hotly disputed. This borderline magic was recourse to 'a vain act' in order to get rid of a spell.

Thus, married couples were in the habit of repeating three

times certain prayers when naked and prepared for the conjugal act. This certainly belonged to the category of vain acts but both the number three and the nakedness savoured of something definitely worse, illegal superstition; but, as no invocation of the devil was involved, lenient moral theologians were apt to allow it. More rigid moralists, however, were very much opposed to permitting the number three to pass in this case any more than in many other vain observances where its magical potency was invoked; it definitely overstepped the mark, while to pray naked was so obviously an indecency as to be blasphemous. In any case, if a vain act works, it cannot be merely vain, it must have some witchcraft hidden in it. This last argument, I confess, seems to me unanswerable.

Sánchez probably voices the majority opinion when he says that if the prescribed exorcisms, sacraments, etc., of the Church fail to bring about a cure, it is as well to assume that God wishes the impediment to continue, and instead of resorting to vain observances – the example he gives is saying a Paternoster into a horse's ear – it is wiser to possess one's soul in patience.

All this wisdom the Inquisitor General and the King's Confessor knew by heart. What they could not know was the answer to the essential specific question: was Carlos impotent through natural causes or through witchcraft? And here was an opportunity of finding out from the one person who must know – God maintaining his habitual silence – namely the devil. They agreed that Don Antonio out in the wilds of Asturias might have the key.

It was not, however, plain sailing. One of the wisest rules of the Church has always been that matters concerning exorcism must always be sanctioned by the would-be-exorcist's bishop, and Don Antonio's bishop was Thomas Reluz, Bishop of Oviedo, whom we have met in the Plaza Mayor of Madrid in the great auto-de-fé of 1680 and who had been the King's Confessor in early days. And Bishop Reluz would have nothing to do with the plan. He repeated what he had always maintained, that there was nothing but nonsense in all this about Carlos's being bewitched; he was merely too subservient to the Queen's will. If the Confessor did not do his job properly, nothing could be hoped for. There was a great need of prayer and more prayer and of telling the

King what a lot of fraud and nonsense there was in all this talk about witchcraft.

Rocaberti and Don Froylan resolved to go behind the sensible bishop's back, but Antonio Arguelles was not going to take any risks. Before he would consent to proceed he insisted on having the Inquisitor General's instructions in writing; to have to exorcize anyone was bad enough but to disobey a bishop in anything to do with exorcism would be fatal if things went wrong; and too often when no unnecessary risks at all were taken, things did go wrong. After all, the devil was powerful, and although he required the permission of Almighty God to accomplish any evil, God's ways were admittedly mysterious, and nobody could ever be certain whether he would withhold his permission from the devil or not.

We know nothing about the unfortunate nuns out of whose spiritual disease this good was hoped for. Nuns were the commonest victims of the devil's whims. A nun would be leading an exemplary life and even be suspected of miraculous gifts or the enjoyment of extraordinary graces and then suddenly the worst would happen. She would howl like a wild animal, blaspheme when she intended to pray, commit unspeakable sacrilege, lose power of speech when devotions ought to have passed her lips, lie distorted like a strung bow, her heels touching the back of her head, vomit horrible things; and her companions would be powerless to help. A devil, seven devils, a whole legion of devils, had entered into her.

Under conditions such as this, men like Arguelles, rushing in at the call of duty where angels could not be blamed if they feared to tread, had to be pure in thought and deed, steadfast in spirit, and thoroughly well trained in the technique of the supernatural duelling which he was undertaking. The Church in its wisdom had issued minute instructions on all points likely to arise.

There were manifest dangers to the person of the exorcist and there were others affecting his soul's health. He might easily commit unpardonable heresy. Take this matter of asking advice or help of the devil. The devil might, in certain cases, be ordered to reveal a fact as a superior orders a slave, but he must never be given a chance of thinking he is being treated as an equal. From very early days there had been unanimous and repeated condemnation of the use of magic, or of the devil's own weapons to achieve any end however desirable, as the destroying of magic or other diabolical powers. And here was the rub in the case of Arguelles and the eminent ecclesiastics. He was being asked by them, and against the wish of his bishop, to come perilously near asking a favour of the devil. No wonder he wanted his instructions in writing signed by the Inquisitor General himself. Even so there must have been some overriding inducement for him to take the risk, something more than a mere desire to help the unfortunate King. What that inducement was will become obvious in due course. For the time being Arguelles agreed to co-operate, but with precautions.

The instructions were to be written in code: the Inquisitor would be alluded to as the *amo*, the master, and Father Froylan as the *amigo*, the friend. This settled, Arguelles was at last willing to begin.

CHAPTER TWENTY-FOUR

THE DEVIL, THE CONFESSOR AND THE INQUISITOR GENERAL

On June 18th, 1698, 'the master', alias the Inquisitor General, requested Don Antonio Arguelles to write the names Carlos and Maria Ana on a piece of paper and, when next he was exorcizing the nuns, to place the paper sealed in an envelope on his chest. At a suitable moment he was to ask the devil whether the persons named on the paper were bewitched.

Any student of the exorcist's art is likely to be astonished at this suggestion and, *pace* the Inquisitor General's shade, one is tempted to claim that it smacks of heresy and vain observance. There is no authority for testing the devil's clairvoyant powers, even if it is possible to justify the request for information.

The belief in the power of the written word and especially of written proper names was of course very strong, and was often used to discomfort the devil in one way or another. Thus Valerius Polydorus Patavinus in his *Practica Exorcistarum*, approved by the Inquisition in 1605, advises their use. He suggests that the following be written on a leaf of paper and, after being suitably blessed, hung round the neck and over the breast of the possessed man to help free him from the devil's vexations.

> In nomine Patris† et Filii† et Spiritus sancti† Amen.
>
> Hel† Heljon† Sother† Hemanuel† Sabaoth† Agla† Tetragrammaton† Aglos† Otheos† Ischiros† Atanatos† Jehovah† Va† Adonay† Sabay† Homousion† Messias† Esereheye† Increatus Pater† Increatus Filius† Increatus Spiritus Sanctus† Jesus Christus Vincit† Christus regnat† Christus imperat† Christus ab omni vexatione Diabolicae perversitatis† te† XYZ, defendat.† Amen.

In suggesting this, however, Polydorus had a very different object in view. The devil was expected to be annoyed by the holy names of God, however wrongly spelt, when they were attached thus to his temporary domicile, and to react in a way favourable to his victim. But the *amo* had quite another objective. He intended not to annoy, but to extract information. Now Canon Law applauded you if you wished to annoy the devil, but gave you no authority to ask any favour of him. Moreover, as was urged later when the whole matter became public, the job of an exorcist is with the possessed victims, and he should not use them to further other ends, such as the King's health, however laudable these ends might be. However, whether this placing of the royal names on the exorcist's person was heterodox or not, it was successful; the devil was forthcoming with relevant information, though it was a long time before he was willing to develop the subject along the lines expected and desired by the politically prejudiced ecclesiastics.

It was a curious moment in history. The succession to the Spanish Throne occupied all Europe's attention, and everybody was seeking a solution by secret means appropriate to his nature. The Inquisitor General and the King's Confessor were engaged in medico-theological researches which might lead to Carlos's having an heir of his body; Portocarrero, who seems to have been quite ignorant of the efforts of the *amo* and the *amigo*, was protecting the King's will in favour of the Bavarian prince; William of Orange was acting in quite a different medium and successfully arranging to carve up the Spanish Empire between himself, Spain's supposed chief friend the Emperor, and her chief enemy France; the Emperor, like everyone else playing a double game, still hoped to get the whole for the Archduke Charles and relied on Maria Ana for this purpose; and finally Louis XIV: what was he doing behind William's back? He was completing 'Le Rond' by working on Maria Ana, ostensibly the life and soul of the Austrian party.

On July 23rd an odd change of political weather was reported by Stanhope from Madrid. In a letter to Mr Yard he passed on a remarkable piece of gossip:

> Here is a report that our new French lady [i.e., the wife of the new ambassador, Harcourt] has sweetened Her Majesty by a proposal that she will still continue Queen of

> Spain by a second marriage in France. It is not impossible, and our Holy Father, the Pope, will not be difficult in granting a dispensation.

and later Stanhope added:

> Her Majesty is now as much in the French interest as she was before in the German, having received all imaginable assurance from Paris, that, whatever may happen here, she shall still continue Queen of Spain, nor do I write this without very good grounds.

Now it is true that not so long ago Maria Ana had been smashing china in her fury against Carlos for signing the will in favour of the Bavarian, and that she and Berlips regarded this will as a concealed machination on the part of Portocarrero in favour of an eventual French succession; but Louis had for some time reasoned that it would not be too difficult to persuade her that she had better look elsewhere, if she wanted to make sure of her future security. Her position was unenviable; sooner or later Carlos must make up his mind to die; for what sort of a widowhood could she hope? Devoted as she had always been to her teeming family in far-away Neuburg and to her brother-in-law the Emperor, she was even more devoted to her own security. She knew that the Spanish people loathed her, and she had few friends elsewhere; what then would happen to her when Carlos died?

Louis had no illusions about human nature and took great pains to use the hopes, and particularly the fears, of his adversaries for his own purposes. He therefore chose at this juncture the right type of man as his new ambassador in Madrid, and, as usual, gave him careful secret instructions. He was to make the best use possible of the natural uneasiness with which the Spanish Queen must be considering her future. Her anxieties had been increased by a minor matter: her steadiest friend and councillor among the Spanish nobility had always been the Almirante de Castilla and at this time the Almirante entered into a second marriage. Maria Ana showed herself remarkably put out by this and in consequence the rumours that he had been her lover were redoubled, while, what was more important, she began to have doubts of his loyalty to her cause.

To add to the confusion, nobody knew if Carlos's will was still in existence and, for that matter, only a handful of people knew what it contained. Finally the Emperor's ambassador, Harrach, was a tactless and stupid man, quite incapable of countering French worldly wisdom. The French ambassador, Harcourt, therefore had things all his own way, and by pandering to the Queen's greedy acquisitiveness and playing on her fears for the future, immobilized her German inclinations, even if he did not make her altogether a Francophile. She was encouraged, however, to see herself the future wife of a French monarch as soon as Carlos had given her the desirable gift of widowhood.

We may be sure that poor Carlos was informed neither of the assistance now being asked of the devil, nor of the plans of his future widow. He would not have been pleased with either, but they would not have caused him as much bitter rage and sorrow as the devious transaction now near completion elsewhere and upon a somewhat larger canvas. In Spain, political theory, in so far as any might be said to have existed, at this time, had not evolved; but in Europe the march of events was bringing new theories to replace such anachronisms as Hapsburg dynasticism and even the older type of French imperialism. William of Orange represented the Maritime Powers, and their growing strength brought with it the newer political theory, that of Balance of Power.

The problem as William saw it was simple: there were three claimants to the Spanish succession; Europe was free for the moment from war; all the nations were almost equally exhausted; the Maritime Powers needed nothing but prolonged peace to gain paramount strength in Europe; yet, when Carlos died, war was inevitable if any one of the three claimants succeeded to the whole Spanish Empire.

The rivals were three children, Philip Bourbon, Louis XIV's younger grandson and Duke of Anjou, who was nine years old, the Archduke Charles, thirteen, and José Fernando of Bavaria, six. The Bourbon claimed through Philip IV's older daughter, Maria Teresa, Louis XIV's wife. It is true that Philip had made her renounce all claims for herself and her descendants when he handed her over in 1660 to Louis on the Isle of Pheasants; but the French, we will remember, made one condition, namely that her dowry should be paid. This one had not been paid, and therefore Louis claimed that the renunciation was not valid.

The Archduke Charles was the Emperor Leopold's son by his second wife and claimed as the direct male descendant from Charles V. As for José Fernando of Bavaria, he was, as we have seen, the great-grandson of Mariana and her choice. There were others, but hardly anyone except Oropesa took seriously the Portuguese King's claim, put forward on the ground that he too had the misfortune to have been descended from Juana la Loca, nor the claim of the Duke of Savoy.

On October 11th, 1698, France, England and the States General agreed secretly on a partition. Spain, the Low Countries and their colonies were to go to the Bavarian claimant; the Emperor's son was to get Milan, and France to get Naples, Sicily and some Spanish border territory.

Of course the secret treaty must be kept secret until Carlos was dead, and of course the secret leaked out within a very few days. Indeed October had not ended before the Spanish ambassador in London knew all about it. Carlos found that his friends and enemies had met together to commit what he considered the worst of all possible sins.

While all this had been going on, Father Antonio had received the Inquisitor General's letter and replied that the request to assist in such high matters was not altogether a surprise to him, since the devil had told him some time before that God kept him for important business, and that it had seemed to him that some superior would give him orders, but what they would be he had no idea. He had now exorcized the nuns, putting their hands upon the altar, and the devil had sworn to God that it was true that the King was bewitched: 'and this was done to destroy his generative organs, and to render him incapable of administering the kingdom.'

The charm had been made by moonlight and was renewed every moon, being particularly powerful at each new moon. It had been administered in a drink when he was fourteen years old. All this the exorcist reported in the devil's own words and added on his own account that the King should be given fasting, half a pint of olive oil duly blessed according to the ritual of exorcism prescribed in such cases. Moreover, he must eat more slowly, and all that he ate or drank must be blessed. The King was very severely infested, and it was a miracle he was still alive. No time must be lost, the danger was great.

We may well believe that the *amo* and the *amigo* were dismayed to receive these instructions, for the poor King was in no condition to drink pints of oil, however good and truly blessed: 'his ankles and knees,' Stanhope reported on June 25th, 'swell again, his eyes bag, the lids are as red as scarlet and the rest of his face a greenish yellow. His tongue is *trabado* as they express it, that is, he has such a fumbling in his speech, those near him hardly understand him' – this last symptom reminds us of the Emperor Charles long ago, from whom or through whom all this ghastly inheritance has passed.

And now, to these reasonable, almost routine, interrogations were added certain questions which were to put a very different face on the whole matter. Names and very dangerous names were to be introduced. The devil was to be asked to play party politics. Was the Queen also bewitched? What persons bewitched the King and how? Had the sorcery been renewed since he was fourteen?

On the receipt of this letter, Don Antonio began to have very great scruples indeed. It was not the remarkable situation wherein the two most eminent theologians in Spain asked him to act as intermediary between them and the devil and to get them the devil's opinion about theological matters. That may very well seem odd to us, but it should be remembered that anything that the devil said was with the permission of Almighty God, and the *amo* and the *amigo* might well suppose that this was the mysterious way in which God had decided to give them vital information. But it was less healthy to introduce political matters. Don Antonio wrote, begging to be excused. He felt, he said, that the Church had not provided for, nor taught the propriety of asking such questions. It was plainly his desire to be free of all this business of asking the devil's advice, but he saw that the *amo* and the *amigo* would resent a mere priest's refusing to comply with their wishes, and he could hardly argue the theological impropriety of his superior's requests; and so he forestalled them in a spirited attempt to shift the blame for the lack of progress in helping the King.

They had asked him for the devil's opinion as to whether

Carlos would benefit from a change of residence, but they were not paying attention to the devil's advice. Things had become desperate; we learn from Stanhope's letter to Lord Chancellor Methuen on July 9th that the King's condition was now apparently hopeless, 'though the Queen lugs him out abroad every day to make people believe he is well till her designs are ripe.'

A great deal more information was now demanded of the devil. There must be a pact of some sort between witch and the devil and there must be some outward sign of it. What was this sign? Where was it? How could it be discontinued? Was it hidden inside or outside the palace? And then there was the symptom that above all dismayed the royal sufferer: the other law in his members so that the thing he would he could not do. What devilish force was responsible for these interior effects? How were they to purify the infested place?

No wonder the *amo* and the *amigo* wanted quick action; from another of Stanhope's letters written the same day as the other we gather that the medical profession was trying new remedies, apparently in ignorance of the theological treatment being carried out rather half-heartedly at the same time. 'They talk of a diet of hens and capons, fed with viper's flesh, but the King looks like a ghost, and moves like an image of clockwork.'

This accounts for the sense of urgency in the letters to Arguelles which stung him to reply once more that the *amo* and the *amigo* said they wanted to cure the King, yet they were not doing what, on the best authority – that of the devil, speaking of course with God's consent – they were told to do. Clearly the King would get worse daily, especially at New Moon, and what on earth would be the good of moving him to Toledo if his illness went with him? Why don't they do justice? The ministers of the Divine Power had already told them all they wanted to know for the cure and they did nothing. Frankly they would not be blameless in God's eyes if the King died.

The Inquisitor's secretary replied even more hotly. How dare a mere priest presume to know more than the *amo* and the *amigo*? How dare he attribute the King's condition to them, merely to excuse himself from further work? The *amo* and the *amigo* considered this in very poor taste. They could not approve of it. Let him get on with questioning the devil. God had begun to reveal the truth and was now being frustrated by his refusal to continue. He was much to blame. Let him get on with the questions without any more answering back at them.

The poor exorcist was now faced with the imminent displeasure of the Inquisitor General, a most unhealthy position to find oneself in in seventeenth-century Spain. By September he had resolved to risk anything rather than to continue on the Inquisitor's black list and on the 9th he wrote:

> continuing the questioning on oath I asked him in what the charm had been given the King. He replied, 'In chocolate on April 3rd, 1675.' I asked of what it had been made. He replied, 'Of the members of a dead man.' How? 'Of the brains to deprive him of health; of the kidneys to corrupt his semen and prevent procreation.'

It appears that the very transparent euphemism here was the devil's own.

> 'Is there the original charm or an exterior sign that could be burned?'
>
> 'No, by the God which created thee and me.'
>
> 'Was it man or woman?'
>
> 'She is already judged.'
>
> 'Why did she do it?'
>
> 'To reign.'
>
> 'When?'
>
> 'In Don Juan de Austria's time; who was snatched away from this life by similar charms only stronger and able to end him sooner.'

Everybody could see that the devil, without naming her, was accusing the Queen Mother Mariana of Austria. In a sense he had steered Don Antonio round a dangerous corner, for it was certainly less perilous to attack the dead Queen Mother than the living Queen Consort.

At this point Don Antonio tried to break off. What the devil said was to the last degree unlikely. Almost anyone indeed would have been more likely to harm Carlos in this way than his mother. Clearly then the devil was acting in a quite irresponsible manner, and there was no knowing what names he would mention next.

No wonder Don Antonio wanted to get back to his proper duty of exorcizing the nuns. As was brought out later by Froylan's opponents there was no warrant in Canon Law or anywhere else for using the possessed as mere lines of communication to their tormenting spirits. Moreover, it was clear by now that the *amo* and the *amigo* had not yet got what they wanted.

However, the devil vouchsafed a little more information about remedies. He recommended what the Church prescribed, holy oil as a beverage, fasting, anointing the torso and head with oil, a purge as prescribed in the manual of exorcisms; and separation from the very sight of the Queen. And he added: 'That is all I know, and that is all I will say.' It was unfortunately for Don Antonio just one sentence too much.

The storm however was to come later; at present the Queen was unaware that the devil was interfering with her marital arrangements. Moreover, the doctors themselves were in favour of a little enforced celibacy on the theory that, if the King was made to wait, his natural concupiscence might be geared to more satisfactory results. How far the devil's other advice was taken is not clear but, after the July crisis, as autumn drew nearer, Carlos was decidedly better.

Stanhope, who still of course knew nothing of the rival systems of treatment secretly being followed, had his own sturdy English explanation:

> The favourable change in the King is attributed to a plaster an Aragonese doctor has supplied to his stomach, which is renewed every week, and has much strengthened his digestion. Or rather what I believe has done it more is that he has of late drunk two or three glasses of pure wine every meal, whereas he has never taken anything before in all his life but water boiled with a little cinnamon.

Soon the doctors began to consider whether he might be allowed to renew co-habitation with the Queen.

Meanwhile the *amo* and the *amigo* had returned to the attack. It was useless for the devil or his go-between to try and break off correspondence; they knew what they wanted and were determined to get it; in their next letter we find a further budget of questions and a more direct hint as to what they wished to be told.

Was there no subsequent bewitching after that of 1675? How was it that the King found difficulty in acting freely as he wished, but found it easy to act against his will, as if a superior power was controlling him and denying him free will? It was hard to believe that all this stemmed from the 1675 witchcraft, especially as the original witch, according to the devil, had since died.

The exorcist replied on September 24th that the King was bewitched by means of a dead body and that the witch responsible was still alive. The devil swore this by God three times. There was no charm outside his body 'and you hold up God's handiwork by withholding the remedies ordered, and the King gets less able to profit by them daily and less fit to govern.' If they did not use the remedies, what was the use of knowing the source of harm? As far as curing him was concerned, they could succeed without telling him the cause. They need only tell him he had melancholic blood. God demanded that they attended to what was necessary, and not to what was superfluous, and God was quick to help if they did not neglect the remedies. The letter ended by saying, 'Thus far the Devil, and in this there is nothing of mine.' Poor Arguelles was clearly struggling to keep within his depth.

Why were the *amo* and the *amigo* apparently so anxious to find out whether there has been a further bewitching since the 1675 occasion? And why have they brought up once more this matter of a tampering with the King's free will? And why has the devil changed his mind and stated that the witch is still alive? It is not surprising that the exorcist emphasizes that what he has written is the devil's opinion and not his own. He must have had a suspicion that he knew what they wanted the devil to say and that he was going to be quite certain that the devil rather than himself should be held responsible if he said it. He tries stalling once more: what is needed, he insists, is not to know the cause of the harm but the remedies for the harm. Arguelles may wish to confine his researches to therapeutics, but the *amo* and the *amigo* are after something far more dangerous.

On October 22nd, nearly a month later, came their reply: it was a direct request for the name of the witch, her residence, the name of the person who asked her to perform the spell, and of anyone else who had intervened and their purpose.

This request Arguelles tried to ignore, but the demands were repeated and enlarged upon. Who is the person who made the first charm, her name, her station in life, where does she live; has she any children alive or dead, and who gave her orders? Who helped her make the charm, who were the intermediaries; in what place was the charm made; who brought the corpse, who extracted the parts used, was it the same person who carried them to the witch; who put the confection in the chocolate; who gave it to the King and did he who gave it know what it was, what persons knew or had wind of it or that it was ordered or given?

The exorcist replied on November 9th, with some definite information: the woman who first made the charms *by the order of the Queen Mother* was called Casilda; she was married, and had two children, but she was already a widow and her children did not live with her. *Valenzuela was the go-between acting under Mariana's orders.* It was he who ordered the chocolate. The witch herself made the charm with no accomplice but the devil; she also looked for and found the corpse of a criminal. She gave it to the already-named confidant, and no one else knew of the wicked transaction.

And now comes the final plunge into the sea of politics: *the charm was repeated on September 24th, 1694 and was given to the King by one who wanted to have the Fleur de Lys come to Spain.* The devil swears he cannot give the name but that they can guess it.

Now who was the devil accusing? It could not be Maria Luisa, since by 1694 she had been dead five years. Maura says it was Maria Ana of Neuburg and that the devil was making a mistake when he called her one of the French party. This seems most unlikely. Maura seems for once to have nodded. The devil was unquestionably of the French party and would not be likely to implicate one of his own allies, and Maria Ana was not and never had been anxious to bring the Fleur de Lys to Spain — unless of course the devil had got hold of the very recent rumour that Harcourt was promising her a French husband.

There is no evidence that the devil at Cangas went so far as to accuse the Queen Regnant; that was to come later and from another devil, or from the same devil in a new mood; for it is a fact interesting to students of the effect of environment that the devil, speaking through possessed people, tempers his tune to the aspirations of the locality in which contact is made with him.

It is by no means certain who was intended by the devil at this time; the phrase about the Fleur de Lys is censored in the published account of these events and is only to be found in the numerous contemporary manuscripts, such as that in the British Museum. The Countess of Soissons is one candidate for the honour, and when public gossip became the arbiter of hidden truth an enthusiastic effort was made to saddle the crime on Berlips. But Berlips had never been heard of at the time these malices were said to have begun.

CHAPTER TWENTY-FIVE

THE DEVIL PLAYS POLITICS

THE devil can hardly be blamed for being confused about people and events at this time, for the chaos at the court of Madrid had become almost indescribable. The behaviour of Berlips and the rest of the Austrian crew was past bearing. The Almirante de Castilla, having come to the conclusion that the Austrian cause was lost, was lending his weight to a *rapprochement* between Maria Ana and the Most Christian King Louis, and to a break between her, Berlips, and Father Gabriel Chiusa, her Confessor. The lifelong enemies Portocarrero and Oropesa were putting their heads together to concert the permanent exile of these disasters and their compatriots, the tailor and the castrato. To do this the King was to be spirited away to the Escorial, unknown to the Queen, and there subjected to as much bullying as was necessary for him to agree to exile the Almirante and all the Austrian camarilla. He was not to be allowed to see the Queen until the latter were on the high seas bound to Italy.

In the midst of these plots and counterplots while Harcourt was intriguing successfully to gain all Spain for the French party, he received a dispatch from Louis which must have astounded him. Louis announced the signing of the Partition Treaty.

This changed the emotions of everybody: month by month Carlos was unmoved by the neglect and dishonesty, the laziness and incompetence which were bringing material ruin to all his kingdoms, but when the fantasy of the seamless garment was assailed, even he became for the moment a man of action.

His health improved. It may have been the oil and other sacred treatments prescribed by the devil, as the few ecclesiastics in the secret may have thought; it may have been the chicken fed on viper's flesh or renewed intercourse with his wife, as the doctors thought; or with Stanhope we may give credit to the wine. But the factor which stirred the languid will was unquestionably the act which on October 11th, 1698, carved up the sacred body of Spain for consumption by rival hungry potentates. On November 11th, 1698, Carlos responded:

> I will that when God removes me from this present life, Prince Joseph Maximilian be called and be King in all my kingdoms, Estates and domains, notwithstanding any renunciations made for lack of just cause.

So great was the confusion that people attributed the motive power to the most varied sources, to individuals so opposed to one another as the Queen, Portocarrero and the Almirante, while the true instigator, Oropesa, was scarcely thought of. Everybody was turning his coat so fast and so often that all was mere guesswork. Only Portocarrero remained where he had always been. The Queen did not even know what was contemplated, and when she discovered she was virtually disarmed because Oropesa had been crafty enough to award her a very fat pension in one of the clauses.

When it became known that the King had made a will, had signed a scrap of paper as he could have done at any moment for many years, there was an explosion of national pride, hope and joy. Somehow Spain felt herself again. It was even forgotten that Carlos had all his life been a weakling. Their King appeared to them a King indeed, almost another Philip II or Emperor Charles. Enormous bullfights were ordered, and illuminations, and military splendour. Even the grandees and councillors forgot their miserable bickerings. The national unanimity and sense of self-sufficiency had been brought about by one thing: a small boy was to inherit All; there was no fear now of the seamless garment being torn in pieces. The small boy's portrait was painted beckoning arrogantly to a ship in full sail, anchors up, ready to take him to Spain. That was in December 1698. Five weeks later the small boy was dead.

It was as if the one iron band holding together a crumbling ruin had suddenly broken; the mystical joy gave way to very material discontent. The population which had been exalted by patriotic fantasy into a state of euphoria that bore no relation whatever to their daily experiences, now saw life as slow starvation, with bread and all other foods scarce and dear, fields without crops, frontiers without protection, existence without hope. Even when there was almost nothing to eat Spaniards could feel themselves well-fed if they could believe in their dream; once the dream vanished, all crumbled away. José Fernando of Bavaria had been the point around which fantasy could weave compensating patterns of national dignity, at his death the insubstantial fabric disappeared.

This reaction reached a culmination on April 28th, 1699, when the Madrid or Oropesa Riot took place. Compared with many popular uprisings both in Spain and elsewhere both before and since it was almost nothing, but it seems to have inspired so much horror that it was branded into the memory of the generation which witnessed it. Moreover, it contained elements so typical of the Spanish character that it sums up in its brief chronicle the mentality of a whole people. Stanhope, Dr Geleen and various ambassadors gave accounts written on the following days and therefore not concordant with one another in many details. We shall follow Dr Geleen. Corn and bread had risen to outrageous prices, and when the police official arrived in the Plaza Mayor for his routine inspection of the market the large crowd was in despair; the general scarcity spelt empty stomachs in many homes that night. A poor woman, seeing the official, told him that she had nothing to take home for her husband and six children and what was she to do? The official replied with a brutal joke: 'You'd better castrate your husband so as not to have so many children.' The woman screamed obscene epithets at him, threw dead pigeons in his face, and several bystanders including a priest turned on him and menaced him so seriously that he took refuge in a near-by convent.

This incident acted as a catalyst; a winged spirit looking down on the great square would have seen it animated into new life, like a nest of ants into which a stone has been dropped. Thousands of black figures swarming around the stalls and barrows swirled about into a new pattern of movement, and soon an angry crowd estimated at ten thousand poured out of the square in the direction of the palace crying 'Death to Oropesa, death to the Almirante, death to the Corregidor.'

Arrived at the palace, the leaders attempted to enter, but

Benavente, showing considerable courage, met them on the main stairs and tried to pacify them with money and even handed them the gold star off his uniform; but they continued to cry out and to gesticulate with the specimens of almost uneatable bread they had brought with them. At last Benavente advised them to address their complaints to Oropesa, the President of the Council, and, as one man, the crowd turned and marched to that unpopular stateman's palace crying 'Death to the dog who has brought us to such misery.' It was clear that they meant to destroy and burn Oropesa's palace and to injure him, their anger being increased by a rumour, probably untrue, that he had recently sold large quantities of wheat to Portugal at great personal profit.

In due course the Duque's servants answered the volleys of stones with fire, and at least one of the crowd was killed, although the defenders claimed that they had intended to fire in the air. The rage of the crowd now knew no bounds, and monks of various religious orders came to the rescue by exposing the Blessed Sacrament and crucifixes on the palace balconies. To these supernatural reinforcements the attackers offered no opposition, but their rage was not appeased. Carrying the dead man, they retreated from Oropesa's spiritual defences only to return to the royal palace, which they approached with the traditional Spanish cry of 'Long live the King, death to the bad government, death to the dog, Oropesa.' They now demanded the dismissal of the Corregidors and the appointment in their place of their favourite, Ronquillo.

The King acceded to their demand, and Ronquillo, mounting a horse and carrying a crucifix in his hand, led them back to Oropesa's palace where, after four hours' wrangling, he was able to assure them that orders would be given for the reduction of all prices of bread, wine and meat. Not yet satisfied, most of the crowd went back to the royal palace. The Queen, with tears pouring down her cheeks, appeared on a balcony and promised that their demands should be obeyed. They would not listen to her. This is not surprising considering her unpopularity.

At last the King himself appeared, and at once the atmosphere changed. Demands, threats, menaces ceased on the instant; the crowd became stilled and their leaders respectfully begged the King to pardon them all. 'Yes,' replied Carlos, 'I pardon you, and you must pardon me also, because I did not know your need, and now I will give the necessary orders to have it remedied,' and as he said this he twice removed his hat, an unparalleled act of courtesy. The crowd melted away, but as night fell, notices appeared on the walls and houses threatening that if the Government were not immediately changed, Oropesa, the Almirante, Aguilar, the unspeakable Berlips, and an unnamed fifth person would be executed by the people. Nobody failed to identify this anonymous object of hatred with the Queen. However, Ronquillo set about fining the monopolists who were responsible for the high prices, and almost at once bread and meat became cheaper. For the moment things quietened down; but no problem had been solved; Spain was no less sick.

So much for the effect on the Spanish people of the death of José Fernando. What was happening in the European courts? It is doubtful whether Carlos's will had had much effect outside of Spain: Louis protested and threatened war in the legitimate cause of his grandson; the Emperor took it more peacefully, summing up his attitude in one sentence – 'After all the electoral prince is my grandson.' England and Holland were pleased, because the decision made war less likely and would not interfere with their commercial progress. But the child's death was a far more serious event in the eyes of the powers because it not only made nonsense of Carlos's will, but of their Treaty of Partition. Once more the whole question had to be thought out from the beginning.

The dreary negotiations which ended in the Third Partition Treaty were to drag on until just before Carlos's death, and meanwhile great changes in Spanish political thought had made the new accord almost meaningless. But we must return once more to the Inquisitor General, the Confessor and the Devil.

We left them in September 1698 embarking on the stormy sea of politics. It is noteworthy that just when opinions in Madrid were shifting and an air of uncertainty surrounded the Queen's attitude, the devil seems to have become cautious and uncertain in the information he was prepared to give. It is hard to avoid the suspicion that the devil or some lesser character was anxious not to say too much until opinion in Court circles had somewhat settled down.

The exorcist's increased caution was not at all pleasing to the *amo* and the *amigo*, and Arguelles received a further reprimand. They were grateful for the trouble he had taken but frankly disappointed at the diminished clarity of the devil's answers. Much that he had told them could not, upon inquiry, be verified. Thus the first witch mentioned, Casilda, was supposed to live in the Calle de los Herreros, but no such street existed in Madrid; and as for the second witch, Maria, said to live in the Calle Mayor, to look for the right Maria there was like looking for a needle in a haystack. The devil must give surnames and *say if the person who ordered the second charm was a person in authority. Let him give this name in cipher, if need be.* Evidently things were becoming highly inflammable and resistance very great. The devil must be conjured in God's and the Virgin's name and, for final weight in the tug-of-war, the name of the King's protector, St Simon, Patriarch of Jerusalem, should be thrown in as well.

The exorcist made more excuses. On November 28th, he reported that the devils inhabiting the nuns were more rebellious than ever. When he placed the nuns' hands on the altar and began the interrogation, the devil had gone so far as to say that all that had been so far stated was lies and that the King was not bewitched after all. He had gone on exorcizing for two hours until overcome by exhaustion, but with no success whatever. At the end, the demons had burst out into conversation again and advised him not to tire himself further, as the Mother of God had already decreed that he would come out victorious at the appropriate time.

A shrewd observer might have seen that Arguelles was now about to state his own terms. At present he was doing all the work, and we can surely not blame him for feeling that a labourer was worthy of his hire. Here were two leading theologians, both in high and powerful office, using a poor priest, condemned to live in very much of a backwater. Don Antonio was bound sooner or later to define his *quid pro quo*.

That is one way of putting things; but it is perhaps an altogether too modern way, out of key with the subject matter with which we are occupied. To a watchful contemporary what was happening would be only too clear: the devil was beginning to possess Don Antonio. However well he had equipped himself for the struggle, he had left weak places in his spiritual armour. To begin with, he was a disappointed man, a university-trained scholar condemned to a backwater in remote Asturias with no company except a few badly educated nuns and the local villagers – and all this through no fault of his own. It is a strong character indeed that in such circumstances remains free from envy and frustrated ambition. No doubt the devil saw this very early and planted a poisonous seed when he hinted that Don Antonio had been reserved for great things.

And then the Inquisitor General and the Confessor had tempted him and he had fallen: nobody could pretend that he was conducting the exorcism along proper lines. His one and only objective should have been the restoring of the poor nuns to good health and, instead, he was using them for quite another purpose. What more likely than that God should deliver him over to the Bestia Bestialisima, to the Tempter.

In his next letter he repeats that there is complete rebellion on the part of the demons and that the devil says he has been told to keep silence, but that all will be known in due course. He makes an attack on the royal physicians, who are all disloyal and false as also are the pharmacists. The King must elect one scientific doctor; and all his bedding, furniture, clothes, and if possible his place of residence must be changed and the remedies continued. On other points, the devil says he must still be silent, but that there is much more involved than has yet been revealed.

By December 10th, the Confessor had agreed to continue the remedies. Don Antonio repeated his accusation against the doctors in stronger terms, so much so that his correspondents, while still refusing to agree, said they would watch them more closely. Moreover, the advice to change the King's personal linen and to send him off on a journey was carried out on the excuse of visiting the body of San Diego; and a new doctor was brought in. Contemporary observers, ignorant of the true cause, were very puzzled to account for these innovations.

On December 16th, the devil said that the surname of Casilda was Perez and that the Calle Herrajeros had formerly been called Herreros.

Replying on December 31st, the *amo* and the *amigo* complained that the devil was so confusing; first he had said the witch was dead, now that she was alive. He must be forced to make himself clear. The King was much better, and they hoped that with brief care on the part of Don Antonio he would be completely restored.

The slightly better atmosphere seems to have emboldened Don Antonio, for a week later he came out into the open and made clear the preferment which was his just price for further interpreting between Inquisitor General and Devil. He was certainly tired of being relegated to a remote village and wanted to be back at the centre of things. Fortunately the devil was in agreement with him, and two days running swore by the triune God that the information still missing could only be revealed in the Chapel of Our Lady of Atocha. Meanwhile the work which had been begun must be ended and the remedies continued. This declaration was repeated in subsequent communications, and the devil explained that the reason he would only speak in the fashionable Madrid church was, first, that the devotion to the Sacred Image of our Lady of Atocha was showing signs of languishing, and he wished to do something to restore it; and second, that Don Antonio 'may rise up from slavery to the throne, as did Bardecheus [*sic*] in the time of Haman'. This can only be described as very handsome of the devil, since he had nothing to thank Don Antonio for and even less call for gratitude to Our Lady of Atocha.

By the end of April the deadlock was complete, the *amo* and the *amigo* complained that no trace of either witch had been found, and Don Antonio, backed by the devil, said in so many words: no Atocha, no more exorcisms. Alas for Don Antonio's hopes of preferment; by May, Queen Maria Ana had through her spies at last found out most of what was going on and, worse still, in June the Inquisitor General Rocaberti died.

CHAPTER TWENTY-SIX

RIVAL EXORCISTS

THE long-drawn out conferences between Inquisitor General, King's Confessor and Devil were not the only transaction of a paranormal nature carried out at this time. Both Carlos and his Queen were supplementing the treatment ordered by their doctors – bleedings, purges, enemas, medicines – with the treatments recommended by the Church. They were being exorcized in exactly the same way as the nuns in Asturias and according to the rituals prescribed by the Church, the only difference being that they were exorcized as bewitched persons rather than as possessed persons.

From time to time they would have a good new exorcist recommended to them, just as we might hear of a good new psychiatrist in Harley Street. Thus, in December 1698, a Jeronimite friar of great popular reputation exorcized Maria Ana specifically to make her fertile. In spite of his good references his conduct was most indiscreet and at last led to his disgrace. He was busy praying by the Queen's bedside when he suddenly became ecstatic, gesticulating and leaping in a way that terrified the Queen, who jumped out of bed and out of the room screaming 'as if Luzbel himself were after her'. Doctor Geleen, who was out of sympathy with exorcists, recounted the incident to the Elector John William of Neuburg and prophesied the same fate for a Bernardine friar who was at that time exorcizing the King.

It would be quite wrong to suppose that these recourses to spiritual forms of healing were unusual among the royalty of those days: indeed the Hapsburgs and Wittelsbachs had had a good deal of trouble one way and another with the devil. Several of Maria Ana's relatives had had to be very extensively exorcized. John William Palatine himself dabbled in magic and alchemy and was quite certain from an early date that the devil was responsible for his cousin Carlos's trouble. His own first wife had been forced to miscarry by the devil's personal intervention. John William went further: in his opinion the whole House of Austria was comprehensively bewitched because it was the cornerstone of the Catholic Church, a fact which had led the devil to arrange premature deaths for the Emperor's first two wives. Nor was he so wide of the mark. Though the term bewitchment is not now part of the vocabulary of psychiatry it was indeed true that the Hapsburgs suffered the misfortune understood by that term in those days. But it was not because they were the cornerstone of Catholicism; it was because the inbreeding of bad stock had concentrated in them a number of hereditary poisons.

John William took special precautions to avoid a further accident to his wife should the devil attack her in any future pregnancies; but in spite of all he could do she died childless only three years later.

It is perfectly clear indeed that neither Carlos nor his Queen objected to exorcism as such. Frankly, it was less unpleasant than the remedies of 'natural magic' prescribed by the doctors. But in the manoeuvres of the Inquisitor General, now dead, and of Froylan Diaz, there had been much more than religion; there had been politics – and particularly distasteful politics from the Queen's point of view.

Maria Ana therefore devoted all her energies to revenging herself on Froylan Diaz and the Inquisitorial Council, whom she wrongly supposed to be involved in the plot. Her first step was to seek out her friend Antonio Folch de Cardona, Commissioner General of the Franciscan Order, and to ask him to find out from his brother Lorenzo Folch de Cardona, a councillor of the Inquisition, if the Council had been unanimous in implementing this devilish interrogation.

A very curious conversation took place between the two brothers.

> 'What was the date of the last letter you had from the Devil and what news have you from Hell?' said the Commissioner General, breezily.
>
> 'What the devil do you mean?' replied his brother, the Councillor of the Inquisition.

The Commissioner quoted specimens of the correspondence, with which he had been supplied, and told his brother he need have no scruples about revealing Inquisitorial secrets. Lorenzo continued to say he had no idea what his brother was talking about and begged him to stop joking.

What Lorenzo then learned astounded him, and he swore on his conscience as a priest that he knew nothing whatever about it, and that the whole Council was certainly as ignorant as he. This surprised and delighted Don Antonio Folch de Cardona since it weakened Father Froylan Diaz' position very considerably, but his approach to the problem proved over-impetuous. When he asked Don Lorenzo whether he would hold Father Froylan an offender against the Faith in this matter, Don Lorenzo would not give a definite answer. He agreed that so much conversation with the devil did not seem good. Without any doubt such familiarity was delicate and dangerous. He would, however, hesitate in pronouncing Father Froylan *reo de fé*, as this was a matter for theological experts to pronounce on, that is to say, for the official Censors of the Inquisition. However, he was quite sure that Father Froylan had been most injudicious to enter into such long conversations with the devil without first procuring for himself a full licence from the Council.

Don Lorenzo Folch seems to have been a highly intelligent man, for it is he that is responsible for the detailed and animated account of these devious transactions from which we have been quoting. When due allowance has been made for the fact that he is our only authority for his own acts, he seems to have behaved very sensibly. He is to be admired too, for his fairness to political opponents like Portocarrero, and for refusing to join in the persecution of Froylan Diaz, although this was Maria Ana's chief obsession and he was of her party.

Meanwhile, Midsummer Day had come and, partly due to the Queen's exceedingly ugly mood, Carlos took a turn for the worse. Stanhope reported:

> His Catholic Majesty grows every day sensibly worse and worse. Thursday they made him walk in the public solemn procession of Corpus which was much shortened for his sake. However, he performed it so feebly that all who saw him

> said he could not make one straight step, but staggered all the way; nor could it otherwise be expected, after he had had two falls a day or two before, walking in his own lodgings, when his legs doubled under him by mere weakness. In one of them he hurt one eye, which appeared to be much swelled, and black and blue in the procession; the other being quite sunk into his head; the nerves, they say, being contracted by his paralytic distemper. Yet it was thought fit to have him make this sad figure in public, only to have it put into the Gazette how strong and vigorous he is.

And now the gossip got about. Doubtless the mentidero buzzed with it. Stanhope put it down to the rascally doctors, who, poor fellows, were more like to be the victims of the exorcist than his instigators: 'The doctors, not knowing what more to do with the King, to save their credit, have bethought themselves to say his ill must certainly be witchcraft, and there is a great court party which greedily catch at and improves the report, which, how ridiculous soever it may sound in England, I can assure you is generally believed here, and propagated by others to serve a turn. They, finding all their attempts to banish Madame Berlips fruitless, think this cannot fail, and all possible endeavours are using to find out any colourable pretence to make her the witch. Nor is it the first time that game has been played here, and with success.'

That summer in Madrid was one of the hottest in memory. Yet the King, so cold was his body, had to be covered with several blankets in his bed to stop him shivering.

Now matters took another turn. Don Antonio and Father Froylan had both had enough of it. Without Rocaberti to shelter behind they were afraid of the consequences of their alliance with the devil. They stopped asking him questions. But it seems that they had reckoned without the devil, who continued to make his contributions.

Not many days after Don Lorenzo and Don Antonio had had their brotherly conversation, the Emperor Leopold's ambassador received a letter with remarkable intelligence. The Bishop of Vienna had informed the Emperor of what the devil had said during an exorcism of some possessed people in the Cathedral of

St Sophia. Carlos was indeed bewitched; but on this occasion the devil (who may have been quite another one from the much interrogated devil of Cangas) gave the witch's name as Isabel and her address the *Calle de Silva* in Madrid. But what made this new announcement much more interesting than all that Don Antonio Arguelles had extracted, was the announcement that the charm involved would be found partly under the floor of the palace and partly in Isabel's house.

The ambassador sent these papers to the King. On the advice of Father Froylan, who had had enough experience to teach him to play for safety, Carlos sent them to the Council of the Inquisition. The Council ordered inquiries to be made to discover Isabel's house and the position of the charms in the royal palace, but all attempts failed. So they dug at random: first, the floor of a room in the palace and then the lintel of a door in the Calle de Silva. Having dug to a certain depth, they found in both places a number of objects which included dolls transfixed with nails, and packets of miscellaneous material, all unpleasant. The experts and theologians who saw them, pronounced them of extraordinary importance, and burned them on consecrated ground in accordance with the ceremonial laid down in the Roman Missal. This was in the last days of July and the beginning of August 1699; and on August 15th, Stanhope wrote home:

> His Catholic Majesty is well again, almost to a miracle. So far as I am able to judge ... he has the very same looks I remember him in the time of his best health. Upon this unexpected recovery the Queen and her party have resumed new courage and strength.

It looked as if the magical decontamination had worked.

We may well ask how the dolls and other charms came to be where the casual diggings took place. Were they clandestinely dropped by the diggers and recovered by them in triumph? Or was this sort of superstition so common that wherever the diggings had taken place something would have been found? Or was it a parapsychological fact that was thus unearthed? Whatever the truth, the moribund King had a temporary relapse into something like health.

Carlos was naturally delighted with his supernatural treatments, and the Queen had for the time being to contain her fury against Father Froylan, but soon things once more took a fresh turn, one which inevitably must increase her wrath. There came on the scene a very mysterious character.

It would seem that the activities of the devil, or perhaps the desire to be implicated in the treatment of the King, was spreading all over Europe. We have just seen that the Emperor Leopold had been able to make a contribution from Vienna. It was now the turn of Amadeus II of Savoy.

At the Court of Savoy, there lived a practising exorcist, a Capuchin monk named Mauro Tenda. His reputation was immense. As long ago as 1696 Satan had told him to go to Spain where he could play an important part in curing the King of his numerous deficiencies. Not until 1698 did he succeed in overcoming the difficulties involved in such a journey; but in the summer of that year he arrived at the Court and was welcomed by Carlos himself.

This was very like carrying coals to Newcastle, for, as Maura says, though many things in Spain were in short supply, there were plenty of clerics and friars who specialized in dealing with the devil.

Maura makes the very plausible suggestion that Mauro Tenda's arrival in Madrid is best explained by a glance at the character and political needs of Victor Amadeus II. This minor potentate, he says, 'has passed into History with the well-earned reputation of having been the most Machiavellian sovereign of his time'. He was a claimant, though not a very hopeful one, to spoils, when Spain should be dismembered; and he was therefore more than likely to want a good diplomatic vantage point from which to meddle in the incessant intrigues at Madrid. This was denied him as far as the usual diplomatic channels were concerned, as his representative could not claim anything but a back seat with a very poor view compared with that enjoyed by the ambassadors of larger potentates.

For a shrewd man placed at this disadvantage there was a good way out. Monks and religious officials enjoyed rather greater ease in crossing national boundaries than other men, and all sorts of monarchs including Louis XIV had found it convenient to use them as spies or unofficial diplomats. It is most probable therefore that besides his spiritual therapy Mauro Tenda was expected by his sovereign to indulge in other activities in Spain.

However that may be, it was at the King's request that Mauro Tenda came. Carlos had made up his mind to be thoroughly exorcized. No longer was he to be treated as a sufferer from a mere charm, but as one possessed, or at any rate requiring severer treatment.

Mauro Tenda had developed a technique of his own for dealing with the devil. It was not that he offended against orthodoxy in any way, but that he supplemented the manuals of exorcism by what might almost be called controlled experiment. Count Aloisius de Harrach, the Emperor's ambassador, is our chief authority, for the Emperor Leopold was interested in every detail of Carlos's bewitchment, and Harrach wrote long accounts which we may assume reflected the true state of affairs.

One of Harrach's dispatches (undated but almost certainly of September 1699) repeats what Carlos's Confessor, Froylan Diaz, has told him under oath of secrecy. When Father Mauro had been exorcizing various women, the devil, concealed in one of them, declared that the Queen was bewitched also, and that she wore round her neck a small bag containing some of the King's hair mixed with earth, which she put under her pillow when she slept. When asked who was responsible for this charm, the devil accused Berlips and another lady, who had mixed the ingredients with their saliva and given it to the Queen.

The devil absolved the Queen's Confessor, Father Gabriel Chiusa, from responsibility for this, but said he had made another charm with hairs on his own account which enabled the Queen to get what she wanted. Father Froylan regarded it as his duty as Carlos's Confessor to get hold of the little bag, but this could only be if the King would steal it from under the Queen's pillow while she slept. In this he could not get co-operation from the Inquisitor General, because that official wanted to keep in with the Queen in the hope that she would procure him a Cardinal's hat. It would be easier to get hold of a certain store of charmed tobacco, and when that was out of the way the King would cease to be bewitched as he had been ever since his mother's death. For Harrach, the proof of witchcraft was the King's Bavarian will and the Queen's treachery to the House of Austria; and he now hoped that they would both return to their senses and therefore to their loyalty to the Emperor and his family.

On September 20th, 1699, Harrach gave the Emperor many more details. By now there were two rival supernatural agencies in full swing, one contributed by the Emperor Leopold, the other by Amadeus. The Emperor was taking the devil's statement in Vienna very seriously and requested that the whole matter be put before Portocarrero, the Inquisitor General and the King's Confessor. The Queen gave Harrach permission to do this, provided he did not mention her or her Confessor; since in the universal muddle it was no longer possible to assume that the Council of the Inquisition would take kindly to further collaboration with the devil, whatever view might be taken by the Inquisitor General.

The most interesting thing about Mauro's methods was this taste for controlled experiment, which led however to an over-simplified method of testing for the devil's presence in Carlos's body. It resembles a badly designed experiment by an incompetent modern psychical researcher. He told the devil to pinch Carlos in one hand, and Carlos shouted out at once that he had felt it. He then ordered the devil to transfer his activity to the King's shoulder, and at once Carlos felt a pain there. If we were told that Carlos was prevented in some way from hearing these orders to the devil, the test would be very much more significant.

These experiments had one definite result: they dispelled any doubts Carlos had about being possessed. The way in which the devil obeyed Father Mauro when told to move around in his body seemed much more conclusive than the contradictory news from Cangas. When the devil obeyed orders to pinch his knee, he agreed to confess and communicate every two days and to be exorcized every third day; but in spite of his renewed enthusiasm found excuses for putting off the next visit for fifteen days. When Father Mauro returned, the Queen refused to attend, and only his Confessor witnessed events. These were promising, the devil showing himself in an exemplary mood and obeying all commands, 'passing from one foot to the other and from the shoulder to a hand'.

It was at this stage that they managed with the Queen's help to get the little bag away from the King's pillow, and it was found to contain eggshells, toe nails, hair and 'all the things usually employed in witchcraft'. It seems, therefore, that both the royal couple had little bags, and that while Carlos stole Maria Ana's, she stole his. No doubt both were believed to contain relics, which for that matter would not have necessarily been very different from the actual contents. It was decided not to burn this bag, since when the one taken from Philip IV had been burned, that monarch died immediately after.

Carlos improved rapidly, and Father Mauro said the cure was almost complete. He was careful to turn the tables nicely on the doctors, who had given up, blaming their failure on the supernatural character of the King's sufferings. He told Carlos to cross himself three times, without pausing, over the place where he felt pain and to order the devil in the name of the All Powerful to leave him alone. If he was still in pain he would know that the cause was natural and that it was the doctors' business to cure it.

In spite of this, Father Mauro warned Harrach that if the doctors failed, he would have to proceed to exorcisms of a far more disagreeable nature, which would possibly frighten Carlos to death. But Father Mauro was not destined to embark upon heroic methods; an unexpected and ludicrous episode led to his disgrace.

One day in September a woman entered the palace, and, rushing past the guard in a wild fury, demanded an audience; but, as she seemed mad, her entry was opposed. She screamed. The King heard and ordered her to be admitted to his presence, where she broke out into dislocated phrases and looked more like a fury than a woman. Fortunately the King always carried a piece of the True Cross which he now held between her and himself, and his attendants were enabled to remove her to the corridors on their shoulders. Little did anyone know, but nemesis in the shape of a crazy woman had called for Father Mauro Tenda.

CHAPTER TWENTY-SEVEN

MARIA ANA HITS BACK

THIS incident was more than enough to disturb the dithering royal nerves, and Carlos ordered the woman to be followed and everything about her investigated. It was quite impossible, in his opinion, to ignore anything or anybody connected with the devil, and it was clear that the woman had come as the devil's emissary.

Don José de Olmo, the chief clerk of the works, was sent immediately to trace her homeward-bound footsteps. What he found was truly terrifying; she lived with two other women and all three of them, at least to José de Olmo's eyes, were possessed, probably by several legions of devils. One of them went so far as to claim that the King had really taken up residence in their room, where they kept him shut up in a box, feeding him and subjecting him in all things to their will. How they explained the simulacrum up at the palace, we are not told. Don Lorenzo, with his usual caution, describes this woman as 'agitated by the evil spirit or by her own madness', but Carlos, upon hearing Don José's report, was quite certain that once more the devil was in it. The best thing to do was to send the professional Father Mauro Tenda to make sure.

He, of course, unhesitatingly pronounced all three to be energumens, and then and there set about exorcizing them with his usual vigour. The sessions were numerous, and at some of them Father Froylan attended. It would have been better for him had he kept out of it all, and he was certainly foolhardy, after his earlier experience, to suggest certain questions for Father Mauro Tenda to ask of the devils responsible.

'Who bewitched the King?'
'A beautiful woman.'

'Is it the Queen?'

'Yes.'

'Who made the charm for the Queen?'

'Don Juan Palia.'

'Of what country is he?'

'Of those attached to the Queen.'

'In what was the charm given?'

'In snuff.'

'Is there any left over?'

'Yes, it is kept in a writing desk.'

'Which Queen gave the charm to the King?'

'The one that died.'

'Is there any more charm besides what you said this morning?'

'Yes.'

'Who made it?'

'A woman called Maria de la Presentación.'

'Where does she live?'

'In the upstairs room of this house.'

'Who ordered this woman to make the charm?'

'Antonia de la Paz.'

'Was the material removed from the threshold of the door in the Calle de Silva a charm?'

'Yes.'

'Of what was it made?'

'Of a dog's bone.'

Later the devil denigrated the living Queen and the Almirante de Castilla, and others; but always in a confused way as if not quite certain of his part in the complicated situation.

This naturally infuriated the Queen yet more against Father Froylan, especially when Carlos confirmed that he was the chief conspirator and was trying to destroy her by implicating her in the witchcraft. She determined to have Father Froylan publicly accused by the Inquisition as *reo de fé*, and to extract a public denial of everything the Father of Lies had said.

To achieve her ends the Queen sought to have one of her party step into the dead Rocaberti's shoes. With a sympathetic Inquisitor General there would be no difficulty in having Father Froylan well and truly punished. Rocaberti had had to go behind the backs of his own Council to take action in the matter of the Cangas exorcisms, and if there was an Inquisitor General who did not believe in the supposed witchcraft, let alone in her complicity in it, there was bound to be agreement between him and the Council. Father Froylan would be doomed.

Maria Ana therefore chose Antonio Folch de Cardona for the post, and we owe to his brother Lorenzo a lively account of what followed. The King was experiencing one of his short periods of good health, or rather of sufficient relief to be able to have a mind of his own for a few days. Naturally he attributed this to the exorcisms, now in full swing, and nothing would induce him to take any step which might bring them to an end. They were a drug of addiction. He had enough sense at that moment to see what his wife was after, and he was determined not merely to oppose her choice, but to choose someone who would continue an enthusiastic campaign against the devil.

Carlos knew what he wanted and even set about trying to get it. He sent secretly for the Cardinal de Córdoba and told him he was to be Inquisitor General and that a request for the necessary Papal Bull was already on its way to Rome.

According to Lorenzo Folch, who may have heard of it from the Cardinal himself, since he and even his brother were on very good terms with the rival candidate, there followed a moving scene. The Cardinal fell on his knees and, kissing the King's hand, swore to do all that he should in his new office. 'That I believe,' said Carlos, 'and see the confidence I place in you; since I place in your hands my health and my life. Many tell me I am bewitched, and I well believe it; such are the things I experience and suffer: and when you are Inquisitor General you will do justice to all and to me also, delivering my heart from this depression which torments me so.' Whereupon both King and Cardinal wept.

The Cardinal indeed was so moved that he was determined to find out the truth about the witchcraft then and there. He at once consulted with Father Froylan, who told him all about the Cangas revelations, the exorcisms of Mauro Tenda, and the devil's Viennese contribution.

The Cardinal passed on all this information to our Lorenzo Folch, telling him that, from what the devil had said at Cangas and from the other revelations, it was quite clear that the Almirante de Castilla was implicated. Moreover, the King had once more begun to feel very ill after his short-lived amelioration, so that no time must be lost in putting a stop to the evil machinations.

The Inquisition of Granada, where the Almirante was at present living in banishment, should be ordered to arrest him and put him in a decent prison suitable to his rank. His whole household should then be arrested as well, and all his papers confiscated and brought in sealed boxes to the Court for investigation. No doubt, sufficient corroborative evidence would be found for the devil's statements, and he could then be investigated by the Inquisition. As men accustomed to luxury were always weak, he would certainly break down under torture and confess his dealings with the devil against the poor King.

He explained to Don Lorenzo that he had told him all this so that the Council could act, he being unable to do so until the Papal Bull arrived, which would mean a delay of at least a month.

Don Lorenzo — we have of course only his own account to go on — was astonished at the Cardinal's rashness. You could not arrest people of the Almirante's position unless you had a practically cast-iron case against them, particularly if you were the Inquisition. The Cardinal might lose all his well-deserved reputation if things went wrong. Where would he be if nothing was found among the Almirante's papers? He had nothing but the devil to go on, and the devil's evidence was muddled, self-contradictory and obscure. With the greatest respect for the Cardinal's dignity and person, the Councillors would take no notice of his request until the Bull came, and he really must ask to be excused from summoning them to discuss the matter.

The Cardinal de Córdoba was crestfallen. He tried to alter Don Lorenzo's mind by describing to him the great danger the King was in and the paramount necessity to avoid delay; but Lorenzo would not budge. There followed further conferences between the Cardinal and the exorcists, but nothing could be resolved. The Cardinal went home depressed and feeling rather ill. He called a doctor who prescribed such a bleeding that he was unable to recover from it, and in three days he was dead. Lorenzo leaves dots in his printed account where, in the manuscript, a copy of which exists in the British Museum, he hints at poison, 'of which,' he writes, 'there were many suspicious among his relatives and staff; but I will not be so rash as to affirm it.'

So ended the last attempt to use the devil as an ally, for now the King was in the depths again and without the heart to oppose the Queen's wishes. And she had become rather more tactful and did not again urge her former candidate. The episode of the three possessed old women had depressed Carlos more than ever, and there was little difficulty in getting him to accept the apparently neutral Don Baltazar de Mendoza, Bishop of Segovia, for the vacant post. But Don Baltazar was not so neutral as he seemed. The Queen was careful to tell him privately what was expected of him and promised to influence the King to secure him a Cardinal's hat in exchange for the ruthless persecution of her enemies — the exorcists and others who had tried to implicate her in the witchcraft.

Not that Maria Ana doubted the witchcraft or the efficacy of the exorcisms. What she objected to was the use of these supernatural aids by her enemies. If the devil had not lent himself to party politics on the other side, she would have been happy to have his advice. One can sympathize with her point of view. Even the devil should not mix politics with religion.

The Capuchin Monk, Mauro Tenda, was the first to suffer. The theological crime for which he was tried had nothing to do with the exorcisms, but in the course of his defence he gave full details of what had happened when he had exorcized the three old women in the presence of Froylan Diaz, and thus provided the necessary ammunition for the attack on the King's Confessor. In his speech to the Inquisitors he accused the Queen's Confessor, Father Gabriel de Chiusa, of having manipulated the whole plot against him with the help of 'other persons of the highest rank'; and everybody knew who he meant. The Inquisition did not allow itself to be impressed and condemned him to *abjuración de levi* and perpetual banishment.

Father Froylan Diaz' case did not end so simply. Indeed in fulfilling his promise to the Queen and with the hopes of a Cardinal's hat ever before him, Don Baltazar behaved more stupidly than one would believe possible. He ordered Froylan to appear before the Council of the Inquisition to answer concerning matters arising out of Mauro Tenda's evidence which might be preferred against him.

The Father replied that he could not do so, as these matters pertained to the confessional, and apart from this, the King, whose Confessor he was, had made him promise to keep the whole thing secret. The Council were disposed to be content with this answer, but not Froylan's enemies. The Dominicans and also the Inquisitor General, with his eye on a Cardinal's hat, were determined to destroy him.

A few weeks later a member of their order preferred three charges against him. Two were so frivolous that the Council refused to hear them. The other was concerned with the Cangas transactions and was based on the correspondence which the Dominicans had secured from Arguelles.

Father Froylan defended himself vigorously and claimed that everything he had done was under the orders of Rocaberti. And as for what had later happened with the three possessed women, he had been sent by the King's express order to assist at the exorcisms. José de Olmo witnessed that this was so. Father Froylan submitted learned pleadings based on the behaviour of Saints and Doctors of the Church, including St Thomas Aquinas himself. Once more the accusers were nonplussed.

Don Baltazar and the Queen had secret meetings and agreed that the next step was to dismiss Father Froylan from his office of King's Confessor. For this purpose the Inquisitor General visited Carlos and told him that his much-liked Confessor was a bad man.

Carlos showed surprise and asked whether the new Inquisitor General was quite sure. Quite sure, said the Inquisitor General, and, with a sigh and a shake of the head, Carlos dismissed Father Froylan from his spiritual employment.

As soon as the Queen heard this welcome news, she urged the appointment of Father Froylan's arch-enemy, Father Torres-Padmota, as the new Confessor, and the King, exhausted by so much quarrelling all around him, consented.

Father Froylan was ordered to go to a convent in Valladolid pending trial, but he resolved to escape. When he reached Rome, however, he was arrested and returned to Spain. His case was reopened, and upon the advice of Lorenzo, put before five theologians for greater security. These gave the unanimous opinion that Froylan had done nothing against the Faith and thereupon the Council voted his acquittal *nemine contradicente*.

This meant a complete break between them and the Inquisitor General; the latter, overriding his Council's will and purpose, insisted on Froylan being imprisoned in the secret prisons. On July 8th, 1700, the Council met again, and the Inquisitor General read out a condemnation composed by himself and asked the Councillors to sign. They refused. The most they would allow was the appointment of a further theologian if the Inquisitor General had doubts about the findings of the five. The Inquisitor General said it was too late. Lorenzo said it was never too late to do justice. The Inquisitor General demanded a vote, Yes or No. Lorenzo thereupon voted No, and was followed by all the rest. Within an hour the Inquisitor General had three Councillors, including the two oldest and most respected, arrested. The scandal was immense.

Much later, after the three Councillors and Froylan Diaz had spent years in prison, they were vindicated. But long before this the history of Carlos the Bewitched had come to an end.

CHAPTER TWENTY-EIGHT

'LET'S STAY AND HEAR THE WILL'

SOMETIMES the moving boundary we call the present is the meeting place between a past burdened with fantasies and a future buoyant with a new realism. If humanity is to be saved from tears at such a moment the past must give way. Otherwise an explosive mixture shatters all and maims the future in its cradle.

In May 1700, Europe found itself caught up in such a disaster. Carlos and the Emperor Leopold, symbolic figures of the fantastic past, would not give way, and, by their obstinacy, split the new realistic forces in two, ruined their own countries, and plunged Europe into war. If only Carlos had not died at the worst possible moment, if he had hung on to life for a year or two more, Louis XIV and William of Orange might have brought the future to birth as collaborators, not as deadly enemies, as signatories to treaties, not as leaders in bloodshed.

> By an irony of fate [writes G. M. Trevelyan], cruel alike to Carlos and to Europe, his grotesque sufferings were prolonged year after year, contrary to all expectations. He lingered till November 1700, and died at the precise moment when nothing short of a World War could decide the question of his inheritance.

By 1700, all Europe was exhausted. But there was one vital difference between Louis and the Emperor in the face of their common need for peace. Louis was fully aware of it; the Emperor, still relying on God to stop the interferences of the devil with Maria Ana and Carlos, was not. When peace eventually became impossible, the Emperor went further: he relied upon Spain coming to the rescue of his own weakness, although he knew that Spain was even weaker than himself. In the final analysis, the

Emperor and Spain remained faithful to the fantasies of the past, even though Louis, grown older and wiser, was far more conciliatory than anyone would have expected of him.

When the Bavarian child died, Louis bent all his efforts upon providing a peaceful solution. His policy was based on two assumptions, one of which was false. Quite rightly he knew that the rest of Europe would not allow him to inherit for himself or for his grandchildren the entire Spanish Empire, but he wrongly supposed that it was unthinkable that Spain would make such an offer. Against the opinion of his ambassadors, Harcourt and his successor, Blécourt, he refused to imagine such a possibility. The only solution that Louis could see, therefore, was a new Treaty of Partition. The astonishing historical irony is that by negotiating a partition treaty, Louis brought about unwittingly that Spain was bequeathed in its entirety to his grandson. By the one act which Spain would never forgive or permit, he secured from Spain herself the Spanish Empire. But because this was a solution which the other European powers also would never permit, the result of this unexpected success was precisely what he most wished to avoid – war; and a war which he lost.

The political chaos was even greater than this result alone suggests. So anxious for peace was he, that Louis negotiated a partition which was remarkably generous to his opponents. Thus he accepted William's suggestion that the Austrian claimant should have Spain, the Spanish Netherlands and the Spanish Indies. France was to have Naples, Sicily and Milan (which was to be exchanged for Lorraine later).

It was now that the Emperor made one of the great mistakes which sometimes change history. It was an action which can only with the greatest difficulty be fitted into an 'economic interpretation of history'. He refused to sign the treaty, which gave him almost everything, and he refused because he believed that once the exorcists had brought back the Spanish royal pair to a proper frame of mind, he would get everything. Only the devil could be standing in the way of Austrian pretensions, and God would eventually bring him to heel. Unfortunately, if their objective was to bring back the Spanish King and Queen to their Austrian allegiance, the exorcists failed in their job.

The negotiations between Louis and William came to a head

in March 1700. By then the farcical hope that Carlos might have an heir of his own body was at last abandoned. And by then Maria Ana had lost all her loyalties except to herself. A majority of the Spanish grandees, led by Portocarrero, had made up their minds that the problem of succession was not whether Bourbon or Hapsburg should reign, but how to assure that any successor should be able to keep the seamless garment intact. And Europe at that time proved to be divided into those who concentrated on the political and economic struggle which was to dominate the future, and those who remained faithful to a mystical religious conception which with them at least had dominated the past.

It was the moment of truth for Carlos. All the nice distinctions between frigid and bewitched were put in the background; gone too were all the false pregnancies and pretences of future renewals of honeymoon behaviour. Nothing remained but the need to defeat partition. It no longer mattered who it was that took his possessions, provided he took all. At last it was clear that death was knocking at the door.

On June 6th, 1700, Carlos ordered the Council of State to meet. He himself refused to be present, so that their conclusions would be unquestionably their own. They came to the almost unanimous conclusion that the best way of keeping the Spanish Empire intact was to give it to the prince most likely to defend it. That the new urge towards Balance of Power demanded partition did not influence them at all; they looked to a far higher authority than Louis or William to settle their destiny. Portocarrero's '*voto*' expressed the opinion of all except perhaps the Conde de Aguilar, who clung to Austria to the last: if the prince who could aid and defend them could have been the Archduke, said the Cardinal-Archbishop, that would have pleased everyone most, for to Austria all their tradition and upbringing bade them turn. But they could not be influenced in this matter by preferences or affections nor any feeling of good will. Therefore the only choice was one of the King of France's grandsons. Some, like Santeste-ban, added that the King must not submit to the partition plots, but if necessary Spain must go down fighting for her unity rather than submit. Fresno advised a mediator, preferably the Pope, and said if the French claimant was to be preferred, it must be on the understanding that the two kingdoms should never be joined.

Medina Sidonia simply repeated the need to keep the Spanish Empire intact as it had been kept 'so many *happy* years', a strange description of the preceding miserable fifty years.

Carlos wrote to the Pope, and in his letter showed not only his faith in that functionary but his ignorance of any limitation of his powers. He spoke of the Pope's infallibility and asked him in the light of that infallibility to pontificate about the Spanish succession. The Pope was too wise to accept such an extension of the dogma, and contented himself with advising Carlos to do whatever his Council wished. His reply reached Madrid on July 6th, 1700.

On July 20th, Blécourt wrote to Louis, and once more mentioned almost for the last time, rumours that the Queen was pregnant, rumours which meant no more than that Carlos seemed not quite so ill as usual, rumours which no longer were honestly believed by anyone except possibly the unteachable Harrach.

Throughout August, Louis was engaged in complicated diplomacy throughout Europe, in the midst of which he found himself on the horns of a dilemma. With the utmost secrecy he was asked by the Spanish ambassador to give a categorical answer to a very awkward question: 'If the Spanish Empire was offered to his grandson, would he be willing to accept?'

Louis regarded this secret request as a deliberate attempt to embarrass him. If he said no, then Carlos would undoubtedly make the Archduke Charles his heir; if he said yes, he would be guilty of perjury, since he had signed a partition treaty with William. He refused therefore to answer, and Carlos was left in doubt as to whether any will he might sign would be accepted. If he left the Empire to the Austrian candidate, the rest of Europe would rise to prevent the will being implemented; if, as he so little desired, he left it to the French, there was no knowing that his objective would be achieved; Louis might be faithful to William of Orange rather than to the wishes of Spain. He might divide the Empire so as to placate those who were determined to prevent him inheriting it intact.

And so August passed without a will; Carlos remained powerless to act because of the uncertainty of Louis's response. But at last, things became urgent, for as September advanced it became certain that this time death was really in earnest. Harrach fought on and begged his friends to force Carlos to sign a will making the Archduke Charles his heir, but even his most pro-Austrian friends told him that this would be impossible. The alternatives were no will or a will in favour of the Bourbon. At present the first seemed most likely, since poor Carlos was paralysed by Louis's equivocal attitude.

At the end of September San Isidro and San Diego were brought to the palace, and though they had sometimes achieved a temporary rallying of some dying royal person, they usually presaged an end. Moreover, October was generally regarded as fatal to Spanish Kings. Everybody was frantic. Father Gabriel Chiusa told Harrach that he was doing all he could to get Father Nicolas, the King's new Confessor, to hint indirectly – the matter could not be approached directly – that the time had come when no further delay in signing could be allowed; and Harrach still imagined that the heir would be the Archduke. He went so far as to say that Portocarrero himself favoured it.

On September 29th, Blécourt told Louis that Carlos was dead, and corrected the false rumour next day. On October 1st, Harrach told the Emperor that the will had not been signed, but that it was quite impossible that the heir could be other than the Archduke Charles. On October 2nd, Doctor Geleen wrote that the will was signed, but nobody knew the contents. On October 6th, Harrach said that the King's illness could not be natural, and it was clearly witchcraft, but the Inquisitor General had forbidden exorcism. On October 7th, Blécourt told Louis that the will had been signed three days earlier and that the Duque de Medina Sidonia, who had been present, said it was in favour of the Bourbon.

What had actually happened was that on October 2nd, Carlos had authorized Portocarrero to have a will drawn up in the form of Philip IV's will, leaving all the important names blank. Next day in his presence and in that of Portocarrero an official wrote in the vital clause:

> And recognizing as a result of several consultations with Ministers of State and of Justice that the reason why Doña Ana and Doña Maria Teresa, Queens of Spain, my aunt and sister, renounced succession to those kingdoms was to avoid the prejudice of uniting them to the Crown of France, and

recognizing that, this fundamental motive no longer existing, the right of succession subsists in the nearest relative, in accordance with the laws of these kingdoms, and that today this condition is fulfilled by the second son of the French Dauphin, therefore, in obedience to these laws, I declare my successor to be (should God take me without leaving heirs) the Duke of Anjou, second son of that Dauphin; and as such, I call him to the succession in all my Kingdoms and dominions, without exception of any part of them.

The Duc de Berry, the first son, was named second in succession; after him, and here lay the sting, the Archduke Charles. But whoever the inheritor, it must be 'without allowing the least dismemberment nor diminishing of the Monarchy founded with such glory by my ancestors'.

And so Louis was faced fair and square with a disagreeable alternative – either he must accept the will and perjure himself in the eyes of his co-signatories to the Treaty of Partition, or he must see the whole Spanish Empire go to his rival, the Austrian Archduke. To the last he had never believed that he would be faced with this dilemma. A letter of his crossed the one from Blécourt giving him the news of the will. In it he said it was quite impossible to imagine that the Spanish grandees or Maria Ana would submit to having a Bourbon on the Spanish throne; but when the unexpected happened, he deserted his alliance with William of Orange, which was to bring him only a part, and supported the succession of the Duke of Anjou to the whole. The result was Oudenarde, Malplaquet, Blenheim and the rest.

As for Carlos, as usual the effort of coming to a decision had a good effect on his health. On October 8th, Doctor Geleen said the King was wellnigh dead, with two hundred and fifty motions in nineteen days, but on the 16th the doctor reported an improvement. Harrach believed he would recover enough for them to undo the Cardinal's treachery over the will; and five days later he went so far as to say the King's recovery was so complete that there might still be hope for an heir. Harrach must go down in history as one of the most optimistic fools who was ever an ambassador.

But Carlos's mind was even now not at rest. The conflict

between dead mother and living wife persisted, and he added a futile codicil to his will, saying that he hoped that in the interests of universal peace the Duke of Anjou might marry an Austrian Archduchess. It was his last effort to reconcile the interior conflicts which had dominated his life. And one last request concerned an act of piety which he had always intended to perform but somehow had always left undone – in view of the great advantages likely to accrue to his beloved country, he requested his successor to appoint Santa Teresa de Jesus co-patron of the Kingdoms of Spain.

There remained to him only a week more of his intolerable existence. The Queen fed him by hand on milk of pearls; he became stone deaf; they put cantharides on his feet and freshly killed pigeons on his head to prevent vertigo. At nine on the night of the 29th they tried to keep him warm by putting the steaming entrails of freshly killed animals on his stomach; he became voiceless; the inevitable Agua de la Vida was applied and made him sweat for four hours and slightly revived his power of speech; and then at 2.49 p.m. on November 1st he died.

They opened him up according to custom: his heart was the size of a small nut, three large stones lay in his liver, his kidneys were full of water instead of blood, his intestines were putrid. 'The general opinion,' wrote Harrach, 'is that the death is due to witchcraft, an opinion which agrees with what the devil said in Vienna and in Madrid.' So ended the Hapsburg dream of conquering the world by marriages. So died the last Spanish Hapsburg descended from poor Juana la Loca.

BIBLIOGRAPHICAL NOTE

THE life of Carlos Segundo, *El Hechizado*, the Bewitched, as Spaniards call him is chiefly important to English readers for its close connection with the War of the Spanish Succession. But poor Carlos deserves to be considered as a man, as one of those victims of heredity and environment whose very weakness affects the course of history as powerfully as the strength of a Napoleon.

In this book I have dealt with his intimate life. The infirmities with which his forbears saddled him were accentuated by every misery which etiquette and superstition could produce. His importance in the Human Comedy is precisely this, that he is the perfect example of what folly and ignorance can do by way of warping and torturing a human being. As this is my theme, I make no apology for including more details of a medical, biological and psychological nature than are usually to be found in a history.

There has been scarcely any study of Carlos II in English. The last English writer, Martin Hume, worked before most of the documents had become accessible. Recently, English students have been understandably more concerned with the Golden Century of Spanish history and literature than with the decadence.

Since I am writing for the general reader rather than for the professional historian I have regretfully done without detailed bibliographical footnotes, but since the facts are often so surprising and much of the material rather inaccessible, a bibliographical note is essential for purposes of verification and amplification.

The earlier chapters deal with Carlos's disastrous heredity and the results of the Hapsburg policy of accumulating possessions by inbreeding. Unfortunately the three studies of this facet of Carlos's pre-natal life were all written before genetics had been properly established on a scientific basis. They can only be recommended cautiously for their facts and not at all for their theories.

RUBBRECHT, DR OSWALD

L'Origine du Type Familial de la Maison de Habsbourg (Brussels, 1910)

GALIPPE, V.

L'Héredité des Stigmates de dégenérescence et les familles souveraines (1905)

WOOD, FREDERICK ADAMS

Mental and Moral Heredity in Royalty (New York, 1906)

There is a later study in Spanish:

BIBLIOGRAPHICAL NOTE

AGUILAR, DR FLORESTÁN

Origen Castellano del prognatismo en las dinastias que reinaran en Europa; also a later study in German (which I have not seen).

STROHMEYER, W.

Die Vererburg des Habsburger Familientypus (Nova Acta Leopoldina, N.S. V.219)

For the eccentricities of Maximilian I, I am partly indebted to a most interesting little book:

WAAS, GLENN EDWARD

The Legendary Character of Kaiser Maximilian (New York, 1941)

For an appraisal of Juana la Loca, Henry IV, the Emperor Charles V, Philip IV and their effect on their descendants:

MARAÑON, DR GREGORIO

Ensayo Biológico sobre Enrique IV de Castilla y su tiempo (Madrid, 1941)

El Conde-Duque de Olivares (Madrid, 1936)

PFANDL, LUDWIG

Juana la Loca: su vida: su tiempo: su culpa (Madrid)

Dr Marañon has also written a number of essays and annotations which throw much light on the medical and psychological problems involved in the life of Carlos.

The obstetrical and medical details of Philip IV's family and the general medical ideas which dominated Spanish life in the seventeenth century are illuminated by a rare book:

DR GASPAR BRAVO DE SOBREMONTE RAMIREZ

[proto-medicus of Philip IV and of the Inquisition]

Resolutionum Consultationum Medicorum (Lugduni, 1662)

(These invaluable case histories and theses are only to be found in the Third Edition of Dr Bravo's immense folios, a copy of which exists in the Wellcome Medical Historical Library.)

Those who are interested in the effect of infant training on character will derive pleasure and profit from an exhaustive study of royal infancies in Spain:

ECHÁNOVE, LUIS CORTÉS

Nacimiento y Crianza de Personas Reales en la Corte de España 1566-1886 (Madrid, 1958)

(By the way, the author states that Carlos had even more wet-nurses than I, following the Duque de Maura, have allowed him.)

BIBLIOGRAPHICAL NOTE

The brief mentions of Sor Maria de Agreda will, I hope, tempt readers to refer to the splendid edition of her letters.

Cartas de la Venerable Madre Sor Maria de Agreda y del Señor Rey Don Felipe IV, procedidas de un bosquejo histórico por D. Francisco Silvela, 2 vols. (Madrid, 1885)

I have quoted, for details and gossip of palace life, the inveterate gossip-writer Barrionuevo and his anonymous successor published in four volumes:

PAZ Y MÉLIA, A.
Avisos de D. Jerónimo de Barrionuevo 1654-1658, 4 vols. (Madrid, 1892)

Further details about superstitions concerning the sacrament of baptism and the 'mazapan' will be found in:

THIERS, JEAN-BAPTISTE
Traité des Superstitions qui regardent tous les sacremens, 4 vols. (Paris, 1704)

This work also contains a great deal of interesting information about the Church struggle to prevent the sacrament of marriage being degraded by the superstitions surrounding the hazard of psycho-sexual impotence.

The rather scandalous details of Philip IV's intrigue with La Candelara are only to be found clearly stated in:

BERTAUT
Journal de Voyage d'Espagne (1659) published in Rev. Hisp. vol. 47, 1919, p. 1 seqq.

The best account of Maria Luisa's coming to Spain is that published in Bull. Hisp. vol. 4:

GUERRA Y VILLEGAS
Relación de la jornada ... en las Reales entregas de la Reyna N.S^a^. D^a^. Maria Luisa de Orléans.

Two classics referring to Spain during his first marriage:

VILLARS (MARQUÉS DE)
Mémoires de la Cour d'Espagne de 1679, jusqu'à 1681 (Paris, 1893)
Lettres de Madame de Villars à Madame de Coulanges (Paris, 1868)

No one would recommend the writings of Madame d'Aulnoy except for entertainment.

The whole of chapter fourteen describing the auto-de-fé of

1680 is taken from the contemporary account which was republished at the beginning of the nineteenth century.

With chapter fifteen the theme of Carlos's impotence begins to claim our attention. The sources for contemporary opinion on this problem are inexhaustible. As I have suggested in the text, psycho-sexual impotence seems to have been a universal concern in earlier centuries. Besides Dr Bravo, already mentioned, I have used:

SÁNCHEZ, THOMAS DE CÓRDOBA
de Matrimonio (My edition is 3 vols. folio 1300 pages, 1665; a rather late Lyons printing.)

This, by a Spanish Jesuit, is of course a favourite with later writers who, as is usual with such literature, copy and appropriate whatever they find useful.

The terrible story of La Cantina is excellently told from the original documents by the Duque de Maura. When we come to the ambassador Rébenac and the tragedy of Maria Luisa's death we have to compare two very different sources:

LEGRELLE, A.
La Mission de M. de Rébenac à Madrid et la Mort de Maria Luisa: Reine d'Espagne 1688-89 (Paris, 1894)

Maura's preoccupation is to tilt at all French romanticists and historians and to defend Spain from the charge of having murdered one of her Queens. This he does in:

MAURA GAMAZO, DUQUE GABRIEL DE
Maria Luisa de Orléans: Reina de España (Madrid, no date)

He attacks Legrelle whose monumental four-volume: *La Diplomatie Française et la Succession d'Espagne* is known to all political historians and puts his scholarship beyond cavil, whatever opinion we may form of Rébenac. Maura, however, gives credit to Legrelle for having discovered and published the essential documents about the death and post-mortem. The only complaint that Maura has against Legrelle is that he regards the question of poison as an open one, whereas he, Maura, is certain that poison can be ruled out.

I have used for the antidote triaca the very rare:

CAMERARIUS, JOACHIM
Libri duo de Theriaca et Mithridatio

This work gives a number of different recipes for making triaca, some of them with fifty and sixty ingredients.

On poisons in general the admirable Spanish Doctor Laguna should be consulted. His commentaries on the sixth book of Dioscorides discuss the whole incidence of poisoning. The edition in Spanish which I have used is relatively late, 1635, and would certainly have been in the hands of the Spanish Court in the time of Maria Luisa.

From chapter eighteen to the end of the book one of the most important sources is the admirable:

ADALBERTO DE BAVIERA Y GABRIEL MAURA GAMAZO
Documentos Inéditos referentes a las Postrimerias de la Casa de Austria en España

This vast collection was published in the Bulletin of the Spanish Academy of History and later a few off-prints were made and published in five volumes (1927-35) containing over two thousand pages. I have to thank my friend Sr Sala Badal for finding me a set, and scarcely a page from chapter eighteen to the end has not benefited by these or the other vital source:

Proceso Criminal, Fulminado contra el Rmo P.M. Fray Froylan Diaz de la Sagrada Religion de Predicadores Confesor del Rey N. S. D. Carlos II ...

This anonymous account written by Lorenzo Folch de Cardona was published in three parts (though Maura only mentions two and Pfandl one). The first was published by Blas Roman, 1787, the second by Antonio Espinosa, 1788, and the third by Joseph Doblado, 1788, all in Madrid.

There seem to have been a large number of manuscript copies passed round, and I have consulted the one in the British Museum (Add. MS. 10241) which has only slight textual variants and two short passages later expunged from the printed book.

The textbooks of exorcism popular at the time went much further than the forms laid down in the *Rituale Romanum*. Among those which include exorcisms for male impotence and which are likely to have been in the hands of Carlos's theological advisers, I have consulted (in each case the dates given are those of my own copies):

BIBLIOGRAPHICAL NOTE

NOYDENS, P. BENITO REMIGIO

Practica de Exorcistas (Barcelona, 1675, date of censura, 1665)

This is the work relied on by Maura and very widely used, judging by the many editions published in various parts of Spain.

GOMEZ LODOSA, P. F. DIDACUS

Jugum Ferreum Luciferi seu Exorcismi terribiles ... (Valencia, 1676)

VICECOMES, F. ZACHARIAS

Complementum Artis Exorcisticae (Venice, 1636, preface dated 1615)

The general sources for witchcraft are too well known to mention. When I quote Martinus Delrio: *Disquisitionum Magicarum: Libri Sex* it is from the Moguntia 1603 folio edition. Delrio was a Spaniard and this added in Spain to his universal popularity elsewhere.

The polygraph Menendez y Pelayo claims that Spain in the seventeenth century (and for that matter in all others too) was the least superstitious part of Europe. This can certainly be disputed, but it should be remembered that while Catholics vied with Calvinists elsewhere in the number of witches they burned, Spain and her Inquisition had an excellent record for near-common sense in this matter, as H. C. Lea in his well-known works has emphasized. Recently two Spanish studies have appeared which will give the reader an insight into the intellectual background, against which the events described here, should be seen.

CIRAC ESTOPAÑÁN, SEBASTIÁN

Los procesos de hechicherías en la Inquisición de Castilla la Nueva (Madrid, 1942)

An admirably documented epitome of all witchcraft cases heard by the Inquisitions of Toledo and Cuenca with chapters on the most notorious. More information will be found here of the Santiguadores, one of whom treated the dying Queen Mother Mariana.

BAROJA, JULIO CARO

Las Brujas y Su Mundo (Madrid, 1961)

An uneven account, valuable for its emphasis on the comparatively humanitarian treatment of witches by the Spanish Inquisition.

For those who would like to see the evidence against Menendez y Pelayo's claim, there are two admirable sources.

CERVANTES

El casamiento engañoso y El coloquio de los perros (Critical edition of Don Agustín de Amezúa, Madrid, 1912)

BIBLIOGRAPHICAL NOTE

Amezúa's lengthy introduction is still almost the best account of Spanish beliefs about magic and witchcraft and better than can be found in most other European languages.

Best of all:

FEIJOÓ FR. BENITO GERONYMO

Theatro Critico Universal ... para desengaño de errores comunes (Best edition Madrid, 1769, 8 vols., original publication began 1726)

It is impossible to overestimate the good sense and persuasiveness of this Benedictine, who did more than anyone else to raise his countrymen out of the intellectual morass into which they had slid by the beginning of the eighteenth century. Particularly relevant to the subject of this book are: vol. 1, No. 5 'Medecina', No. 8 'Astrologia Judiciaria'; vol. 2, No. 3 'Artes divinatorias', No. 5 'Uso de la Magia'; vol. 3, No. 1 'Saludadores', No. 6 'Milagros supuestos'; vol. 4, No. 9 'Transformaciones y transmigraciones magicas'; vol. 8, No. 6 'Demoniacos'. These *Discursos* give us a clear picture of what ignorance and bigotry existed at the time, no less, even if not more, in Spain than elsewhere. Their reception also shows the hidden stores of Spanish good sense waiting for encouragement.

The funeral sermons of the period are innumerable and very much the same in character. The two publications I have quoted on the death of Mariana are:

JORGE DE PINTO

Llantos Imperiales de Melpomene Regia ... (Madrid, 1696)

Panegirico funeral en las Exequias de la Serenissima Reyna Madre Doña Mariana ... que celebró la excelentissima Ciudad de Barcelona ... (Barcelona, 1696)

For the daily life of Carlos and his Court in the last and most interesting years there is one outstanding source in English:

MAHAN

Spain under Charles II or extracts from the correspondence of Alexander Stanhope (1690-1699) (London, 1846)

The bluff common sense of a close observer who nevertheless stood outside the Spanish dream is invaluable. Another English source of less value is:

BIBLIOGRAPHICAL NOTE

DUNLOP, J.

Memoirs of Spain during the reigns of Philip IV and Charles II 2 vols. (London, 1834)

It will not be necessary to describe the more usual sources for historical information available. I have of course referred to a number of them. There is a poor bibliography in Pfandl, and in the first edition of Maura many original documents are either printed or listed. It is sufficient to refer to three modern writers who have been indispensable in the writing of this book:

PRINCIPE ADALBERTO DE BAVIERA

Mariana de Neoburgo Reina de España (Madrid, 1938)

This is the Spanish translation and is little more than a faithful epitome of the collection of original documents already mentioned. It has a most valuable bibliography.

PFANDL, LUDWIG

Carlos II (Madrid, 1947)

The Spanish translation of the German work. According to Maura, Pfandl had not read all the published sources and was ignorant of nearly all the unpublished ones. He does not seem to have known any but the first volume of the indispensable collection already mentioned. His account of the bewitching and exorcisms is quite unreliable. Nevertheless his book is very readable and sometimes a needed corrective to the patriotic bias of the chief authority who is, of course,

MAURA GAMAZO, DUQUE GABRIEL DE

Carlos II y su Corte, 2 vols. (Madrid, 1911-15)
Vida y Reinado de Carlos II, 3 vols. (Madrid, 1942)
Maria Luisa de Orléans: Reina de España (Madrid, no date)
Supersticiones de los Siglos XVI y XVII y Hechizos de Carlos II (Madrid, no date)
Fantasias y Realidades del Viaje a Madrid de la Condesa d'Aulnoy (Madrid, no date)

The Duque de Maura's work on Carlos II has had a tragic history. It was first thought of as a de luxe publication, and the first volume on beautiful paper with many illustrations and splendid apparatus of notes and appendices appeared in 1911. It was dedicated to King Alfonso and had all the points to be expected of a scholarly conservative royalist's lifework. Shades of the First World War are already visible in the second volume in 1915, and a series of world and Spanish events prevented any further volumes from being published. Foreign archives became inaccessible, King Alfonso went, production prices soared, the Duque's school of thought became unfashionable. He tells us that he set himself the task of collecting all the unpublished data, with a view to a definitive complete edition, only to see his papers destroyed in the Spanish Civil War.

Meanwhile the collaboration with Prince Adalbert of Bavaria altered his plans and nearly ended his intention to publish further, but the publication of Pfandl's work decided him to proceed, since German and French historians, he writes, cannot understand Spanish psychology and falsify, often without intending to, Spain's past, and thereby confuse disastrously Spain's future.

The result is a disappointment, largely because changed economic circumstances are responsible for a format difficult to read and without all the interesting *apparatus criticus* of the earlier work.

It will be agreed that a historian who considers all foreign writers incapable of understanding their subject matter is liable to lay himself open to criticism by those writers. Though Maura is meticulous with his facts, his interpretations must sometimes seem perverse to a foreign reader. Nevertheless, his second work on Carlos is quite indispensable, and my debt to it is gratefully acknowledged. The third book is valuable for its original documents but loses value because so large a proportion of it is a polemic against certain French authors who scarcely merit Don Gabriel's attention. The fourth book is much more interesting but tends to reveal the same exaggerated *españolisma* as the other. The fifth book is an entertaining analysis of the falsehood and truth in the Spanish excursions of Madame d'Aulnoy.

My thanks are due to the Barcelona Central Library, the British Museum Library, the London Library, the Wellcome Medical Historical Library, but especially to Sr Sala Badal, Bookseller, Calle Boters, Barcelona, who has helped me accumulate nearly all the necessary books, and I have to thank Mr H. S. Vere Hodge for his painstaking and critical reading of the manuscript.

INDEX

INDEX

INDEX

LEE COUNTY LIBRARY SYSTEM
DISCARD
3 3262 00021 1398

DISCARD
LEE COUNTY LIBRARY
SANFORD, N. C.